Social representation
development of knowledge

Social representations and the development of knowledge

Edited by
Gerard Duveen
Department of Education, University of Cambridge

and Barbara Lloyd
School of Social Sciences, University of Sussex

The right of the
University of Cambridge
to print and sell
all manner of books
was granted by
Henry VIII in 1534.
The University has printed
and published continuously
since 1584.

Cambridge University Press

Cambridge
New York   Port Chester
Melbourne   Sydney

CAMBRIDGE UNIVERSITY PRESS
Cambridge, New York, Melbourne, Madrid, Cape Town, Singapore, São Paulo

Cambridge University Press
The Edinburgh Building, Cambridge CB2 2RU, UK

Published in the United States of America by Cambridge University Press, New York

www.cambridge.org
Information on this title: www.cambridge.org/9780521363686

First published 1990
This digitally printed first paperback version 2005

A catalogue record for this publication is available from the British Library

Library of Congress cataloguing in publication data
Social representations and the development of knowledge/edited by
Gerard Duveen and Barbara Lloyd.
    p.   cm.
Based on papers from a symposium which was held at the 1987
Annual Conference at the British Psychological Society.
Includes indexes.
ISBN 0 521 36368 3
1. Social perception in children – Congresses.   2. Social
perception – Congresses.   3. Social role – Congresses.   I. Duveen,
Gerard.   II. Lloyd, Barbara B. (Barbara Bloom), 1933– .
III. British Psychological Society. Conference (1987: Brighton,
England)
BF723.S6S66   1990
155.4′ 18 – dc20   89–33178   CIP

ISBN-13 978-0-521-36368-6 hardback
ISBN-10 0-521-36368-3 hardback

ISBN-13 978-0-521-02103-6 paperback
ISBN-10 0-521-02103-0 paperback

Contents

v

Contents

Figures

Tables

List of tables

Contributors

Felice Carugati
Università di Parma

William A. Corsaro
Indiana University

Maria D'Alessio
Università degli studi di Roma 'La Sapienza'

Paola De Paolis
Université de Genève

Julie Dickinson
University of Sussex

Gerard Duveen
University of Cambridge

Francesca Emiliani
Università degli studi di Bologna

Nicholas Emler
University of Dundee

Barbara Lloyd
University of Sussex

Luisa Molinari
Università degli studi di Bologna

List of contributors

Serge Moscovici
Ecole des Hautes Etudes en Sciences Sociales, Paris

Jocelyne Ohana
Ecole des Hautes Etudes en Sciences Sociales, Paris

Kalliroi Papadopoulou
University of Sussex

Gün R. Semin
University of Sussex

Acknowledgements

The idea for this book developed from a symposium which we organised at the 1987 Annual Conference at the British Psychological Society. We are grateful to the British Academy for their support, which enabled Serge Moscovici and Paola De Paolis to participate in the symposium. During the time in which we have prepared the book our work has been supported by a grant from the Economic and Social Research Council (No. C00232321). We should also like to thank our secretary, Karen Wraith, for all her assistance. We are grateful in addition to Jeanette Rodd and David Lloyd for their help.

1

Introduction

Gerard Duveen and Barbara Lloyd

Social representations as a perspective in social psychology

The concept of social representations introduced into social psychology by Moscovici and his collaborators has had a chequered reception in the English-speaking world. It is in *La Psychanalyse, son image et son public* that Moscovici (1976a) elaborated the concept of social representation most fully, both theoretically and empirically. In the absence of a translation, even Moscovici's own English presentations of the concept have an abstract, general or programmatic character, since they introduce a theoretical perspective without the benefit of a clear demonstration of its value for empirical research (see Moscovici, 1973, 1981, 1983, 1984, 1988; Moscovici and Hewstone, 1983).

In calling the first chapter of his book 'Social representation: a lost concept' Moscovici implies that social psychology has become disengaged from a concern with the situation of psychological processes in social life. The concept of social representation is intended to restore to social psychology an awareness of the social by providing the means for comprehending social life from a psychological perspective. Such a perspective is a necessary prerequisite for understanding the influence of social relations on psychological processes.

Moscovici defines social representations as

system(s) of values, ideas and practices with a twofold function; first, to establish an order which will enable individuals to orient themselves in their material and social world and to master it; and secondly to enable communication to take place among the members of a community by providing them with a code for social exchange and a code for naming and classifying unambiguously the various aspects of their world and their individual and group history.
(*Moscovici, 1973, p. xiii*)

This definition establishes social representations as particular kinds of structures which function to provide collectivities with intersubjectively shared means for understanding and communicating. As well as referring to social representations as structures in this way, Moscovici also uses the term to designate the process through which such structures are constructed and transformed. (If the English language were more flexible one could refer to this process as *social representing*, but to avoid such solecisms we shall use the singular form without an article to refer to social representation as process, and the singular with an article or the plural to refer to a social representation or social representations as structures.) As process, social representation is not bound by the canons of logical discourse, nor is it regulated by procedures of empirical verification or falsification. Rather, social representation is construed as being composed of two complementary functions, anchoring (whereby the unfamiliar or remote is absorbed into the familiar categories of everyday cognition) and objectification (whereby representations are projected into the world, so that what was abstract is transformed into something concrete). These two functions are interdependent, in the sense that a representation can become securely anchored to the extent that it is also objectified, and *vice versa*, that objectification would be impossible unless a representation were anchored. Nevertheless, they can be analytically distinguished as two moments in the process of social representation.

Moscovici's conceptualisation of the process of social representation is related to his distinction between the consensual universe of social representations and the reified universe of scientific discourse which respects the laws of logic and whose products are open to empirical investigation (1981). His purpose in making this distinction is not to propose a particular philosophy of science, but to point to a central phenomenon of our own society whereby the category of scientific understanding is distinguished from the category of everyday or common-sense understanding. What is proposed, then, is that these two universes, the reified and the consensual, correspond to a particular social representation in which the realm of the scientific is distinguished from that of common sense. The distinction is, nevertheless, a powerful one, as Moscovici notes. Science 'attempts to construct a map of the forces, objects and events unaffected by our desires and consciousness. [Social representation] stimulates and shapes our collective consciousness, explaining things and events so as to be accessible to each of us and relevant to our immediate concerns' (Moscovici, 1981, p. 187). Social psychology, in this view, is concerned with the analysis of the consensual universe, for which the theory of social representations provides the conceptual apparatus.

Social representations thus provide the central, integrative concept for a distinct perspective on social psychology, a perspective which is not an entirely new departure but one which recovers and enriches traditions which had become marginalised in the discipline. It shares with both Piagetian theory and other constructivist trends in psychology and the social sciences an epistemological basis in treating the subject and object of knowledge as correlative and co-constitutive and rejecting the view that these terms designate independent entities. The ontological corollary to this position is that social representations are constitutive of the realities represented, a constitution (or construction) effected through anchoring and objectification. Thus the *content* of what is constructed is accorded the same significance as the process of construction, and hence Moscovici's dictum that social representations are always the representation of *something* (Moscovici, 1976a, 1984).

In this respect the theory of social representations is not a psychology of cognitions about social life, but rather a theory in which psychological activities are located in social life. Indeed, social representations can be contrasted with social psychological theories based on narrower definitions of psychological activity focussed on notions of attitudes or attribution. In such theories social cognition is viewed as cognitive processes in relation to social stimuli, but these 'social stimuli' are taken as given, since social life itself remains untheorised. The effect of this theoretical lacuna is to present a view of social cognition as the activity of individual minds confronting the social world. For social representations, on the other hand, attitudes and attributions arise as consequences of participation in social life; they form, as it were, the visible tip of an iceberg whose submerged portion comprises the very structures which enable the subject to construct meaningful attitudes and attributions. As Moscovici notes, the concept of social representations may be difficult to grasp because it occupies a 'mixed position, at the crossroads of a series of sociological concepts and a series of psychological concepts' (1976a, p. 39). The focus for this perspective is the systems of social representations through which groups construct an understanding, or theorise, social life. Thus as well as being always the representation of something, social representations are also always representations of *someone or some collective* (for example, Moscovici, 1976a, 1984). The interdependence between social representations and the collectives for which they function means that social life is always considered as a construction, rather than being taken as a given.

The duality of social representations in constructing both the realities of social life and an understanding of it recalls a similar duality in Piaget's conceptualisation of operational structures. Piaget's task was facilitated by the availability of a knowledge of physics, mathematics and logic. These sciences describe a reified universe which provided him with a perspective from which it was possible to understand and interpret the behaviours of subjects at different levels of development. Without access to the logic of class inclusion it would have been difficult for him to have understood the attempts of children to answer the question whether there were more flowers or more roses in a given collection.

In the consensual universe of social life there is no privileged vantage point which offers an objective perspective from which to orient any investigation. In some circumstances it is possible for investigations of social representations to locate a point of reference comparable to the 'objectified' perspective available to Piaget. Moscovici's (1976a) study of psychoanalysis, for instance, takes the body of psychoanalytic theory originating in the work of Freud as an objectified point of reference from which to compare and contrast the social representations of psychoanalysis constructed by different social groups. He was able to observe the transformation of this body of knowledge as it was reconstituted in the network of representations held by the different groups. Again, without access to the corpus of psychoanalytic theory it would be difficult to understand and interpret the responses of members of different social groups to questions about psychoanalysis.

The study of social representations of psychoanalysis is an example of the way in which the reified universe of science is represented in the consensual world of everyday understanding. But not every social representation originates as a body of knowledge in the reified universe of scientific discourse. Indeed, most of the studies presented in this book concern social representations of themes drawn from within the realm of the consensual universe. In dealing with themes such as gender or the emotions a primary task for the investigators is to locate a perspective from which to organise the investigation. In some of the chapters the investigators have been able to use a knowledge of the social representations among adults as a point of reference for analysing the development of these representations through childhood. This is the case, for example, in the chapters by Lloyd and Duveen on gender, Corsaro on rules of social interaction and Semin and Papadopoulou on reflexive emotions. But in other cases the perspective from which to organise an investigation is more difficult to locate. In the studies of social representations of childhood by D'Alessio and by Emiliani and Molinari, for instance, no specific social group provides a fixed point of orientation. These studies resolve the issue by focussing on the object, childhood, and comparing the ways in which different groups represent this object. Similarly, both Carugati's study of the social construction of intelligence and De Paolis' analysis of social representations of psychology illustrate this perspective focussed on the object.

The issue outlined here is methodological in the sense that it concerns the relation of an epistemological position to empirical investigation. It is a strategic problem for research on social representations rather than a question of specific techniques. In each case the researcher has to proceed by identifying what Lucien Goldmann describes as a *significant structure* (Goldmann, 1976, 1980), by which he means a structure which has a functional necessity for a particular group. Social representations as significant structures identify both the group which constructs a representation and the content which is represented. The notion of social representations as significant structures also helps to distinguish this theory from other recent attempts to construct theories concerning the social psychological analysis of social life in terms of ordinary explanations (Antaki, 1981), linguistic repertoires (Potter and Wetherell, 1987) or rhetoric (Billig, 1987). What all of these approaches share is that they identify particular processes independently of any specific content, so that, again, the particular characteristics of specific aspects of social life remain outside the theory. While certain forms of ordinary explanation or particular linguistic repertoires or rhetorical devices all describe identifiable features of social discourse, these are also all features of the discourses of particular groups about specific aspects of social life, and thus draw on underlying social representations. Although they may provide useful analytical tools for investigating social representations, without explicating their implicit references to social representations, the analysis of these features of discourse cannot describe the social-psychological representation of social life. These features describe formal structures which it is difficult to locate in concrete social-psychological terms bound to some particular content. In this sense it can be said that these features do not constitute significant structures.

Social representations as a genetic theory

A genetic perspective is implied in the conception of social representations, in the sense that the structure of any particular social representation is a construction and thus the outcome of some developmental process. The works of Piaget and Goldmann again offer a comparable point of view. Both of these authors insisted on describing their approach as a *genetic* structuralism in which a structure is always viewed as a particular moment in development. A structure is the relatively enduring organisation of a function, while the realisation of a function implies its organisation in a structure. For similar reasons the theoretical perspective of social representations can be described as a *genetic social psychology*. Even if social representations as structures do not meet the strict formal criteria proposed by Piaget (1971), they nonetheless constitute organised wholes with the specific function of making communication and understanding possible.

Conceived in this way the concept of social representation appears to have a general application as a means of comprehending the way in which socio-epistemic structures exercise a psychological influence. But to grasp the complexities subsumed in this concept it is useful to distinguish three types of transformations associated with social representation. There are processes of *sociogenesis*, which concerns the construction and transformation of the social representations of social groups about specific objects, *ontogenesis*, which concerns the development of individuals in relation to social representations, and *microgenesis*, which concerns the evocation of social representations in social interaction.

Sociogenesis

Sociogenesis is the process through which social representations are generated. Moscovici's (1976a) study of psychoanalysis is an example of the diffusion of scientific knowledge through the community as it is reconstructed by different social groups. But, as we noted above, it is not only knowledge originating in scientific discourses which gives rise to social representations: other themes also circulate in society through the medium of social representations. In recent years social representations of gender, for instance, have clearly been undergoing transformations, providing another example of a sociogenetic process. One chapter which clearly touches on issues of sociogenesis is De Paolis' comparisons of the social representations of psychology held both by psychologists and other professional groups working in the field of mental health.

Sociogenesis takes place in time, so that even when social representations are investigated at a particular moment in time, the resulting description needs to be viewed in a diachronic perspective. Moscovici's study, for instance, was originally published in 1961, and describes the structure of social representations of psychoanalysis at that time. Clearly the sociogenesis of these representations had taken place over the years since Freud's work began to appear. In the intervening years since Moscovici's study the theory of psychoanalysis has itself evolved and the characteristics of many social groups has also changed. A comparable study undertaken today might reveal transformations in the social representations of psychoanalysis. Sociogenesis thus also points to the historical dimension of social representations.

Ontogenesis

Human infants are born into a social world constructed in terms of the social representations of their parents, siblings, teachers, etc., representations which also structure the interactions of these others with the child. If, as Moscovici asserts, the society into which children are born is a 'thinking society', it is social representations which constitute the 'thinking environment' for the child. Developing the competence to participate as actors in this thinking society implies that children can acquire access to the social representations of their community. It is this process which we refer to as the ontogenesis of social representations, although ontogenesis as a process is not restricted to childhood, but occurs whenever individuals, children or adults, engage with novel social representations in order to participate in the life of a group.

An adequate account of ontogenesis needs to describe how social representations become psychologically active for individuals. Elsewhere (Duveen and Lloyd, 1986) we have suggested that ontogenesis is a process through which individuals re-construct social representations, and that in doing so they elaborate particular social identities. It is as social identities that social representations become psychologically active for individuals. Thus we can say that in expressing or asserting a social identity individuals draw on the resources made available through social representations. As this formulation implies, there is a distinction between social identities and social representations. Our own research on gender has shown that the same social representation can support distinct social identities. As we note in our chapter, in many respects boys and girls develop similar representations of gender, but they do not behave in similar ways.

The influence exercised by social representations on individuals can take different forms. Some social representations impose an imperative obligation on individuals to adopt a particular social identity. This is the case, for example, with representations of gender or ethnicity where individuals are constrained to construct the corresponding social identity. In such cases there is an external obligation which derives from the ways in which others identify an individual in terms of these social categories. In other instances the influence of social representations is exercised through a contractual obligation rather than an imperative one. In these cases an individual joining a social group contracts to adopt a particular social identity. Social representations of psychoanalysis provide an example of such a contractual obligation. As a body of knowledge psychoanalysis exercises no external obligation on individuals to interiorise the categories of analytic thinking as psychologically active constructions. But entry to some social groups (principally that of psychoanalysts themselves, but also other social groups for whom an analytic perspective forms part of their world-view) is dependent upon individuals contracting to construe the world in terms of psychoanalytic categories.[1]

Microgenesis

A third genetic aspect of social representations is in social interaction, where individuals meet, talk, discuss, resolve conflicts – in short, communicate with one another. Social representations are evoked in all social interactions through the social identities asserted in the activity of individuals. Social identities, however, are not fixed attributes which individuals carry into each interaction and which remain invariant through the course of interaction. Rather, particular social identities are constructed through the course of social interaction, or through the successive encounters which make up the history of a particular interpersonal relation. There is a genetic process in all social interaction in which particular social identities and the social representations on which they are based are elaborated and negotiated. It is this process which we refer to as the microgenesis of social representations.

The evocation of social representations in social interaction occurs first of all in the ways in which individuals construct an understanding of the situation and locate themselves and their interlocutors as social subjects. In many circumstances, of course, there will be a mutuality in the understandings constructed by different participants which will obviate the need for any explicit specifications or negotiation of social identities, though one can still describe the course of such social interactions as the negotiation of social identities in the same sense as one speaks of a ship negotiating a channel. But where the mutuality of understanding cannot be taken for granted, or where an assumed mutuality breaks down, the negotiation of social identities becomes an explicit and identifiable feature of social interaction. In these circumstances the negotiation of social identities may involve the co-ordination of different points of view and the resolution of conflicts. In every social interaction there is a microgenetic process in which social identities are negotiated and shared frames of reference established, processes for which social representations provide the resources. Corsaro's chapter gives a vivid illustration of the microgenetic process and presents a view of ontogenetic and sociogenetic dimensions.

Language is, of course, a central medium through which social interactions are conducted, and recent studies in sociolinguistics have emphasised the construction of social identities in discourse (Gumperz, 1982) as well as the role of social representations (Rommetveit, 1974, 1984). Through the course

[1] We are grateful to Serge Moscovici for suggesting these particular terms, imperative and contractual obligations, to characterise this distinction.

8

of social interaction participants may come to adopt positions distinct from those with which they entered the interaction, and in this sense microgenesis is always a process of change. In many instances the changes which can be observed through the course of social interaction are transitory rather than structural as individuals adopt particular social identities in order to pursue specific goals or accomplish specific tasks. Yet social interaction is also the field in which social influence processes are most directly engaged (see Moscovici, 1976b), and in some instances the influences at work in social interaction may also lead to structural change in the representations of participants. These changes may be ontogenetic transformations in the development of social representations in individual subjects (see Doise and Mugny, 1984), but they may also be sociogenetic transformations resulting in the restructuration of social representations.[2]

Some examples may help to illustrate the possible relationships between these three types of genetic transformation of social representations. Consider first of all the scientist who proposes a new theory, and let us assume that we are dealing with an Einstein or a Freud proposing a radical new interpretation of the human situation or human experience. Through various forms of social interaction (publications or lectures) the scientist tries to communicate this theory to colleagues. The communication will have been successful to the extent that other scientists will have understood the concepts being proposed and also accepted that these concepts are well founded and not in error. The outcome will be ontogenetic transformations in the representations held by these scientists as individuals, as well as a sociogenetic transformation in the representation held by the scientific community as a social group.

By contrast, consider the developing child as they grasp some social representation of their community, gender or nationality, for example. For this development to occur the child needs to receive some communication, whether through interaction with other children or adults or from the public representations presented in the media. These microgenetic processes will have led to ontogenetic transformations in the child's representation of the world, but the social representations of their community are unlikely to be influenced by these particular microgenetic processes. In this case there is ontogenesis without sociogenesis, a state of affairs which is a characteristic feature of childhood given the negligible influence which children are able to exert on the representations held by their community.

In both of these examples ontogenesis and sociogenesis are the consequence of microgenetic processes. Indeed, microgenesis constitutes a motor, as it were, for the genetic transformations of social representations.

---

[2] Lucien Goldmann makes a similar point when he notes that there may be information which can be communicated to either groups or individuals only on condition of a transformation in their socio-psychological structures (Goldmann, 1976).

References

Antaki, C. (ed. 1981). *The Psychology of Ordinary Explanations of Behaviour.* London: Academic Press.

Billig, M. (1987). *Arguing and Thinking.* Cambridge: Cambridge University Press.

Doise, W. and Mugny, G. (1984). *The Social Development of the Intellect.* Oxford: Pergamon.

Duveen, G. and Lloyd, B. (1986). The significance of social identities. *British Journal of Social Psychology,* 25, 219–30.

Goldmann, L. (1976). *Cultural Creation in Modern Society.* Saint Louis: Telos Press.

　(1980). *Essays on Method in the Sociology of Literature.* Saint Louis: Telos Press.

Gumperz, J. (1982). *Language and Social Identity.* Cambridge: Cambridge University Press.

Moscovici, S. (1973). Foreword to C. Herzlich, *Health and Illness.* London: Academic Press.

　(1976a). *La Psychanalyse, son image et son public.* 2nd edn. Paris: Presses Universitaires de France.

　(1976b). *Social Influence and Social Change.* London: Academic Press.

　(1981). On social representations. In J. Forgas (ed.), *Social Cognition.* London: Academic Press.

　(1983). The coming era of social representations. In J. P. Codol and J. P. Leyens (eds.), *Cognitive Analysis of Social Behaviour.* The Hague: Martinus Nijhoff.

　(1984). The phenomenon of social representations. In R. Farr and S. Moscovici (eds.), *Social Representations.* Cambridge: Cambridge University Press.

　(1988). Notes towards a description of social representations. *European Journal of Social Psychology,* 18, 211–50.

Moscovici, S. and Hewstone, M. (1983). Social representations and social explanations: from the 'naive' to the 'amateur' scientist. In M. Hewstone (ed.), *Attribution Theory.* Oxford: Blackwell.

Piaget, J. (1971). *Biology and Knowledge.* Edinburgh: Edinburgh University Press.

Potter, J. and Wetherell, M. (1987). *Discourse and Social Psychology.* London: Sage.

Rommetveit, R. (1974). *On Message Structure.* London: Wiley.

　(1984). The role of language in the creation and transmission of social representations. In R. Farr and S. Moscovici (eds.), *Social Representations.* Cambridge: Cambridge University Press.

2

The underlife of the nursery school: young children's social representations of adult rules

William A. Corsaro

Introduction

There has been a definite trend in theoretical work on human development towards the acceptance of what has been termed a constructivist approach. This view, which is most often associated with the theoretical work of Piaget (1968), stresses the active role of the child, arguing that children interpret, organise and use information from the environment and, in the process, construct mature skills and knowledge. Although these developments are clearly in the right direction, they still cling to what Harré (1986) referred to as the doctrine of individualism.

An adherence to individualism is evident in two respects. First, understanding of children's interactions remains at an interpersonal level; interpersonal alignments (for example, adult–child versus peer) are contrasted to show how they differentially affect individual development. But how interpersonal relations reflect cultural systems, or how children, through their participation in communicative events, become part of and collectively reproduce these interpersonal relations and cultural patterns is not seriously considered. Second, the adherence to individualism is also seen in the overwhelming concern with the endpoint of development, or the movement from immaturity to adult competence. For example, work on social cognition focusses on identifying stages in the abstract conception of friendship. Children's conceptions are elicited through clinical interviews and their underdeveloped conceptions are compared to those of competent adults (Selman, 1980; Youniss, 1980). Yet, few scholars study what it is like to be or have a friend in children's social words or how developing conceptions of friendship get embedded in peer culture.

Theories of children's social development must break free from the

11

individualist doctrine that sees social development solely as the private internalisation of adult skills and knowledge. Childhood socialisation must be understood also as a social and collective process. In this view, it 'is not just that the child must make his knowledge his own, but that he must make it his own in a community of those who share his sense of belonging to a culture' (Bruner, 1986, p. 127).

This approach extends the emphasis on children's activities in constructivist theory, stressing that such activities are always embedded in a social context and always involve children's use of language and interpretive abilities (Cicourel, 1974). The approach is essentially interpretive, stressing that children discover a world that is endowed with meaning and help to shape and share in their own developmental experiences by their interactive responses (Cook-Gumperz and Corsaro, 1986; Corsaro and Rizzo, 1988).

Only recently have cross-cultural studies in developmental sociolinguistics documented the importance of these collective productions (Corsaro, 1988; Ochs, 1982; Schieffelin, 1986). They demonstrate how children's participation in specific interactional routines is central to their acquisition of language and culture. Routines are recurrent and predictable activities that are basic to day-to-day social life. The habitual, taken-for-granted character of routines provides actors with the security and shared understanding of belonging to a cultural group (Giddens, 1984). On the other hand, this predictability empowers routines, providing frames within which a wide range of socio-cultural knowledge can be produced, displayed and interpreted (Goffman, 1974).

Children's participation in cultural routines is an essential element of the interpretive approach. In adult–child interaction children are frequently exposed to social knowledge and communicative demands that raise problems, confusions and uncertainties that are later readdressed in the routines that make up peer culture (Corsaro, 1985; Corsaro and Rizzo, 1988). Through their participation in peer activities children are attempting, in the words of Moscovici (1981), to make the unfamiliar familiar. They are attempting to transform confusions and ambiguities from the adult world into the familiar routines of peer culture. In fact, children's production and participation in a wide range of peer routines, including role-play routines where various adult roles are enacted and expanded (see Corsaro, 1985; Garvey, 1977), spontaneous fantasy routines within which characters from children's fairy tales and films are brought to life (see Corsaro, 1985, 1988), and routines produced to circumvent adult rules (see Corsaro, 1985 and below), provide evidence that young children have internalised many adult social representations (Moscovici, 1981). Furthermore, the actual production and maintenance of peer culture is essential in children's development of social representations. The development of social representations (like other aspects of the culture) is seen as a collective process involving children's interactions with adults and peers.

The interpretive approach views development as a process of children's appropriations of their culture. Children enter into social systems and, by interacting and negotiating with others, establish understandings that become fundamental social knowledge on which they continually build. Thus, the interpretive model refines the linear notion of stages by viewing development as a productive–reproductive process of increasing density and reorganisation of knowledge that changes with the children's developing cognitive and language abilities and with changes in their social worlds.

A major change in children's worlds is their movement outside the family. In interacting with playmates in organised playgroups and schools, children produce the first in a series of peer cultures in which childhood knowledge and practices are gradually transformed into the knowledge and skills necessary to participate in the adult world. In my research, I have focussed on peer culture in the pre-school years. This involves the micro-ethnographic study of peer interaction of nursery school children in the US and Italy. I have identified several stable features of peer culture and have described basic patterns of cultural production and reproduction in children's peer activities (see Corsaro, 1985, 1988; Corsaro and Rizzo, 1988).

In this chapter I focus on a specific routine in peer culture in which children mock and attempt to circumvent adult rules. In the production of the routine the children produce a wide variety of what Goffman (1961) has termed 'secondary adjustments'. Secondary adjustments are 'any habitual arrangement by which a member of an organization employs unauthorized means, or obtains unauthorized ends, or both, thus getting around the organization's assumptions as to what he should do and get and hence what he should be' (Goffman, 1961, p. 189).

Secondary adjustments are seen by Goffman as forming the 'underlife' of social establishments. Goffman identified a number of types of secondary adjustments in his documentation of the underlife of an asylum, a highly restrictive institution. Goffman argued, however, that his work in an asylum led to findings regarding the individual's relation to organisations that apply in some ways to all institutions. Furthermore, Goffman believed that the individual's tendency simultaneously to embrace and to resist institutional rules is a central feature of personal identity or self.

Although pre-school children do not have a stable sense of self or the cognitive skills necessary to infer the implications of both embracement and resistance of organisational rules for personal identity, they do have a clear notion of the importance and restrictiveness of the adult world as compared to children's worlds. At this age, children have made a distinction between adults ('grown-ups') and children. In fact, children can, and often do, distinguish between the adult world and their own peer world.

Although membership and participation in the adult world is important to nursery school children, their developing sense of who they are is also strengthened through their active resistance of certain adult rules and expectations regarding their behaviour. In this sense, the children's joint recognition of adult rules, and their mutual resistance to certain of these rules, can be seen as reflective elements of peer culture.

There are two distinct points about the relationship between children's secondary adjustments and their development of social representations that I will stress throughout this chapter. First, the analysis of children's secondary adjustments provides evidence that the children share a basic understanding of adult social rules. Secondly, secondary adjustments provide a forum in which children are able to elaborate their own peer culture, their own set of social representations. In the process of acquiring a sense of adult social structure, children simultaneously come to produce their own unique peer culture.

In the following sections of this chapter I examine the importance of the underlife of the nursery school for children's social representations of adult rules. In the analysis I will: (1) discuss the importance of the routine of mocking adult rules in peer culture and describe several different types of secondary adjustments of American and Italian nursery school children; (2) present and discuss examples that demonstrate how children, in the course of the production of the routine, address individual as well as group interests; and (3) discuss how the children's creative production of their shared social representations of adult rules in the routine can be seen as a first step in their acquisition and eventual reproduction of adult social representations.

Ethnographic context and data-collection procedures

The data for the following analysis of peer routines were collected in two long-term micro-ethnographic studies of peer interaction in nursery schools. The first study was conducted in a nursery school in the United States which is part of a child study centre for education and research staffed and operated by a state university. The school is located in a large metropolitan city near the university campus. There were two groups of children at the school, with approximately twenty-five children in each group. One group attended morning sessions and ranged in age from 2.10 to 3.10 years. The second group (which had been at the school the year before) attended afternoon sessions and ranged in age from 3.10 years to 4.10 years at the start of the school term. The majority of children came from middle- and upper-class families; their parents ranged from blue-collar workers to professionals.

Detailed discussions of field entry and data-collection procedures for this study are presented elsewhere (see Corsaro, 1981, 1985); therefore, I will provide only a summary of the data-collection process here. Data collection moved through a series of phases. The first phase involved unobtrusive monitoring of activities in the school from a concealed observation area. These observations were important in learning a great deal about the children (for instance, their names, play activities, frequent playmates and so forth) and the schedule and normal routine of the school day. This phase was followed three weeks later by about three months of participant observations. I utilised what I term a 'reactive' method of field entry, allowing the children to react to and define me and gradually draw me into their activities. This strategy was successful in that the children came to see me as an atypical adult and in many ways as a 'big kid' (many of the children referred to me as 'Big Bill').

My participation during this phase was primarily peripheral. Although I never initiated activities, I responded when the children asked me to take on certain roles in their play; for instance, I pretended to eat sand cakes and pies and helped build constructions with blocks. It was clear that I was not a full participant, and I was not seen as a peer; however, I was accepted into the children's culture and routinely included in activities that the children did not produce in the presence of the teachers and other adults. In fact, the children frequently called my attention to and included me in their secondary adjustments to school rules (see Corsaro, 1985, and below). As a result, I was privy not only to the existence of the underlife, but also to its complexity and significance in peer culture.

During my fifth month at the school I introduced video equipment. For the next five months, an assistant videotaped peer interactive episodes twice a week while I remained involved with the children. Interactive episodes are defined as those sequences of behaviour which begin with the acknowledged presence of two or more interactants in an ecological area and the overt attempt(s) to arrive at a shared meaning of ongoing or emerging activity. Episodes end with physical movement of interactants from the area which results in the termination of the originally initiated activity. The basis of this definition of the sampling unit (interactive episode) was the interplay between theoretical assumptions about basic units in face-to-face interaction and the background information collected in the settings under study (see Corsaro, 1985 for a discussion of the generation of the definition of 'interactive episode' and other details).

On days when we did not videotape during this period, I continued my participant observation and the collection of field notes. Overall, I recorded 633 interactive episodes in field notes and 146 episodes on videotape (around twenty-five hours of video data). Although I collected some episodes of teacher-directed activities, most of the data focussed on peer play and culture. These materials were supplemented with informal interviews with the teacher, parents and the children throughout the ten-month period.

The second study was conducted in a *scuola materna* in a large city in northern Italy. The *scuola materna* is a pre-school education programme that exists throughout Italy and is usually administered by local governments (see Saraceno, 1984 for a detailed discussion of child-care policy in Italy). It provides child care and educational programmes for children aged three to six. Attendance in the *scuola materna* system is high: in the city of the school I studied in 1983, over 90 per cent of the children aged three to six attended regularly. The *scuola materna* I studied was staffed by five teachers and attended by thirty-five children for approximately 7 hours each weekday (9.30 a.m. to 5.30 p.m.), although some children returned home at 1.00 p.m. The general methodological procedures, which involved participant observation, audiovisual recording and microanalysis of peer interaction, were similar to those used in the American study.

In some ways, field entry was more easily accomplished in the Italian setting because of my earlier experience in the American school. In addition, my limitations regarding conversational Italian (my comprehension was good and improved, but I made numerous grammatical and pronunciation errors when speaking Italian) led the children to see me as an incompetent adult. Over time, however, it became apparent to the children that I could communicate better with them than with the teachers. As a result, the children saw themselves as having a special relationship with me – a relationship that was different from the one I had with the teachers. They would talk with me and I with them with little difficulty, but it was apparent to them that this was not true regarding my communication with the teachers. In short, the children saw my relationship with them as a partial breakdown of the control of the teachers. Such a breakdown is an important aspect of peer culture (see Corsaro, 1985). As a result of these aspects of field entry, I was able to establish myself quickly as a peripheral member of the peer culture in the *scuola materna*. As was the case with the American school, the Italian children readily included me in their secondary adjustments to school rules. In fact, I became a valued member of the peer culture when, during my second week at the school, I was jokingly corrected by a teacher for talking during 'quiet time'. My unwitting violation of a school rule and the resulting reprimand resulted in my quick entry into the underlife of the *scuola materna*.

While in the *scuola materna*, I collected some 325 interactive episodes in field notes over a six-month period. In addition, I collected forty episodes of peer interaction on audio- or videotape during the last few months of this period and fifteen additional episodes on videotape during a six-week return visit to the school a year later. These materials were supplemented with informal interviews with parents, the teachers and the children.

Nursery school children's secondary adjustments to adult rules

Although peer culture was manifested in a variety of ways in the American and Italian nursery schools, two central themes appeared consistently in the children's peer activities: the children made persistent attempts to *gain control* of their lives and to *share* that control with each other (see Corsaro, 1985, 1988). These two themes of control and sharing are apparent in the children's resistance to school rules. In the process of resisting adult rules, the children develop a sense of community and a group identity. In addition, the children's evasion of adult rules through co-operative secondary adjustments enables them to gain a certain amount of control over their daily lives.

The children's resistance to adult rules can be seen as a routine because it is a daily occurrence in the nursery school and is produced in a style that is easily recognisable to members of the peer culture. Such activity is often highly exaggerated (for instance, making faces behind the teacher's back or running around) or is prefaced by 'calls for attention' of other children (such as 'look what I've got' in reference to possession of a forbidden object, or 'look what I'm doing' to call attention to a restricted activity).

Although recurrent, predictable and recognisable in terms of its general nature, specific instances of the routine of resisting adult rules are often highly complex and dynamic. In the nursery school children run up against a range of rules that from their perspective seem arbitrary and unfair. Over time the children develop a shared sense of the injustice of these rules and then proceed to concoct an impressive repertoire of types of resistance.

Once children begin to see themselves as part of a peer group the mere doing of something forbidden and getting away with it is highly valued in peer culture. Making faces behind the teacher's back and leaving one's seat or talking during 'quiet time' when the teacher leaves the room become commonplace over the course of the school year. Even the youngest of the children quickly develop an appreciation of this simple form of the routine that can be seen as *exaggerated violation* and *mocking* of school rules. Here there is violation of the rule solely for the sake of violation – to challenge directly and to mock the authority of the teacher.

Other varieties of the routine are more complex and more fully in line with Goffman's notion of secondary adjustments. Here the children go beyond violation for violation's sake to employ authorised or unauthorised means to obtain unauthorised ends. A frequent secondary adjustment involves the use of *subterfuge*. For example in both the United States and Italy there was a rule that prohibited (or severely restricted) the bringing of toys or other personal objects from home to school. Such objects were attractive to other children because they were different from the everyday materials in the school. As a result, the teachers were constantly settling disputes about sharing the personal objects. Therefore, the rule specified that such objects should not be brought to school and, if they were, they must be stored in one's locker until the end of the day. In both the American and the Italian school the children attempted to evade this rule by bringing small personal objects that they could easily conceal in their pockets. Particular favourites were toy animals, Matchbox cars, sweets and chewing gum. While playing, a child would often show his or her 'stashed loot' to a playmate and try to share the forbidden objects without catching the attention of the teachers. In Italy the children would often say to me, 'Guarda, Bill!' ('Look, Bill!') and show me a toy car or hand me a sweet. Sweets were a preferred choice because the child and his or her peers could share the forbidden objects and then go on to consume the evidence, often with teachers close at hand.

The teachers were, of course, often aware of what was going on, but would simply chuckle to themselves and ignore these minor transgressions. The children, on the other hand, felt they were fooling the teachers. In fact, these secondary adjustments were not minor or trivial deceptions in the children's eyes, but rather important moments in the sharing of peer culture.

Other types of secondary adjustments involved the children's use of what Goffman has referred to as 'make-dos' to get around certain rules. That is, the children would use 'available artifacts in a manner and for an end not officially intended' (Goffman, 1961, p. 207). For example, there were no toy weapons in either school and there was a general rule against the use of pretend weapons. However, boys would often shoot at each other from a distance simply by pointing their fingers and cocking their thumbs. Children would also convert objects like sticks and broomstick horses to swords or guns and would actually construct weapons with building materials like Lego.

Some examples of 'make-do' were highly ingenious. In the American school there were several rules regarding the use of play materials. Play with certain toys like blocks, dishes or toy animals was restricted to the areas in which the materials were located. Children often violated these rules by subterfuge, simply concealing objects on their persons during transport. On one occasion, however, a boy, Daniel, took a suitcase from the playhouse, carried it to the block area, and filled it with blocks and toy animals. He then carried the suitcase outside, dumped the blocks and animals in the sandpit, and buried them. Shortly thereafter, a teacher noticed the suitcase in the sandpit and told Daniel to return it to the playhouse. Daniel did so without protest, but then quickly returned to the sandpit to play with the blocks and animals. At clean-up time, Daniel abandoned the secretly transported objects and went inside. When a second teacher discovered the objects in the sand during clean up, she asked two children in the area how they got outside. They responded with the typical pre-school child's answer: 'We don't know.' Which in this case was true, but not believed by the teacher.

Similar examples occurred in the *scuola materna*. When the children went to the outside yard to play in the afternoon, the teachers used a large plastic milk carton to carry play materials. Not surprisingly, some of the children found the carton to be a more attractive play alternative. On one occasion a child placed the carton on her head and chased after several other children. She eventually fell and suffered a minor injury. After this incident, the children were forbidden to play with the carton. However, one day several children placed a bucket filled with rocks in the carton. Then two children, one at each end, picked up the carton and marched with the others around the school chanting: 'Arriva la banca!' ('Here comes the bank!') The children had created a whole new dimension in banking, a bank which makes house calls. A number of other children immediately responded, asking for money. Soon the teachers became involved, encouraging the children to count out the money (rocks) carefully and follow normal banking procedures. After about half an hour of orderly banking a dispute broke out and several children struggled over the carton. At this point one of the teachers noted the transgression of playing with the carton, and as one child noted, that was: 'Finito la banca' ('That's the end of the bank').

A final type of secondary adjustment that I saw in both schools involved the active co-operation of several children. These secondary adjustments can be seen as extensions or elaborations of 'existing sources of legitimate satisfaction' for private ends. They are what Goffman has referred to as examples of '*working the system*' (1961, p. 210). Many of these secondary adjustments were employed to avoid helping at 'clean-up time'. Clean-up time usually occurs at transition points in the nursery school day (for example, before snacks or meals, meeting time, etc.). There is a general rule that children stop play when clean-up time is announced and help the teachers put play areas back into order. It does not take the children long to begin questioning the necessity or logic of clean-up time. I once overheard a child,

Richard, in the American school argue against putting toys away during clean-up time because 'we'll just have to take'em out all over again!'.

The children came up with a range of strategies to evade clean-up time. These strategies include: relocation (immediately moving to another area of play upon hearing the announcement of clean-up and claiming you are not responsible for the disorder in the new play area); pretending not to hear the announcement (simply ignoring the command to obey the rule for as long as possible); and personal problem delay (claiming you cannot help clean up for one of a number of personal reasons). This last strategy is particularly interesting. Children report a plethora of problems such as feigned illness or injury ('I got a stomach ache', 'I hurt my foot', etc.), pressing business (for instance, helping another teacher clean up in another part of the school, going to the toilet, etc.), or role-play demands (e.g., a mother needs to finish feeding her baby, a fire-fighter has to put out a roaring blaze, etc.).

Once in Italy a child, Franca, told one of the teachers that she could not help clean up because I was in the process of teaching her English. There was some truth in this since children often asked me how to say certain words in English and Franca and several other children had made such requests earlier in the day. However, we were quite clearly not involved in such activity when clean-up time ensued. Fortunately, I was not brought into the dispute because the teacher rejected Franca's excuse out of hand. Nevertheless, during the course of this debate a good deal of the work of clean-up was performed by other children. In fact, all of the strategies to avoid clean-up are partially successful for this reason. Because of organisational constraints (i.e., teachers' needs to get the children to lunch, to begin meeting time, etc.) any delaying tactic is somewhat effective. It does not take long for children to learn this and to 'work the system' accordingly.

Overall, it is clear that the children's resistance to adult rules is an important feature of peer culture in the nursery school. The children's secondary adjustments are innovative and collective responses to the adult world. By collectively resisting adult rules, children come to develop a group identity that is important in their acquisition of a sense of social structure (Cicourel, 1974). By sharing a communal spirit as a member of peer culture, children come to experience how being a member of a group affects both themselves as individuals and how they are to relate to others. Through secondary adjustments, children come to see themselves as part of a group (in the nursery school, pupils sharing a peer culture) which is in some instances aligned with, in others opposed to, other groups (in the nursery school, teacher rules and adult culture). At the same time children also begin to develop an awareness of how communal bonds and values can be used to address personal interests and goals; a subject we turn to in the next section.

Children's pursuit of personal goals within secondary adjustments

Over the course of the school year the children's creation and participation in a wide range of secondary adjustments led to the development of what I have termed (in line with Goffman, 1961) an underlife in the nursery school. The underlife exists alongside of and in reaction to those organisational rules of the nursery school which impinge upon the autonomy of the children. In this sense the underlife is an essential part of the children's group identity.

However, the children also come to discover that 'this sense of group identity' itself can be used as a resource to pursue individual goals within peer interaction. Clear evidence of this discovery can be seen in the children's attempts to control the behaviour of their peers by offering them the opportunity to share the use of forbidden objects which had been smuggled into the nursery school. On one occasion in Italy I saw an older boy, Luca, fail repeatedly at getting a younger child, Matteo, to play a board game the 'correct' way. Although exasperated with his younger playmate's refusal to follow directions, Luca would not give up. Finally, Luca abandoned the game momentarily and took a small car from his pocket. He then rolled the car towards Matteo, who picked it up, looked it over and rolled it back. After playing with the car for several minutes, Luca returned it to his pocket and suggested that they return to playing with the board game. This time the younger child played 'correctly'. After a few minutes, however, Matteo asked to see the car again, but this time Luca said: 'Basta cosi!' ('Enough of this!') and left Matteo sitting alone at the table.

On some occasions children devise elaborate schemes to evade school rules which also involve attempts to achieve personal goals. Consider the following example that I tape-recorded in my work in the *scuola materna*.

The scheme:

> Felice (F) and Roberto (R) are playing in the outside yard. Felice has a small plastic container that another child had brought to school and given him to play with. Felice shows the container to Roberto, which triggers an idea of bringing water from inside the school to the outside play area. Such transportation of water is normally not allowed by the teachers.

F–R: Guarda, l'ho chiusa.

(Look, I closed it.)

R–F Ehi, se mischiamo con la terra e facciamo un castèllo di sàbbia? Tu prendi l'acqua con quello. E dopo quando c'hai la pipi lo dici – lo dici alla maestra che te lo fa. E poi non puoi sempre dirlo tu e allora me lo dai e lo dico io. E poi 'tum'. Te lo do e lo dice lui, eh? Cosi portiamo l'acqua per fare il castèllo di sàbbia.

(Hey, what if me mix it with dirt and make a sandcastle? You get water with that. And when you have to wee-wee you tell – you tell the teacher and she lets you do it. And since you can't always be the one asking, you give it to me and I'll ask. And then 'tum'. I give it to you, and then he asks, OK? (Points to another child, Tony.) This way we get water to make a sandcastle.)

F–R: Eh?

R–F: Dai, vai a dire che c'hai la pipi.

(Come on, go and say that you have to wee-wee.)

F–R: Eh no, adesso no.

(Oh no, not now.)

In this example Roberto's seeing Felice playing with a forbidden object results in his concoction of a highly elaborate scheme to make sandcastles. The idea is not very practical since it would require a great deal of water to make enough sand to carry out the plan. However, Roberto carefully develops his scheme, whispering at times to create a sense of intrigue. Roberto's plan also clearly anticipates the possibility that the teachers might catch on ('since you can't always be the one asking' to go to the toilet), and, therefore, includes the devious participation of himself and another child, Tony, who was playing nearby. Finally, the plan involves Felice's giving up the toy container to Roberto, who would then have ample time to inspect and play with it when he goes inside to get the water. From the video it was clear that Felice was tempted by the scheme, but the requirement of giving up the container to Roberto may have led him to decide against participation.

This example displays nicely the intertwining of group and individual interests in the peer culture. It also displays the children's detailed knowledge of organisational features of the nursery school (i.e., 'working the system' by obtaining the water during a ratified trip to the toilet, taking turns at asking permission to go to the toilet so as not to arouse the teachers' suspicions, etc.) and the complexity of negotiations in the underlife. Finally, this example illustrates the importance of the micro-ethnographic method in uncovering the existence of this and other features of peer culture.

Towards a reproduction of adult social representations

So far in this chapter I have described children's routine resistance of adult rules in the nursery school and discussed the importance of such resistance in the peer culture. I have suggested that the children's collective construction of an 'underlife' (composed of a wide range of complex secondary adjustments) demonstrates their intricate knowledge of organisational features of the nursery school. However, I have said little about how children's creation and participation in peer culture (of which the 'underlife' is but one aspect) affects their acquisition or appropriation of adult social representations of norms or rules.

In line with the interpretive approach to socialisation described earlier, children's development of social representations of adult rules can be seen as a productive–reproductive process. Children are exposed to the existence of school rules directly by teachers. The children, then, through innovative secondary adjustments, infuse meaning in the rules in line with their own productive peer culture. As a result of these activities in the peer culture the children's social representation of the adult rules have changed. The children no longer see the adult rules simply as arbitrary restrictions of their behaviour; the social organisational complexity of the rules become more apparent.

Some specific examples can help to illustrate these theoretical claims. Consider the rule that prohibits children from bringing personal objects to school. As I noted above, the children get around this rule by bringing small objects that they can easily conceal. However, they are not satisfied with simply 'breaking the rule' by having the objects at school. It is important that the violation and secondary adjustment to the rule be shared with other children. In this way the individual child's reaction to and attempt to make sense of the adult rule becomes (to use Moscovici's term) anchored in the collective security of the peer culture. However, once anchored in this way the social representation is now also objectified (again Moscovici's term) in activities in the peer culture, shared activities that are subject to the practical constraints of interpersonal interaction.

We noted earlier that the teachers are aware of the children's secondary adjustment to the rule regarding personal objects. The teachers overlook these violations because the nature of the secondary adjustment often eliminates the organisational need to enforce the rule. The children share and play with smuggled personal objects surreptitiously to avoid detection by the teachers. If the children always played with personal objects in this fashion, there would be no conflict and hence no need for the rule. Thus, in an indirect way the secondary adjustment endorses the organisational need for the rule.

The children become aware of this complexity of the relation between rule and secondary adjustment when conflict over the use of smuggled objects inevitably arises. For example, a girl, Luisa, brought a small plastic replica of Superman to the *scuola materna* in her pocket. At one point she showed the toy to a boy, Franco, with whom she was trying to cultivate a special

23

friendship. Franco was very impressed and the two children played together in the outside yard, passing Superman back and forth without incident for over half an hour. However, at one point, Luisa complained that Franco was getting Superman dirty, keeping the toy in his possession too long, and not sharing properly. Franco dismissed these complaints and continued to play with the toy.

Luisa now found herself in a quandary. She knew that if she reported Franco's refusal to share to the teachers, she herself would be reprimanded for bringing the toy to school in the first place. Therefore, Luisa waited patiently until Franco returned the toy to her. She then placed it back in her pocket and said that Franco could not play with it any more. Franco protested, but, like Luisa, he realised that he could not go to the teachers. Resigned to the circumstances, he went off to play with some other boys, leaving Luisa alone with her Superman.

We see that the very anchoring of developing social representations in the security of the peer culture enables their objectification and use in interaction. This objectification in turn often results in interpersonal conflicts whose resolution leads to further social representation. The productive–reproductive nature of the process is apparent.

The process was also present in the children's secondary adjustment to other school rules. We saw earlier in the example of 'Arriva la banca!' that the children were able to create an activity where the normal restriction of play with a potentially dangerous object was relaxed. That is, the creative use of the plastic carton as the key aspect of the innovative 'travelling bank' temporarily suspended its threat to the general welfare of the children. However, once a struggle over the carton occurred, its potential danger reappeared and the teacher reasserted the rule without protest from the children. This example is also interesting because it illustrates the children's exposure to the sometimes 'fuzzy' boundaries of moral and conventional rules (cf. Shweder, Mahapatra and Miller, 1987; Turiel and Smentana, 1984).

It was also clear in the analysis of secondary adjustments that organisational features of children's social lives can be quite complex. Given particular features of a given social situation the children find that adults may react differently to their secondary adjustments. We saw, for example that in some cases the teachers ignored obvious secondary adjustments to school rules (for instance, the rule regarding bringing personal items to school), while in others the teachers actually encouraged the children to play with an object that had been previously forbidden (the 'travelling bank' example). These examples display the complexity of culture contact between adult and child worlds.

In a sense the teachers themselves appear to be engaged in a kind of secondary adjustment to their own rules. The teachers are aware of and see positive functions in certain elements of the peer culture. For example, the travelling bank involved developmentally constructive activity (counting, co-operation, etc.) from the teachers' point of view and was, therefore, encouraged for some time despite the use of restricted material. However, the teachers' tolerance seemed to be reached when this particular secondary adjustment threatened the general order which they wished to maintain.

It would seem, then, that the analysis of children's secondary adjustments not only illustrates a great deal about children's representations of adult rules, but also reveals the existence of adult representations of children's peer cultures. Although such adult representations are not the focus of this chapter, they do seem to impinge on children's secondary adjustments in two ways. First, teachers' enforcement of their rules is moderated by their recognition of the importance of peer culture so that they give some scope to children for the elaboration of secondary adjustments. Secondly, the ambiguities of teachers' rule systems allow children to circumvent some rules (for example, to use the plastic carton as a bank) by exploiting others (engaging in constructive activities from the teachers' point of view).

We see, then, that in the course of these and other secondary adjustments the children are learning a basic feature of all rules. Knowledge of the content of a rule is never sufficient for its application; rules must be applied and interpreted in social context (see Wootton, 1986). In this sense children's social representation of adult rules does not involve simply thinking (or cognition) about social life; rather it involves children's psychological activities in their social lives (see Duveen and Lloyd, Ch. 1 in this volume).

Children's social representation of adult rules and culture is initially, in line with Vygotsky (1978), always a collective process. Social representations become psychologically active for individual children as a result of their reconstruction of prior shared cultural experiences with adults and peers. To understand fully children's ontogenesis of social representations it is necessary for researchers to be willing to enter children's worlds and peer cultures.

References

Bruner, J. S. (1986). *Actual Minds, Possible Worlds*. Cambridge, Mass.: Harvard University Press.

Cicourel, A. (1974). *Cognitive Sociology*. New York: Free Press.

Cook-Gumperz, J. and Corsaro, W. (1986). Introduction to J. Cook-Gumperz, W. Corsaro and J. Streeck (eds.), *Children's Worlds and Children's Language*. Berlin: Mouton.

Corsaro, W. (1981). Entering the child's world: research strategies for field entry and data collection in a preschool setting. In J. Green and C. Wallat (eds.), *Ethnography and Language in Educational Settings*. Norwood, N.J.: Ablex.

(1985). *Friendship and Peer Culture in the Early Years*. Norwood, N.J.: Ablex.

(1988). Routines in the peer culture of American and Italian nursery school children. *Sociology of Education*, 61, 1–14.

Corsaro, W. and Rizzo, T. (1988). *Discussione* and friendship: socialization processes in the peer culture of Italian nursery school children. *American Sociological Review*, 53, 879–94.

Garvey, C. (1977). *Play*. Cambridge, Mass.: Harvard University Press.

Giddens, A. (1984). *The Constitution of Society*. Cambridge: Polity Press.

Goffman, E. (1961). *Asylums*. Garden City, N.Y.: Anchor.

(1974). *Frame Analysis*. New York: Harper & Row.

Harré, R. (1986). The step to social constructionism. In M. Richards and P. Light (eds.), *Children of Social Worlds: Development in a Social Context*. Cambridge, Mass.: Harvard University Press.

Moscovici, S. (1981). On social representations. In J. Forgas (ed.), *Social Cognition*. London: Academic Press.

Ochs, E. (1982). Talking to children in Western Samoa. *Language in Society*, 11, 77–104.

Piaget, J. (1968). *Six Psychological Studies*. New York: Vintage.

Saraceno, C. (1984). The social construction of childhood: child care and education policies in Italy and the United States. *Social Problems*, 31, 353–63.

Schieffelin, B. (1986). Teasing and shaming in Kalui children's interactions. In B. Schieffelin and E. Ochs (eds.), *Language and Socialization across Cultures*. New York: Cambridge University Press.

Selman, R. (1980). *The Growth of Interpersonal Understanding*. New York: Academic Press.

Shweder, R., Mahapatra, M. and Miller, J. (1987). Culture and moral development. In J. Kagan and S. Lamb (eds.), *The Emergence of Morality in Young Children*. Chicago: University of Chicago Press.

Turiel, E. and Smentana, J. G. (1984). Social knowledge and action: the coordination of domains. In W. M. Kurtines and J. L. Gewirtz (eds.), *Morality, Moral Behaviour, and Moral Development*. New York: Wiley.

Vygotsky, L. S. (1978). *Mind in Society*. Cambridge, Mass.: Harvard University Press.

Wootton, A. (1986). Rules in action: orderly gestures of actions that formulate rules. In J. Cook-Gumperz, W. Corsaro and J. Streeck (eds.), *Children's Worlds and Children's Language*. Berlin: Mouton.

Youniss, J. (1980). *Parents and Peers in Social Development: A Sullivan–Piaget Perspective*. Chicago: University of Chicago Press.

3

A semiotic analysis of the development of social representations of gender[1]

Barbara Lloyd and Gerard Duveen

In this chapter gender is analysed as a semiotic system in which particular values, ideas and practices are associated with the designations 'female' and 'male'. These categories provide the framework for marking a range of material elements, personal dispositions and behavioural styles. These elements, dispositions and styles are in turn comprehended as signifiers of gender and provide the resources which individuals employ to express a social gender identity.

Sign systems function as a means of communication for social groups, and their operation is dependent on the intersubjectively shared representations of group members. In this sense sign systems can be seen as an expression of social representations. We have used the concept of social representations to explore social psychological aspects of gender (Lloyd, 1987; Lloyd and Duveen, 1989). In this chapter a detailed consideration of the nature of semiotic relations provides the framework for a discussion of developmental changes in the construction of social gender identities through a re-examination of material from studies of young children's gender knowledge.

Developmental semiotics

When someone describes a doll as a toy for girls, or a gun as a toy for boys, they are not describing characteristics which are physically inscribed in these toys, but the social markings of these objects. Mugny, De Paolis and Carugati have observed that social marking 'connects relations of a cognitive order

[1] The support of the Economic and Social Research Council (ESRC) is gratefully acknowledged. The work was funded by ESRC award No. C00232113 to Dr Lloyd. Caroline Smith and Adrienne Hirschfeld also worked on this project, and we are grateful to them for their contributions. We should also like to thank John Archer, Lisa Catan, Serge Moscovici and Paola De Paolis for their comments on an earlier draft.

with those of a social order' (1984, p. 137). This connection arises through the use of the same social representation to mark objects as well as to structure the cognitive processes required to comprehend the markings. Thus one can say that, on the one hand, social representations of gender are objectified in the markings of toys as suitable for girls or for boys; while, on the other hand, the comprehension of these markings is made possible through social representations of gender. These are really two sides of the same coin. Social representations establish a common semiotic code for both the marking of objects and the mediation of cognitive processes, and thus provide the connection between the social order and the cognitive order.

The relationship between social representations and social marking emphasises the fact that social representation always involves processes of signification. While the semiotic character of social representations has long been recognised in theoretical accounts (Moscovici, 1976; Jodelet, 1984), analyses of social representations have stressed the processes of anchoring and objectification rather than the nature of signification. For adults and older children this issue may be relatively unimportant, since it can be assumed that they have developed all the cognitive instruments necessary for handling different types of signification (signals, symbols, signs). But in early childhood this assumption cannot be made, since these cognitive instruments develop through the first years of childhood. Indeed, distinguishing between types of semiotic relations is essential for a developmental analysis of the genesis of representation (Piaget, 1951; Wallon, 1970).

From both developmental (or genetic) and semiotic points of view it is necessary to distinguish between signification and representation. As Piaget and Wallon, among others (cf. Barthes, 1967), make clear, not all semiotic relations imply mental representation. The emergence of a capacity for mental representation is the most important cognitive development in early childhood since it frees the child's activity from the constraints of the here and now. The development of the cognitive instruments which make representation possible always occurs within particular contexts. The tradition of cognitive-developmental psychology has insisted on a distinction between process and content in cognitive functioning as the basis for analysing the development of representation. A developmental analysis of semiotic processes provides a perspective for considering the genesis of processes of representation in the context of the social representations of the community into which the child is developing.

It was Ferdinand de Saussure who first suggested the prospect of a general semiology which would be 'a science that studies the life of signs within society' and which 'would be a part of social psychology' (Saussure, 1974, p. 16). In his *Course in General Linguistics* Saussure also recognised other forms of signification apart from signs, and the genetic psychologies of Piaget and Wallon elaborate his work to take account of other ways in which signifiers are related to signifieds. When the field of semiotics is construed as pertaining to all types of relations between signifiers and signifieds there is a problem of terminology, since different authors demarcate the field in different ways (cf. Barthes, 1967). We propose to use three terms (signal, symbol, sign) to mark two distinctions between types of semiotic relations. First, we distinguish semiotic relations in which signifiers and signifieds are undifferentiated (signals) from those where they are differentiated (symbols and signs); and, secondly, within the class of differentiated signifiers we distinguish those in which the relation of signifier to signified is motivated (symbol) from those in which there is an 'arbitrary' relation between signifier and signified (sign). These distinctions correspond to the major divisions in the genetic psychologies of Piaget (1951) and Wallon (1970).

Signification is undifferentiated when there is an immediate relation between signifier and signified. In Piaget's words a signifier 'is not differentiated from its *signifié* [signified]...in that it constitutes a part, an aspect or a causal result of that *signifié*' (Piaget, 1970, p. 53). Thus a signal may be a part which signifies a whole, as in the case of the branches of a tree overhanging a fence which signify the presence of the remainder of the tree occluded by the fence. An example from psychology is the conditioned stimulus which comes to signify (elicit) the appropriate response in Pavlovian conditioning. This last example illustrates an important psychological characteristic of signals: they are always embedded within the context of the subject's immediate field of practical action. In Piaget's terms signals correspond to the sensorimotor level of psychological organisation; a signal is recognised when it is assimilated to a scheme of action, and this knowledge is realised in the execution of the scheme. Thus, in sensorimotor signification the signal signifies a scheme, and the lack of differentiation between signifier and signified procedures the immediate engagement of the scheme. An adult's finger or a pencil may signal the scheme of grasping for an infant, and once recognised as a signal, the grasping follows immediately.

'Representation', Piaget writes, 'begins when there is simultaneous differentiation and co-ordination between signifiers and signifieds' (Piaget, 1951, p. 3). The immediacy characterising the relations between sensory event and action is broken in differentiated signification. Events can be assimilated to 'internal schemes' or concepts; the child can know an object as a finger or a pencil without having to act out this knowledge. Equally, past events can be evoked through internal signifiers (images). One object can now be used as an external signifier, to signify another object. But, as Piaget makes clear, one thing can signify another only on the grounds that it can be assimilated

29

to the same operatory structures. For a child to use a pencil to signify an aeroplane, for instance, they must be able to assimilate the pencil to the concept 'aeroplane'. Here the pencil becomes a symbol for the aeroplane. In symbols there is always a *motivated* relationship between signifier and signified, which in this case is the analogy of shape between the pencil as signifier and the aeroplane as signified. The motivation relating a symbolic signifier to its signified is always some knowledge held by the subject. While this knowledge may be publicly accessible, the characteristic of symbolic signification is that the motivated relationships between signifiers and signifieds are not regulated by a public or conventional semiotic code, but remain private and personal.

The third category of semiotic relations we consider is signs, where signifier and signified have what Saussure described as a purely arbitrary relation to one another. For Saussure the signifier in a linguistic sign is a 'sound-image' and the signified a 'concept', and, thus, between the signifier 'tree' and the concept 'tree' which is signified there is no necessary relationship. Saussure's use of the term 'arbitrary' to describe the relations between signifier and signified in signs has been questioned by Benveniste (1971). For both authors, however, what is central to this relationship is that in signs there is no inherent or necessary link between signifier and signified. For Saussure the term 'arbitrary' indicates this lack of necessity and, the sound-image 'tree' signifies the concept 'tree', but any other sound-image could have been used to signify the concept 'tree'. However, once the association between the sound-image 'tree' and the concept 'tree' becomes fixed in the collective communicative practices of a community the relationship of sound-image to concept loses its arbitrary nature (as Barthes, 1967, points out, no individual member of the community is free to modify this relationship). It was for such reasons that Benveniste preferred the term 'unmotivated' to 'arbitrary'.

This issue becomes clearer when derivative and associated words are considered, such as 'pear-tree', 'apple-tree', 'family tree', where the element 'tree' is *necessary* for the construction of these compound forms. In such words it is no longer possible to speak of a purely arbitrary relationship between signifier and signified. Lévi-Strauss gives the clearest expression of this problem when he notes that 'the linguistic sign is arbitrary a priori, but ceases to be arbitrary a posteriori' (Lévi-Strauss, 1972, p. 91). Thus, we can say that while there is no necessary connection between the sound-image 'tree' and the concept 'tree' *a priori*, communicative practices establish a necessary connection *a posteriori*. Or, to return to the example of the gender marking of toys, there is no *a priori* necessity associating girls with dolls or boys with guns, but social representations of gender establish a necessary association *a posteriori*. One function of social representations is to transform the arbitrary into the consensual, thereby facilitating communication.

Since the conventions of a community create the necessary relations between signifiers and signifieds in signs, these semiotic relations are always public and communicable. A second characteristic of signs follows upon the conventionality of the relations between signifiers and signifieds. Signs do not have meaning when taken singly in isolation, but only in so far as they can be differentiated from other signs. As Saussure puts it, 'in language there are only differences *without positive terms*' (Saussure, 1974, p. 120; italics in the original). Signs, therefore, always appear in systems in which conventions regulate the relations between signifiers and signifieds. Language is the usual example of a system of signs capable of expressing ideas, but other systems have also been considered as signs, such as the food system or the fashion system (see for example Barthes, 1967), and, for our studies, toys.

These types of semiotic relations describe three ways in which signifiers relate to signifieds. It is possible for the same signifier to be comprehended through each type of relation. The sound of a bell, for instance, may function as a signal in Pavlovian conditioning. It may also function as a signal for an infant when it is assimilated to a scheme, or some co-ordination of schemes, as when the infant attends to the sound of the bell, or turns to look at the source of the sound. As a symbol, the sound of a bell may evoke any number of memories for a person, memories which would be motivated by their personal history (cf. Proust, 1981). As a sign the sound of different bells may be associated with different conventional meanings – a telephone bell, a door bell, etc.

The two modes of differentiated signification, symbols and signs, are distinct from undifferentiated signals in that they are no longer completely embedded in the context of the subject's field of practical action. Both symbols and signs pertain to the field of representation and, from a developmental point of view, demand a higher level of psychological organisation than the sensorimotor co-ordinations appropriate for signals. While there is a developmental process involved in the passage from undifferentiated to differentiated signification both Piaget and Wallon note that the use of signs and symbols emerges contemporaneously in the child. It is not possible, therefore, to mark any developmental difference in the psychological organisation required for symbol or sign use (cf. Furth, 1981); both depend on the same cognitive instruments. Our interest lies in the development of sign functioning in children, and we have little to say about the development of privately motivated symbol usage.

We can now consider the framework which this developmental semiotics provides for an analysis of the development of social representations. Social representations establish systematic social markings of objects, events and activities, markings which function as signs. In the field of gender, for instance, not only is the material culture marked in this way, but so are behavioural styles as well as other aspects of social interaction. As a semiotic field, therefore, social representations of gender encompass a wide range of linguistic and non-linguistic signifiers. The development of social representations of gender provides children with the resources both to comprehend these diverse signifiers as signs of gender and to produce signs of gender in their interactions and communications with others.

Our semiotic approach highlights two issues for an analysis of the development of social representations of gender. The first is the need to distinguish between undifferentiated (signal) and differentiated (sign) signification in children's activity. One criterion for doing so follows from the characteristics of signals described above, namely that signals always elicit responses from children. So long as signification remains undifferentiated children are not independently active in the field of gender, but reactive to events and the activities of others. Actively marking gender rather than reacting to gender markings is an indication of differentiated signification.

The second issue concerns the use of signs *per se*. The development of differentiated signification corresponds to the progressive internalisation of social representations. However, the emergence of differentiated signification is not a sudden, all or nothing event, but a gradual process. Initially differentiated signification remains tied to particular contexts of activity, and only later becomes independent of context (a process which Vygotsky refers to as the decontextualisation of semiotic means (cf. Wertsch, 1985)). It is to be expected, therefore, that differentiated signification will emerge first of all in contexts which offer the child some scaffolding (Wood, Bruner and Ross, 1976). An ability to use signs independently of context is a later development.

Evidence of sign use in children's activity corresponds, therefore, to evidence for children's internalisation of the social representations of their community. Empirically the development of a social representation can be traced through an analysis of children's capacity to use signs in accordance with the conventions of their community. It should be possible to analyse first the emergence of children as semiotic actors capable of differentiated rather than undifferentiated signification, and, secondly, the range of signifiers which children comprehend as signs in different contexts.

In the research presented in the following section two kinds of studies are reviewed. First, there are studies of the interactions between very young children and mothers examining the emergence of children as semiotic actors in the field of gender. Secondly, there are studies of children aged eighteen to forty-eight months which examine the development of gender signification in a variety of contexts. In both cases the focus for the research is not so much on the meanings which are signified through social representations as on the processes through which signification is achieved. In these investigations the gender meanings current in the child's community have been determined independently of the observations of the child's action, and, subsequently, these consensual gender meanings have been employed as independent variables in analyses of the development of children's ability to control the signification of these meanings.

Developmental changes in semiotic fields of gender

Entering the gender system

Infants are born into a world where there is already a highly structured semiotic field, defined in terms of their society's social representations of gender. The initial contribution of the infant to the process of gender signification is limited to the presence of biological characteristics, usually external genitalia, which function *for others* in the community as signifiers of membership in a gender category, female or male. The clarity of genitals and the verbal labels 'girl'/'boy' as signs of gender is attested by the different descriptions of female and male infants given by parents on initially viewing their first borns, even when there are no differences in birth weight, birth length or apgar scores (Rubin et al., 1974). Newborns may function as signifiers for others, but gender is not yet meaningful to them as actors.

We have observed the behaviour of women, themselves mothers of first borns between the ages of four and a half and eight months of age, for evidence that the dress and name of infants function as signs of gender (Smith and Lloyd, 1978; Smith, 1982). Specifically, thirty-two women were video-recorded as they played for ten minutes with an unfamiliar six-month-old infant. Half the time the infant was presented wearing a ruffled dress and socks and called Jane and the other half wearing a blue terry 'baby gro' and called John. The 'gender' of the infant was independently manipulated so that half the women interacted with a child whose gender was congruent with their overt dress and name, while the other half were presented with a cross-dressed and cross-named infant. Four different infants (two boys and two girls) were used in this study, and despite our imposition of gender-marked dress and names no differences were observed in their behaviour. At this age children are not yet active in the semiotic field of gender.

Our experimental design allowed us to explore a hypothesis about the chain of signification. Dress and name are presented as signs of gender. In its turn gender signifies differentiated patterns of activity as appropriate to female and male infants, and it is these patterns which can be identified in the observations of mothers. Furthermore, in pilot work we had asked members of the general public to choose, from an array, a toy suitable for a six-month-old girl or boy. In other words we were asking adults which toys signify femaleness and maleness.

The women who played with one of our infants had access to a selection of toys identified in terms of gender signification (two female-marked toys, two male-marked toys and two deemed to be neutral). There was a clear link between the gender marking of those objects and the gender signified by the dress and name of the infants. Regardless of the biological sex of the infant, when the child was presented as a girl women were likely to offer it the doll, but when the same infant was presented with male dress and name, the hammer or rattle was offered first. Across the ten-minute observation period women's use of toys was moderated by the infants' interest. The length of time each of the toys was used by the women was not differentiated according to the gender marking of the object or the assigned gender of the infant. Although these toys signify gender for adults, infant interest in them offers no evidence that they signify gender for six-month-old infants.

The importance of dress and name in signifying gender can also be seen in women's responses to infant activity. By itself gross motor behaviour provides no means for distinguishing between female and male infants; it is a feature of the behavioural repertoire of human infants. But the social representations of gender evoked by the categorisation of the infant as female or male enables gross motor behaviour to be comprehended as a sign of gender. When dress and name signified maleness women offered verbal encouragement to the infant's gross motor activity and responded themselves with further motor stimulation. Yet the gross motor activity of the same infant whose dress and name signified femaleness elicited soothing and calming.

At six months we have no evidence that infants are actors in the semiotic field of gender. Studies of thirteen-month-olds provide some of the earliest evidence that children have entered the semiotic field of gender as actors. Goldberg and Lewis (1969) reported that thirteen-month-olds showed a gender-marked toy preference: girls spent significantly more time playing with blocks, a peg board and two toys with faces, and their play was characterised by its sedentary nature and fine motor manipulative behaviour. Boys were more vigorous in their play, banging toys more than girls. These findings present some of the earliest evidence of differentiations between boys and girls, and point to the beginnings of the internalisation of gender as a system of signs.

Two partial replications were undertaken in our laboratory, but they yielded little evidence of any systematic toy preference which might indicate that toys functioned as signs for these children. The mallet was used more by thirteen-month-old boys, but only in the first study (Smith, 1982). These studies did, however, provide evidence of gender differences in styles of play. In both studies boys engaged in significantly more gross motor activity such as banging, shaking, throwing and pushing. There was a trend for girls to engage in more manipulative play, fitting, placing and handling objects, but we are dealing here with phenomena of different magnitude. Gross motor play was five times as frequent as manipulative activity. Both girls and boys played with the mallet, but boys spent a significantly greater proportion of their time banging it. Object and action are not yet differentiated for these children, just as signifier and signified are not yet differentiated in the signal.

In a second study in this series with thirteen-month-olds, mothers were asked to play with their children for ten minutes after the children had played on their own. The entry of mothers sharpened the marking of gender in their children's activity; the gross motor activity of boys increased significantly. The manipulative play of girls also increased, although this effect was not statistically significant.[2]

At thirteen months children are beginning to mark their activity in a manner congruent with membership of a gender category. The importance of adults in structuring the semiotic field of gender is seen in the increased symmetry between social category membership and behavioural style in the presence of mother. At thirteen months there is little evidence that material culture, toys alone, function as signs of gender for young children; activity and object are just beginning to emerge as signs of gender. The presence of an *adult other* strengthens the signifying chain, though we found no obvious evidence that these mothers responded in a gender-differentiated manner to the gross motor play of their own thirteen-month-old infants (this contrasts with the more stereotypic behaviour of women interacting with unfamiliar six-month-olds reported in the earlier study). Nonetheless, the increase in children's behaviour in a gender-marked direction suggests that mothers are in some way amplifying the gender markings available to children, so that interaction between mother and child is an important vehicle for the internalisation of social representations of gender.

[2] A recent review and meta-analysis has demonstrated differences in the activity levels of boys and girls at this age (Eaton and Enns, 1986). Such differences do not, however, provide a sufficient explanation for our observations. The differences we found pertain to the style of activity, and it is the different styles of activity which are amplified by the mother's presence rather than simply the level of activity.

Participating in the gender system

By the middle of the second year, with the developing use of language, children begin to make rapid progress in the internalisation of gender as a system of signs. In two studies of children aged one and a half to four years we investigated the developing participation of children in the semiotic field of gender. As actors they become increasingly able to co-ordinate both the production and comprehension of signs to signify their membership in a gender category and to respond to others as gendered members of society. In the account which follows we examine the development of different modalities of gender regulation. These include play, language and problem solving. In our first study 120 children aged one and a half to three and a half years were tested individually and observed playing with a familiar peer. Forty children between three and four years were studied intensively in the second.

Children were observed playing in an experimental room supplied with toys chosen to reflect parental ratings for gender (Lloyd and Smith, 1985). Video-records of these sessions were analysed along a number of dimensions. In the first study the children were observed in pairs, either two girls, two boys or a mixed gender pair. In the second study each of the designated actor children played with a same gender partner and a partner of the other gender. Results relevant to gender signification are presented and focus on children's active participation in the gender system.

Duration of play with each toy was coded for each child directly from the video record using a computer-assisted, video-linked keyboard which functioned as a multi-channel event recorder (Smith et al., 1982). In the first study the analysis of duration measures is based upon pair data, i.e. the separately coded scores for each child in a pair added together. These combined scores for play with feminine and masculine toys (Toy Type) were used as the within subjects variable in an analysis of variance with Age and Pair Type as between subjects variables (details of this analysis are reported in Lloyd and Duveen, 1989). A main effect suggesting that masculine toys were preferred by all the children just failed to satisfy conventional levels of statistical inference ($P = 0.053$). The situation was clarified, however, by the highly significant Pair Type by Toy Type interaction which showed that the preference for masculine toys reflected the choices of boys. Boy/boy pairs used masculine toys more than feminine toys and used masculine toys more than girl/girl pairs. A significant three-way interaction involving Age as well as Pair Type and Toy Type suggested that this pattern of preferences was strongest in the older children (two and a half to three and a half years). This provides the clearest evidence for the emergence of children as independent semiotic actors, a development which occurs at about two and a half years.

In the second study only the action play of actor children playing with both a boy and a girl was coded. This design made it possible to differentiate between the effects due to the gender of actors and that of their partners. Duration scores were analysed in a four-way analysis of variance which included Age and Actor's Gender as between subjects variables, and Partner's Gender and Toy Type as within subjects variables. Toy Type was the only significant main effect (F = 59·39; df = 1,36; P < 0·001) and indicated that boys' toys (mean = 408·3 seconds) were played with more than girls' toys (mean = 128·3 seconds). The highly significant Actor's Gender by Toy Type interaction (F = 32·87; df = 1,36; P < 0·001) showed that the difference in toy use arose primarily through a discrimination made by boys, but not by girls. Comparisons between pairs of means showed that boys used boys' toys (mean = 534·8 seconds) significantly more than girls' toys (mean = 46·5 seconds), but that there was no significant difference between girls' use of girls' toys (mean = 210·1 seconds) and boys' toys (mean = 281·8 seconds).

The results of both studies lead to the conclusion that girls and boys use toys differently. Boys use toys to signify their gender category membership by concentrating their activity on boys' toys and avoiding girls' toys; their orientation towards play with toys is to emphasise the differentiation between toys marked for gender. Girls' orientation towards play with toys, however, is not to differentiate between toys in terms of their gender markings.

Duration is a crude measure in the sense that our coding functions so that once children engage with a toy the count begins, and only ceases when the activity stops. In order to reflect children's choice of toy more directly we calculated the number of toy choices made by each child which were congruent with their gender (*paradigmatic* choices) and the number where the choice of toy was incongruent with their own gender (*syntagmatic* choices; a similar distinction was made by Catherine Garvey (1977) in her analysis of the elements of ritual in young children's play).

Toy choice in the first study was analysed by using the number of paradigmatic and syntagmatic choices as the dependent variable in an analysis of variance with Actor's Gender, Partner's Gender and Age as the independent variables. Main effects for both Age (F = 5·99; df = 3, 104; P < 0·001) and for Choice Type (F = 9·01; df = 1, 104; P < 0·01) were significant. The Age effect reflects developmental changes in play and indicates that the number of toy choices made by children increased with age. The Choice Type main effect indicates that paradigmatic choices are more frequent than syntagmatic and is best interpreted in terms of the Actor's Gender by Partner's Gender by Choice Type interaction which was highly significant (F = 11·14; df = 1,104; P < 0·001). This interaction is illustrated in Figure 3.1. The mean comparisons which achieve significance lend further support to the

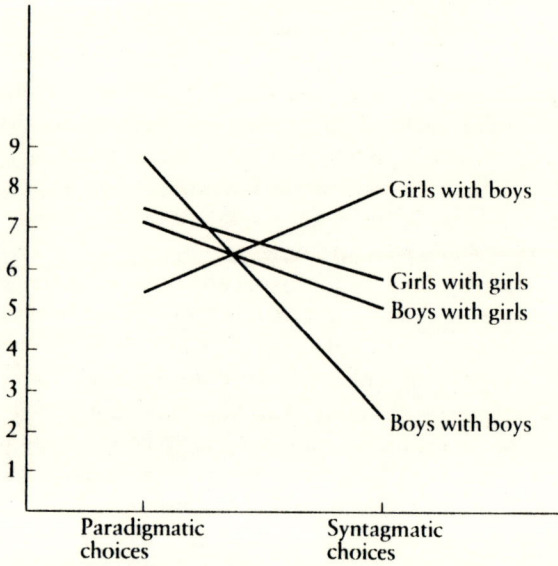

Figure 3.1 Toy choice by gender by partner's gender interaction (first study)

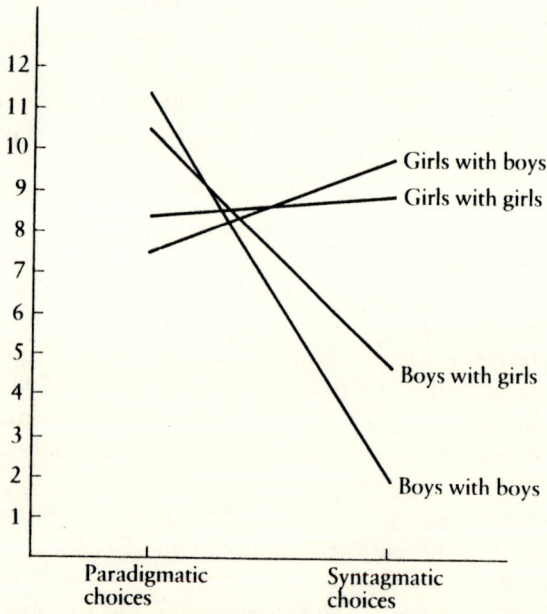

Figure 3.2 Toy choice by gender by partner's gender interaction (second study)

picture which emerged from the analysis of duration measures. The orientation of Actor boys is one of differentiation; playing with boy partners they make more paradigmatic than syntagmatic choices, and playing with girl partners they make fewer syntagmatic choices than their partners. These results reproduce the duration results which indicated that boys use gender-marked toys in a differentiating manner while girls do not mark gender in their use of toys. The three-way interaction also demonstrates that play in girl/boy pairs involves adjustment by both partners. Both girls and boys make fewer paradigmatic (own gender) choices in mixed pairs (the comparison between the means is significant for girls, though not for boys); and both boys and girls make more syntagmatic (other gender) choices in mixed pairs (comparisons between the means are significant for both boys and girls). Nonetheless, these relatively small changes do not obscure the different orientations of girls and boys in their use of toys.

Among the three- to four-year-old children in the second study paradigmatic choices were again significantly more frequent than syntagmatic choices ($F = 10\cdot10$; df $= 1, 36$; $P < 0\cdot01$). Mean comparisons based upon the highly significant Actor's Gender by Choice Type interaction ($F = 21\cdot39$; df $= 1, 36$; $P < 0\cdot001$) showed that boys maintained their differentiated orientation while girls did not employ toys to mark a differentiated identity. Mean comparisons were also undertaken in order to interpret the significant three-way interaction of Actor's Gender by Partner's Gender by Choice Type ($F = 5\cdot48$; df $= 1\cdot36$; $P < 0\cdot05$), illustrated in Figure 3.2. These parallel closely the findings from the play of younger children. Again both girls and boys make fewer paradigmatic choices in mixed pairs (though neither of these comparisons reaches a conventional level of significance) while making more syntagmatic choices in mixed pairs (mean comparisons are significant for the boys, though not for the girls). Comparison of Figure 3.1 and Figure 3.2 emphasises the similarity of the pattern of this three-way interaction between the two studies. In the second study girl actors' paradigmatic and syntagmatic choices with girls and with boys are less distinctive than in the first study. In both studies boy actors differentiate more markedly than girls between paradigmatic and syntagmatic choices.

Overall the results from both studies support the conclusion that boys use toys differentially to signify gender, while girls do not. There is also some evidence that this effect is moderated by the gender of their partner; the most consistent effect is that boys make more *syntagmatic* choices when interacting with girls than when interacting with boys.

In action play children's use of toys is embedded within the context of their practical activity. A second issue concerns children's abilities to employ toys as signs of gender in situations where their play extends beyond the use of toys in practical activity. Pretend play can be distinguished from action play because it involves the introduction of elements extrinsic to the immediate context of action, for example, saying 'This is my baby' while hugging a doll (cf. Nicolich, 1977). Units of pretend play were identified through the use of language indicative of fantasy.

The relative immaturity of these young children becomes apparent when their pretend play is assessed according to these criteria. Pretend play was too rare among the younger children in the first study for any analysis. A four-way analysis of variance with Actor's Gender and Partner's Gender as well as Age and Toy Type was carried out using the number of pretend units for the three- to four-year-olds. Although it produced two significant interactions, Actor's Gender by Age and Actor's Gender by Toy Type, the comparisons between pairs of means failed to reach conventional levels of significance. Although the pattern of toy use in pretend play echoes that observed in action play (see Lloyd and Duveen, 1989), it seems that in general young children's capacity to employ toys as signs of gender remains bound to a context of practical action.

The capacity of young children to employ signs of gender was also investigated through a series of individual linguistic and cognitive tasks which assessed their ability to control gender signification across different representational modalities. In the interviews for the linguistic tasks children were presented with a pair of photographs and a gender-marked linguistic sign (such as LADY or MAN) and asked first to match the graphic and linguistic signs (a recognition task), and second to produce an appropriate linguistic sign for the alternative photograph. Both tasks can be interpreted as evidence that the child is able to attach different signifiers to the same signified, in this case, gender. In the recognition task the child is asked to match a graphic to a linguistic sign, while in the production task the child must provide the linguistic sign.

Sorting tasks provide another way of investigating children's comprehension of chains of signification by presenting them with an array of signs within a single modality, photographs, and asking them to partition the signs according to a particular rule, for instance male here and female there. Two types of sorting tasks were used; in one, children were presented with photographs of people, and in the other, with photographs of toys.

Across the age range we studied, one and a half to four years, performance on the linguistic and sorting tasks improved with age and there was consistency in the order to task difficulty. Recognition was easiest for children of all ages followed by production and then sorting. Gender-marked nouns and pronouns were used in the recognition and production tasks; nouns were easier for children to use in signifying gender. Children found it easier to sort photographs of people according to gender than to assign photographs of toys according to gender. The performances of even the youngest children offered some evidence of gender marking. Improving performance across the range of tasks thus reflects increasing cognitive capacities as well as the increasing influence of social representations of gender.

Children under two years were able to match signs correctly in different modalities 60 per cent of the time when the linguistic signs were the gender-marked nouns – MUMMY, DADDY, LADY, MAN, GIRL, and BOY. Recognition was correct 97 per cent of the time in the three- to four-year-old groups. On the production tasks children made very few errors of gender marking, although they often failed to produce the appropriate part of speech or the precise term sought. By and large children from one and a half years of age are able to produce linguistic signs which mark gender even though their control of the linguistic system is inadequate to meet the most stringent criteria for success.

While these young children were successful in attaching different signifiers to the same signified, more so when we supplied both signs in the recognition task, they experienced considerable difficulty when required to partition an array of signs within a single modality using a particular rule. Children under two years of age were totally unable to sort into gender categories the six photographs of men and women or the six photographs of boys and girls which had been used in the linguistic tasks. By four years of age the proportion of photographs appropriately sorted had risen to 95 per cent for pictures of adults and 87·5 per cent for pictures of children.

In the toy-sorting task children were asked to assign a collection of fourteen photographs of toys whose gender markings had been established by adult judgements. The collection included seven feminine-marked toys (iron and ironing board, comb, brush and mirror set, large white hat, shopping bag, saucepans and stove top, dolls with a cradle, and a tea set), and seven masculine-marked toys (sit-and-ride fire engine, construction trucks, fireman's helmet, briefcase, pegbench with hammer, guns and a garage). Performance increased with age, although even the older children in the second study did not score much above chance levels (on average they successfully sorted 62 per cent of the time). The numbers of feminine and masculine toys sorted appropriately were used as the dependent variables in a repeated measures analysis of variance with Age and Gender as the between subjects variables. In the first study a significant main effect for Age ($F = 13.56$; df $= 3,112$; $P < 0.001$) reflected children's increasing ability to sort the toys appropriately, although the significant Age by Toy Type interaction ($F = 2.79$; df $= 3,112$; $P < 0.05$) showed that this development varied a little for feminine and masculine toys. A main effect for Toy Type ($F = 5.76$; df $= 1,112$; $P < 0.05$) indicated that masculine toys were sorted more successfully than feminine toys. However, a Gender by Toy Type interaction (F = 4·06; df = 1,112; $P < 0.05$) showed that performance differences for types of toy varied as a function of gender. Girls performed equally well for both masculine toys (mean = 3·3) and feminine toys (mean = 3·2), but boys were significantly better at sorting masculine toys (mean = 3·5) than feminine toys (mean = 2·2).

A similar analysis of toy-sorting scores from the second study yielded no main effects for any of the factors, though there was, again, a Gender by Toy Type interaction (F = 6·9; df = 1,36; $P < 0.05$). Although the mean scores suggest that girls performed slightly better with feminine toys (4·65) than with masculine toys (4·0), and that boys were slightly better at masculine toys (4·65) than feminine toys (4·1), neither of these comparisons was significant.

Overall, therefore, it appears that children's ability to respond to the gender marking of toys increases with age, and that certainly by the age of four there are few differences between the performances of boys and girls. The similarity between boys and girls in the second study is emphasised when performances on individual items are examined. Binomial tests on the numbers of children successfully sorting the photographs showed that both girls and boys performed at better than chance levels for the same feminine (shopping bag and doll) and masculine (fireman's helmet) items.

It is instructive to compare children's performances across this range of linguistic and cognitive tasks. All of these tasks present children with material in which gender is marked in a system of signs. For the linguistic tasks the marking is embedded as a feature of language, so that the use of contrasting terms (such as 'woman' and 'man' or 'girl' and 'boy') provides scaffolding for children. In the sorting tasks, however, children were provided with a target photograph of a woman/girl or man/boy, but they were not supplied with a linguistic term which might have facilitated semiotic mediation. All the children found it easier to assign photographs of people to gender categories than to assign objects on the basis of gender markings.

In developing stimuli for the people-sorting tasks a large number of photographs were rated by university students and the items which received the highest scores for womanliness, manliness, girlishness or boyishness were selected. It is likely that these photographs captured aspects of dress, posture and general presentation which embody social representations of gender. The toys were selected on the basis of parental ratings of the gender appropriateness of toys described in published studies as suitable for girls and boys. Photographs of toys offer little or no perceptual support for the social representations of gender which determine their gender marking. Without some scaffolding young children are unable to invoke the social representations available to adults. Even by the age of four, children are performing at little better than chance levels.

These results indicate that the ability of young children to control a set of semiotic relations among gender signs depends upon the context within which the activity is embedded. Where the gender markings are a tangible feature of the context itself they function as scaffolding for children and facilitate semiotic mediation. If the gender markings are not present as a feature of the context, semiotic mediation is difficult even for four-year-olds.

There were very few differences in the performance of girls and boys. It was only in the toy sorting of younger children that any differences were observed. Although the girls performed at about chance level with both feminine and masculine toys, the boys performed slightly better with the masculine toys than with the feminine toys. Even this difference between boys and girls disappeared in the second study, where the performance of both genders improved beyond chance levels.

These linguistic and cognitive results present a very different picture from the analysis of play with toys. Although we studied the same children in both contexts they are very different settings. In play children encounter the gender markings of toys in the context of practical activity, while in the interview measures the gender markings of the materials are no longer embedded in a practical context. This might suggest that performances in play would be developmentally more sophisticated than responses to interviews. Even if this were the case, however, the difference between the two settings cannot itself explain the different *patterning* of results in the two data sets.

The difference between the social identities displayed by girls and boys in their play cannot be ascribed to a difference in their knowledge of social markings. As we noted, girls and boys appear to have a similar knowledge of gender markings. Rather, it seems that the arena of toys is one in which it is imperative for boys to use their knowledge to mark a difference, but one in which girls give no evidence of marking a corresponding difference. Although we have no direct evidence bearing on this point it is difficult to ascribe girls' behaviour to the *lack* of a social identity, precisely because they are in possession of the same resources as boys in terms of their knowledge of gender marking. This suggests that girls express a social gender identity by *not* marking a difference (though there may be arenas other than toy use where girls do assert a social gender identity through differentiated activity).

Social Identities and Social Representations

The semiotic approach adopted here has helped to clarify two issues in the development of social representations. In the first place it has enabled us to distinguish between two forms of social identities, and, secondly, to describe more precisely the relations between social identities and social representations.

The distinction between signals and signs as types of signification corresponds to two kinds of knowledge associated with two forms of social identity. Signals correspond to sensorimotor, practical knowing, and a social identity which is always reactive to events. Children whose cognitive instruments only allow them to use signals are always dependent upon others for a social identity. The child's social identity is held by their community, and in this sense is always an externalised social identity. By contrast signs are always associated with internalised knowing, that is, with representation, and a social identity which can be autonomously asserted. An internalised social identity enables the child to participate as an independent actor in the social order.

As we noted earlier, both Piaget and Wallon recognised a development relation between signals and signs as forms of signification requiring qualitatively different cognitive instruments. The distinction is borne out by the analyses we have presented in the preceding section; externalised social identities associated with signals precede the emergence of internalised social identities associated with signs. In the realm of gender it is about the age of two to two and a half years that internalised social identities become visible. However, while it is possible to assert that a qualitative developmental difference exists between these two forms of social identity, this does not mean that the earlier form simply disappears, to be replaced completely by the later form. In psychological development sensorimotor co-ordinations do not vanish with the development of operatory structures. Similarly, it is likely that many of the behaviours acquired through signal use will persist after the development of the semiotic function so that aspects of externalised social identities may co-exist with internalised social identities. An individual may come to operate with a combination of both internalised and externalised elements (which would be an instance of the 'cognitive polyphasia' discussed by Moscovici, 1976).

The code relating signifiers and signifieds in sign systems is furnished by social representations. While a knowledge of this code is necessary to become an actor in the sign system, such knowledge alone is not a sufficient condition for the development of an internalised social identity. As we noted in the preceding section, while girls and boys appear to have similar knowledge of the semiotic code of gender, they use this knowledge in different ways in their play. Boys orient towards play with toys in such a way as to maximise the differentiation between masculine- and feminine-marked toys, while girls minimise this difference. On the basis of the same knowledge boys and girls adopt different positions in relation to it. Thus the expression of an internalised social identity depends upon both a knowledge of the appropriate semiotic code and the assumption of a position in relation to it.

In another paper we have argued that social identities enable people to situate themselves in relation to social representations (Duveen and Lloyd, 1986). We are now able to clarify this proposition. Social representations furnish a semiotic code, as well as marking out the positions which can be adopted towards it. In this sense the same social representations contain the material for the construction of different social identities. Distinguishing between codes and positions as components of social identities allows us to elaborate Mugny, De Paolis and Carugati's (1984) proposition concerning social marking. While social marking does indeed connect relations of a cognitive order with those of a social order, it is a connection which is mediated by social identities. In circumstances where children are only asked about their knowledge of the semiotic code of gender girls and boys display a similar competence. Investigations of activities which draw on both code and position reveal the different social identities of girls and boys, social identities which mobilise resources available within the same social representation of gender.

References

Barthes, R. (1967). *Elements of Semiology*. London: Jonathan Cape.

Benveniste, E. (1971). *Problems in General Linguistics*. Miami University Press.

Duveen, G. and Lloyd, B. (1986). The significance of social identities. *British Journal of Social Psychology*, 25, 219–30.

(1988). A note on the effects of age and gender on children's social behaviour. *British Journal of Social Psychology*, 27, 275–8.

Eaton, W. O. and Enns, L. R. (1986). Sex differences in human motor activity level. *Psychological Bulletin*, 100, 19–28.

Furth, H. (1981). *Piaget and Knowledge*. Englewood Cliffs, N.J.: Prentice-Hall.

Garvey, C. (1977). *Play*. London: Fontana.

Goldberg, S. and Lewis, M. (1969). Play behaviour in the year old infant: early sex differences. *Child Development*, 40, 21–31.

Jodelet, D. (1984). Représentation sociale: phénomènes, concept et théorie. In S. Moscovici (ed.), *Psychologie sociale*. Paris: PUF.

Lévi-Strauss, C. (1972). *Structural Anthropology*. Harmondsworth: Penguin.

Lloyd, B. (1987). Social representations of gender. In J. Bruner and H. Haste (eds.), *Making Sense: The Child's Construction of the World*. London and New York: Methuen.

Lloyd, B. and Duveen, G. (1989). The re-construction of social knowledge in the transition from sensorimotor to conceptual activity: the gender system. In A.

Gellatly, J. Sloboda and D. Rogers (eds.), *Cognition and Social Worlds.* Oxford: Oxford University Press.

Lloyd, B., Duveen, G. and Smith, C. (1988). Social representations of gender and young children's play: a replication. *British Journal of Developmental Psychology*, 6, 83–8.

Lloyd, B. and Smith, C. (1985). The social representation of gender and young children's play. *British Journal of Developmental Psychology*, 3, 65–73.

Moscovici, S. (1976). *La Psychanalyse, son image et son public.* Paris: PUF.

Mugny, G., De Paolis, P. and Carugati, F. (1984). Social regulation in cognitive development. In W. Doise and A. Palmonari (eds.), *Social Interaction in Individual Development.* Cambridge: Cambridge University Press.

Nicolich, L. M. (1977). Beyond sensorimotor intelligence: assessment of symbolic maturity through analysis of pretend play. *Merrill-Palmer Quarterly*, 23, 89–99.

Piaget, J. (1951). *Play, Dreams and Imitation in Childhood.* London: Routledge & Kegan Paul. (Original edition: 1946).

(1970). *Main Trends in Interdisciplinary Research.* London: George Allen & Unwin.

Proust, M. (1981). *The Remembrance of Things Past*, vol. 1. London: Chatto & Windus.

Rubin, J. Z., Provenzano, F. J. and Luria, Z. (1974). The eye of the beholder: parents' views on the sex of new borns. *American Journal of Orthopsychiatry*, 44, 512–19.

Saussure, F. de (1974). *Course in General Linguistics.* London: Fontana.

Smith, C. (1982). Mothers' attitudes and behaviour with babies and the development of sex-typed play. Unpublished D. Phil. thesis, University of Sussex.

Smith, C. and Lloyd, B. (1978). Maternal behaviour and perceived sex of infant: revisited. *Child Development*, 49, 1263–5.

Smith, C., Lloyd, B. and Crook, C. (1982). Instrument and software report: computer-assisted coding of videotape material. *Current Psychological Reports*, 2, 289–92.

Wallon, H. (1970). *De l'acte à la pensée.* Paris: Flammarion. (Original edition: 1942.)

Wertsch, J. (1985). *Vygotsky and the Social Formation of Mind.* Cambridge, Mass.: Harvard University Press.

Wood, D., Bruner, J. S. and Ross, G. (1976). The role of tutoring in problem solving. *Journal of Child Psychology and Psychiatry*, 17, 89–100.

4

Children's representations of social relations[1]

*Nicholas Emler, Jocelyne Ohana
and Julie Dickinson*

Introduction

How do children make sense of social relationships? How do they represent
the various transactions and exchanges that characterise the social life around
them? How does their knowledge differ from that of the adults in their
community and, perhaps the most fundamental question, what is the process
by which this social knowledge develops? It might be argued that
developmental psychology has now provided much of the answer to such
questions. In this chapter we hope to persuade you that such a conclusion
would be premature. To this end we shall argue that the theory of social
representations generates a distinctive view of the development of social
knowledge, one which is in several important respects at variance with the
prevailing cognitive constructivist interpretation of much current developmental psychology. Our argument and examples will concentrate on the
period of middle childhood, roughly from seven to thirteen years. And we will
consider the knowledge children in this period express with respect to two
specific domains: relations involving formal authority, and wage relations.

The Piagetian revolution

Until the mid 1960s, most psychology texts equated 'social development' with
'socialisation'. Socialisation was about the process by which a child is turned
into a non-disruptive, conforming member of a particular culture. There was
little serious interest in the possibility that to become an effective performer

[1] We would like to acknowledge the support of the ESRC (Great Britain) and the CNRS (France)
in the form respectively of grant Nos. I 01230013, awarded to the first author, and 95 5218,
awarded to Professor S. Moscovici, and the support of the ESRC in the form of a studentship to
the third author.

in society, the child would also need in any sense to understand how that society or any aspect of it functioned. Under Piaget's influence, this view began to change. Today there is little dispute that children do *think* about the nature of the social world they inhabit.

Though Piaget's work on intellectual development was initially regarded as having few implications for social development, from the late 1960s onwards it has been applied increasingly to the development of social knowledge. Today it seems few areas of children's social knowledge have not been examined under the researcher's microscope. But in what way does this research share in a single theoretical tradition?

Most important is the kind of explanation for children's knowledge which lies behind this research, the theory of cognitive development or equilibration. This explanation combines two fundamental assumptions about the relation between mind and experience. One is that experience presents things which be understood, in the sense of being correctly interpreted. Furth makes the following point with regard to the domain of social experience: 'Societal institutions...present themselves as objectively given, with some clear cut rules of how they work. Adults could easily recognize a list of statements relative to business, occupational roles, government or community, that express the logical framework peculiar to these institutions. To understand societal institutions means precisely to understand this framework' (Furth, 1978a, p. 120). The child's progress towards the adult psychological state can be indexed by the extent to which the child also interprets these matters 'correctly', i.e., like adults. And as Piaget has shown us, this development is a very gradual process in which the child's first interpretations are quite unadult-like and far from logical. Much research deals with the sequence in which the various elements of adult-like understanding are assembled in the child's mind.

The second assumption is that this process of assembly is self-generated. Children encounter puzzling experiences, actively try to make sense of them in terms they already understand, and in the course of this activity manage to assemble for themselves further bits of the overall picture. Given sufficient time and experience, they will spontaneously and independently arrive at the point most adults have reached. As Willem Doise (1989) has put it, the child is a kind of DIY constructor of knowledge. What possible objection could there be to this interpretation? Does it not, after all, make sense of the facts?

Children's knowledge: towards an alternative view

An obvious first objection to the above is that much human society persists without extensive correct understanding of things, and indeed that many matters – including such phenomena as economic inequality, crime, institutional arrangements, gender roles, etc. – are not of a kind that is open to a single correct interpretation (Billig, 1987). As to the process by which knowledge is assembled in children's minds, why should it not be acquired simply through active education by adults – a process of inter-generational or social transmission? The position which we believe can be appropriately described as radical cognitive constructivism, the proposition that the individual child spontaneously constructs its own mental representations of the world, involves an apparently reasonable objection to the idea of social transmission. It is that it is clearly not possible to explain all of the things an adult understands to a young child. If nothing else, this confirms the complex structure of dependencies in adult knowledge; understanding A, B and C depends on first understanding D, E and F, which in turn depends on understanding G, H and I, and so on. In this sense it seems entirely appropriate to refer to cognitive development as a constructive process: the pieces have to be put in place in a certain order, one on top of another.

But one can see that the issue is really who does the constructing? Is it largely a do-it-yourself enterprise, or does it involve construction teams drawing upon a range of skills and even prefabricated building-blocks? Radical cognitive constructivists have been more attracted to the former; many report being impressed by occasions on which a child puts pieces of information together and discovers for itself a principle that was previously beyond its comprehension (see, for example, Jahoda, 1984; Furth, 1980). But many also recognise that in this process children are often making use of socially transmitted information, available to them because they happen to inhabit one social group rather than another (Jahoda, 1984). Otherwise it would be difficult to make sense of the wealth of evidence that children do not all acquire precisely the same understandings in precisely the same order in every culture (see for example Dasen and Herron, 1981; Snarey, 1985).

What of the alternative? Our position is as follows: the construction of knowledge in the child is a social process (as is the construction of knowledge *per se*). What is assembled in the child's mind depends substantially upon the society to which that child belongs and the position that child occupies within it.

This is not to say that the child plays a passive role in the construction of knowledge. The child is an active participant in communications with others in its society. Through communication and interaction with both adults and other children the child is subject to (and exerts) social influence towards the construction of concepts shared within the social group to which it belongs. And Moscovici's (1984) theory of social representations provides a starting point from which to suggest how knowledge might be socially constructed within social collectives.

Developing the social representations perspective

In our attempts to clarify what might be distinctive about the social representations perspective, some features of the Piagetian-inspired analyses of social knowledge have come into sharper focus for us. We have begun to see more closely what the differences between these two approaches might be (see also Emler, 1987; Emler and Ohana, forthcoming). It now seems to us that these revolve around four points of emphasis, some more and some rather less obvious. Let us start with the most obvious; it is also the most fundamental.

Social influences on development

Piaget is regarded as having provided a general theory of human intellectual development, and not a story about the peculiar effects on thinking of growing up in Switzerland. Flavell and Ross comment that 'Investigators of adult cognitive processes make the working assumption that the essential features of such processes are universal and invariant within the species. They assume they are studying the way that the class of organisms called "people" comprehend, remember, make social inferences...' (1981, p. 307). Much the same could be said of contemporary cognitive constructivists; they have assumed that there are certain human universals in thought and that it is these cognitive entities their research reveals. Of necessity therefore these cannot be the products of experience in particular cultures, the results of growing up in a particular kind of society. This requirement is reflected in the theory of developmental process: development is a process of adaptation which occurs as the individual child actively reconstructs its understanding of the world. Since that world has certain invariant properties, this reconstructive process brings the child by successive steps progressively closer to an adaptive, rational, coherent and non-arbitrary understanding of reality.

Radical cognitive constructivists take two kinds of position with respect to the possibility of social influences on the development of knowledge. One is to concede that these might occur but to insist they affect only the content of knowledge, not its structure, and then to disclaim any interest in content (Furth, 1978a and 1978b; Kohlberg, 1984). The other is to argue that no social influences of any consequence have been convincingly demonstrated so far as the substance of cognitive development is concerned. Children the world over develop the same concepts – whether of number or causality, justice or property – whatever culture they inhabit and whatever position they occupy in society, and do so according to the same sequence. The only influence that culture can have is to alter the rate of development.

The theory of social representations differs radically on this central claim.

This theory proposes that knowledge, all knowledge, is socially constructed and sustained. Indeed, it takes knowledge to be a social phenomenon and not a property of individuals, manifested in social communication rather than residing in individual heads. The childhood development of knowledge is a process of socialisation in which children are introduced to ways of thinking and understanding which are current in their society. Given the weight of evidence and opinion behind constructivism this is a highly ambitious claim, one for which it would take more than this chapter to provide an adequate defence. We could list some objections to our claim which have proved to be without substance – that social influence cannot generate non-arbitrary, non-relative, rational knowledge (see Emler and Glachan, 1985); that social influence implies the individual is the passive receptacle of culture (see Moscovici, 1976); that social influence can only affect the content of knowledge, not its logical structure (see Doise and Mugny, 1984); that social influence cannot account for developmental sequence or make sense of age differences (it does not need to). But a more basic empirical test can be made: are there in fact differences in the knowledge children display which are relative to the social groups to which they belong? Later in this chapter we shall describe some instances of such differences.

Problem solving or solved problems

Radical cognitive constructivism is broadly a problem-solving model of knowledge, the roots of which can be found in Binet's theory of intelligence, if not earlier. Binet, it will be recalled, developed a practical means for assessing intelligence based on a series of problems which are presented to the child. Behind this strategy lie the ideas that the environment does indeed present us with problems and that intellectual adaptation to this environment is the construction of capacities for solving these problems more or less adequately.

Piaget's own theory of intelligence is really a perfection of Binet's basic idea with the additional insight that the repeated activity of problem solving is itself the engine that drives cognitive growth. Piaget then supposed that the same kind of analysis that he had made of the developing child's relations with the material world could be applied to relations with the social world, at least up to a point. This world likewise constantly presents the individual child with problems and puzzles; the child tries to solve these and in the process gradually transforms the capacities it has available for their solution. These are generally described as mental operations or mental representations of operations.

What kinds of problems are involved? They seem to be of two broad kinds.

51

First, there are problems that arise in social relationships from conflicts of interest. Kohlberg's (1976) research on moral reasoning development concerns problems of this kind, as does work on distributive justice concepts: how should limited resources be divided amongst multiple claimants? Here the development of social knowledge is described in terms of mental operations capable of generating solutions to particular cases (Kohlberg, 1976; Hook and Cook, 1979). Second, there are problems of social description: children are confronted with social institutions and practices much as they are confronted with natural phenomena. And just as they may try to figure out the principle of buoyancy or the laws governing relations in a balance, so also they will try to understand commercial transactions or the principles of interest and profit. Here social knowledge is described in terms of the construction of mental representations of these operations or systems of relationships (Berti and Bombi, 1988; Furth, 1980; Jahoda, 1984).

Notice what else is a part of this model: intelligence is individual problem solving. The theory of social representations differs in three respects here. First, problem solving is a group and not a purely individual activity. Second, solutions are conserved within the collective memory of the group: not all individuals have to start from scratch, re-solving for themselves each puzzle of nature and society. Third, there are few problems, whether of nature or society, that have a single rational answer and so remain decisively and uniquely solved (Billig, 1987).

What does this mean for the development of social knowledge? Most basically, we think it means that if the social environment presents children with problems to be solved, it also presents them with solutions and arguments for solutions. Different social environments can present different solutions, or different arguments, or both. This chapter will provide an example, solutions to income distributions. Thus the development of social knowledge is the development of knowledge about one's social group's stock of solutions and arguments about solutions. This does not mean that the child is simply the passive inheritor of these cognitive entities as a static body of cultural knowledge. On the contrary, these solutions are open to almost endless argument, as Billig (1987) proposes, and the child is a potential participant in that argument.

Knowledge-free versus knowledge-based judgement

Much of the social knowledge discussed by constructivists is paradoxically knowledge-free. It seems to concern problem-solving instruments which operate in the absence of any knowledge about the world except what is immediately observable in the problems to which they are applied. Problem-solvers do not bring with them to new cases any beliefs, implicit or explicit, about the nature of society or its occupants; they bring only a set of mental operations to be applied to the facts of each case.

Let us take a well-documented example. Children judge the culpability of others in terms either of the consequences or the intentions of their actions (Piaget, 1932). The more advanced or sophisticated mental operation is that which weighs intentions rather than consequences. Constructivism treats this kind of moral judgement as a knowledge-free process. Moral judgements involve processing the direct factual evidence of specific cases in accordance with abstract internal principles. Social representations theory assumes that this evidence is also normally processed in terms of knowledge or beliefs that are social in origin. That is, when children or adults make real-life judgements, these invoke or derive from all kinds of beliefs about the people involved. Moral judgements, in other words, are a function of the social representations which people bring with them to each specific case. Two examples examined later in this chapter are the judgements children make of teachers' actions and the judgements they make about income differences.

Agent and object perspectives of the knower

Finally, it seemed to us that constructivists have generally defined knowledge from the perspective of 'knower as doer'. The environment known about is one the actor does things to. Piaget himself was quite explicit about this: knowledge is action; to know something is to include it in a system of action. Hence, the world that is known is the world capable of being acted upon. At the same time it is a relatively inanimate, inert environment that is known in this way. It is an environment of puzzles indifferent to the child's presence within it.

Although the social environment is self-evidently not inert, something of the same emphasis has been carried over into the analysis of social knowledge development. In particular, the perspective of knower as doer remains pre-eminent. And so social knowledge is knowing how to do social things – administer justice, make rules, apportion blame, take the role of the other – how to do things to and in the social environment.

It seems to us that the environment also does things to the individuals who inhabit it; in other words, individuals are subject to the action of the environment and not just the initiators of action upon it. If this is so, then knowledge about the world need not only be knowledge about how to do things to the world. It can also be knowledge about environmental action upon the self, for individuals are also the objects and indeed the targets of environmental action. And with respect to the social environment, this

53

perspective is particularly relevant to children. They more than most groups are targets of social action.

So, the development of knowledge about the social environment is development of knowledge about the kinds of things the environment – both social and material – might do to the self. It is therefore knowledge about social and material hazards, knowledge which explains the actions of parents and other adults, as well as knowledge about how to react to such action.

We now examine these various arguments in terms of two research examples, the first briefly and the second in rather more detail.

Institutionalised relations

Classical social theory hinges on the idea that social life, at least in modern times, has become divided between two broad categories of social relationship, the personal and purely formal. Weber (1947) took the view that the impersonal elements in social relations are best understood in terms of authority relations which underpin them, relations which Weber characterised as 'legal-rational'. Weber distinguished formal or legal rational authority from other varieties in a number of ways, but four are central. The first is that all positions of formal authority exist within a rationally organised hierarchical system – an institution or organisation – and have no legitimacy except in terms of their positions in this system. The second is that each position always has specific, explicit and formally defined and limited spheres of jurisdiction. The third is that holders of such authority can only exercise it in accordance with formally defined, impartial criteria, and not in the service of personal interests. And the fourth is that office holders have formally defined duties and obligations which are likewise distinct from their personal inclinations.

The research of Adelson (1971), Kohlberg (1976) and Furth (1980) suggests that children do not recognise the formal and impersonal elements in role relations until they reach adolescence. They are not initially able to recognise that relations between people could be regulated by anything beyond personal inclinations or preferences. 'Societal decisions are thought to emanate from the free will of a particular person' (Furth, 1978b, p. 251). In other words, the distinction between the formal and the personal is a cognitively complex notion which appears relatively late in childhood. Moreover, the position of Furth and others is that the informal–formal distinction in human relations is an objective feature which children only gradually come to understand in an adult-like way.

Virtually no previous research has been addressed directly to the question of how children come to understand relations of formal authority. However, several studies have revealed that even quite young children perceive authority to have limits (Damon, 1977; Turiel, 1983; Tisak and Turiel, 1984; Piaget, 1932). What these studies show is that children believe any person's authority is limited to what is also morally justifiable, though a couple of cases appear to describe childhood insights closer to Weber's concept of bureaucratic or legal-rational authority. Damon (1977), for instance, uses the example of a football team captain exceeding the authority of this particular position. And Laupa and Turiel (1986) contrast orders given by someone authorised to do so with orders given by people lacking such authority.

Experience in the school, the setting for Laupa and Turiel's (1986) example, might be expected to be particularly formative of children's representations of institutional or impersonal authority. The school is after all the child's first extended introduction to a bureaucracy. It seems sensible therefore to ask how children represent social relations in this context.

Our own investigation (Emler, Ohana and Moscovici, 1987) in this area examined children's representations of the teacher as an organisational role. It involved 123 children from Scotland, and 60 from France, aged six to twelve. The Scottish children were divided almost evenly between middle- and working-class backgrounds, and the French children in a ratio of 2:1, middle class to working class. We asked several questions about the activities of teachers, organising our questions around three areas of role performance: (a) assessing pupils' work; (b) helping pupils with their work; (c) enforcing school rules.

Answers to several questions hinted at a more sophisticated interpretation of organisational roles in this age group than Furth's conclusions allow. For example, by eleven years almost all children recognised that there is a hierarchy of authority in the school and that teachers are in their turn subject to the authority of persons, such as head teachers, above them in this hierarchy. By this age almost all children recognised that teachers did not have the power to alter or ignore any rule, and most also believed it was wrong for teachers to allow their personal preferences to influence decisions about which pupils they would and would not help. In these cases the middle-class children were more likely to show these insights than the working-class, and the French children were more sophisticated about these bureaucratic features than the Scottish.

However, the differences were not all on a single developmental dimension. Scottish and French children had some rather different views about the obligations of office holders. The Scottish children believed teachers were bound to enforce regulations whatever their personal feelings about the fairness of these regulations. This belief was more widespread among the middle-class children and among the older children, and it is tempting therefore to see this as a growing awareness of the objective constraints on officials. The French children disabused us of this temptation. Almost all of them believed the teacher should do what was fair, whatever the regulation required. Likewise, while Scottish children believed it was appropriate for a teacher to justify her actions by invoking the regulations which required them, the French children rejected this idea. Generally, French children seemed more 'sophisticated' about bureaucracy, i.e., recognising its features earlier, but they were also more hostile to it.

Representations of income inequality

We now turn to children's knowledge of wage relations, the exchange of labour for money. Jahoda, Furth and others have documented aspects of their developing insights into the retail and banking systems, in each of which they eventually integrate two parallel processes of commercial exchange. Wage relations are superficially simpler as only one exchange is involved – between employee and employer. And as might be expected therefore, even quite young children understand that work can be exchanged for money (Jahoda, 1979), though there are still several subtleties here, such as voluntary work, and unpaid versus paid domestic work (cf. Duveen and Shields, 1985).

What is more interesting perhaps is the child's theory of labour. In essence, what determines the pricing of work? By eleven or twelve children may understand that a shop-keeper's prices reflect the need to make a profit, but beyond that they are often still hazy about the mechanisms involved in pricing traded commodities (not surprisingly, given economists have difficulties with this too). But various forms of work, like various commodities, attract different prices. How do children make sense of pay differentials, how do they explain them or evaluate them, and for that matter, to what extent are they aware of them?

One possible guide to what we might expect from children is the work on concepts of distributive justice (see for example Piaget, 1932; Damon, 1977; Enright et al., 1980; Hook and Cook, 1979). Piaget described three different strategies children apply to problems of distribution. One is to defer to adults as the appropriate authorities on all such questions. A second is to demand a strict equality of distribution. The third is to make allowance for such matters as age, special needs or previous services rendered. Piaget found these strategies to be roughly ordered according to age. Damon's (1977) own work also pointed to an age ordering, though he found no initial stage of deference to authority. Where their conclusions coincide is on the shift from a preference for equality, in middle childhood, to a preference for distribution according to relative deservingness thereafter.

Hook and Cook (1979) related this age change more explicitly to the principle of equity (Homans, 1961) according to which a distribution of rewards or payments is regarded as fair when it is proportional to contributions. Hook and Cook also relate children's allocation decisions directly to their ability to compute the various logical relations involved. The implications of their analysis are (a) that equity rests on certain cognitive abilities, and (b) that once children understand equity their decisions and judgements will be based on this more logical principle rather than others. Thus with respect to income–occupation relations, children's judgements should be a function only of mental age or intellectual level. In early to middle childhood they should expect everyone to be paid the same. Beyond this they should be increasingly likely to expect incomes to reflect relative contributions.

However, here if anywhere we might anticipate that social group membership will influence beliefs and judgements. Or rather we might expect an influence of membership of distinct social classes, and specifically of middle versus working classes, since these are differentiated in terms of income-earning occupations (rather than, for example, sources of income – capital versus labour).

Very few studies have compared the distributive justice beliefs of children from different social class backgrounds. Enright et al. (1980) found that middle-class children were more likely than working-class children to propose equity solutions, but they interpreted this as a developmental difference; the working-class children had simply yet to develop the more advanced concepts of justice already achieved by middle-class children of the same age.

Research by Connell (1977) and by Leahy (1981, 1983) brings us a little closer to the wage system by asking about inequalities in wealth. Both confirmed that the trend towards equity found in allocation decisions and simple distributive justice problems is also apparent in children's representations of wealth and poverty. But neither found any clear tendency for this to be affected appreciably by children's own positions in the class structure. One of the very few studies which has provided a direct empirical examination of children's beliefs about incomes is Siegal's (1981) investigation of children's perceptions of economic needs. He asked children to divide a fixed sum of money among people in specific occupations, and also asked how much each required for his needs. The usefulness of this study, however, is limited by the fact that the amount of money the children had to divide was very small and bore no relation to real income levels. Moreover, Siegal's study can tell us nothing about the effects of the child's own social class position on these decisions and judgements.

This was the objective of our own work. In a series of studies we asked children from different countries (Britain, France, USA) and social backgrounds about the earnings of people in different occupations (Dickinson, 1987; Emler and Dickinson, 1985; Emler and Luce, 1985; Ohana, 1987).

It seemed to us especially important to ensure that the children were indeed representative of different social groups. From the perspective of social representations theory, if social class does influence beliefs about income–occupation relations it will be to the degree that different social classes constitute distinctive social group environments. Although the social class variable has been widely used in developmental research, including the examples cited above, the studies by Connell, Enright et al., and Leahy, we suspect that the most commonly used index of class, parental occupation, may by itself fail to identify distinct social groups. We believe we were able to achieve such distinctiveness in the Scottish studies by drawing children from state and private schools, and probably in the American study by a similar sampling strategy, but the French study must be treated with more caution in this respect.

In these studies the basic task was to estimate the weekly incomes (monthly in France) of people in different occupations. People were depicted (pictorially) in four different occupations, two of which (doctor and school teacher) were intended to be representative of white-collar or middle-class occupations and two (bus driver and road sweeper, or garbage collector in America) of blue-collar or working-class occupations. We also intended these four occupations to represent a spread in actual incomes. We asked children to indicate income levels by distributing the appropriate amount of 'Monopoly' money to each person.

In addition to questions about the amount earned, we also asked why any predicted differences in income across the four occupations existed, whether such differences were fair, and whether parity of income across these occupations would be preferable.

The first Scottish study (Emler and Dickinson, 1985) was based on a sample of 120 seven- to twelve-year-olds, half from a state school in a working-class city district and half from a private school. The French sample (Ohana, 1987) consisted of 63 children, aged seven to twelve, attending schools in the Paris region; 43 had parents in middle-class occupations, and 20 had parents in working-class occupations. In the American study (Emler and Luce, 1985), children were selected from two state schools, one in a working-class city district, one in a middle-class area, and from an exclusive, fee-paying school. We interviewed a total of 218 children in grades 3–7 (eight- to thirteen-year-olds), 67 from the first school, 71 from the second and 78 from the third.

The first thing to note is that there was considerable consensus in all three countries as to the rank order of incomes across the four occupations, though this consensus became more complete with age and was more extensive

Table 4.1 *Mean ranks of occupations for income estimates as a function of children's social class background and nationality*

	Doctor	Teacher	Bus driver	Road sweeper[a]
Scotland				
Working class	1·71	2·61	2·50	2·89
Middle class	1·47	1·92	3·04	3·48
France				
Working class	1·76	2·30	2·55	3·31
Middle class	1·65	2·11	3·19	3·04
USA				
Working class	1·33	2·51	2·88	3·28
Middle class	1·14	2·45	2·81	3·60
Upper middle class	1·06	2·14	3·13	3·36

[a] 'Garbage collector' for US sample.
Source: Data from Emler and Dickinson (1985), Emler and Luce (1985) and Ohana (1987).

Table 4.2 *Judgements of the fairness of income inequalities as a function of social class background and nationality: percentages judging perceived inequalities to be fair*

	Scotland	France	USA
Working class	69	95	87
Middle class	85	87	87
Upper middle class			88

Source: Data from Emler and Dickinson (1985), Emler and Luce (1985) and Ohana (1987).

among the middle-class children. Table 4.1 summarises the ranks by social class background and nationality. Did these children also regard the differences as fair? Again, there was considerable consensus; in no age, national or social class group did a majority regard the differences predicted as unfair. Again, Table 4.2 summarises the percentages by class and nationality.

The justifications given for the inequalities most frequently referred to differences in the respective inputs of the people in these different occupations. In other words these children were reacting like good equity theorists. There were, however, no age trends; younger children were no less likely than older children to refer to differences in inputs as justification for differences in outcomes. And hardly any children invoked differences in need.

Table 4.3 *Reactions to income equality proposal as a function of social class and nationality: percentages judging income equality to be preferable*

	Scotland	France	USA
Working class	62	63	51
Middle class	40	47	42
Upper middle class			40

Source: Data from Emler and Dickinson (1985), Emler and Luce (1985) and Ohana (1987).

Interestingly, the explanations they gave for income differences were very similar to their justifications. There were very few explanations which did not contain or imply some judgement as to the relative deservingness of individual recipients. Very few children made reference to market forces, and none to competition for particular kinds of job, or to the political power of particular occupational groups in wage bargaining or income protection. Examination of the explanations given by the Scottish children revealed that explanations in terms of references to descriptive characteristics of the work (for example 'He just drives a bus'; 'All he has to do is sweep the road') declined with age, whilst explanations in terms of the importance of the job to society, the difficulty of the work and the qualifications or skills needed increased with age. These changes were not statistically significant, but there were two significant social class differences: greater use of 'descriptive' explanations by the working-class and more frequent reference to qualifications or skills by the middle-class children.

The consensus, evident in the rank ordering of occupations by income and in beliefs about the fairness of income differences, also had limits. When asked, 'Would it be fairer to pay everyone the same?', a clear division opened up, particularly in Scotland and France. Table 4.3 gives the percentages in each social class and national group accepting this proposal; the middle-class children were more likely to resist this proposal than the working-class children. However, responses to this question also varied with age: older children were more likely to reject the proposal.

In the Scottish study we also examined the number of justifications offered by each child in support of judgements about the fairness of income differences, and again we found a significant class difference. The middle-class children appeared to possess a greater range of justifications for inequalities. This finding has been replicated for explanations in a second study in Britain, sampling a slightly higher age range, ten to sixteen years (Dickinson, 1987).

Table 4.4 *Justifications for income inequality: a comparison of Scottish and American children's views*

	Scotland		United States		
Justification[a]	Working class	Middle class	Working class	Middle class	Upper middle class
1. Job demands (effort, difficulty, time)	30	52	37	30	23
2. Social contribution (how much the job helps others)	38	30	33	27	20
3. Qualifications (education, years of study required)	5	13	9	17	25
4. Other (expenses of job, undefined importance, description of job, etc.)	23	5	21	26	30

[a] Numbers refer to percentage of subjects in each national and social class group giving a particular argument as their first justification. Subjects often gave more than one type of argument.
Source: Data from Emler and Dickinson (1985) and Emler and Luce (1985).

Table 4.5. *A further British study of arguments for income differences: percentages using different types of justification by age and social class background*

Age	10–11		12–13		14–15	
Social class	WC	MC	WC	MC	WC	MC
Justification						
Social contribution	74	40	56	54	57	35
Effort	19	70	48	73	42	65
Skills	0	0	17	22	7	28
Study	0	0	7	28	21	65
Qualifications	0	0	9	33	21	43

Notes: Percentages can add up to more than 100 as children frequently offered more than one type of argument. Generally, older children offered more types of argument.
Source: Dickinson (1984).

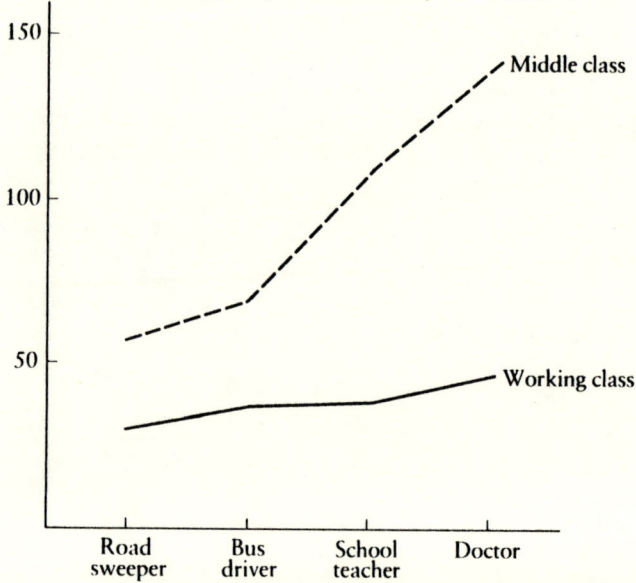

Figure 4.1 Scotland: estimates of *weekly* incomes in £ as a function of social class background (ages 7–11)

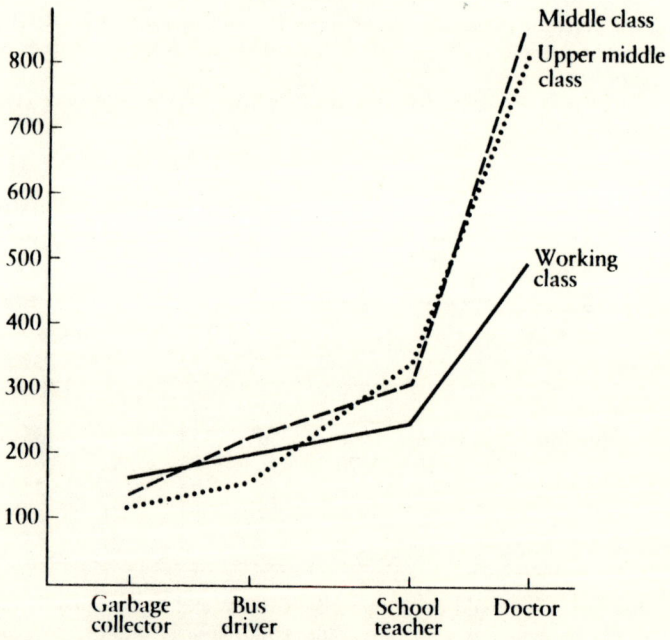

Figure 4.2 USA: estimates of *weekly* incomes in $ as a function of social class background (ages 8–13)

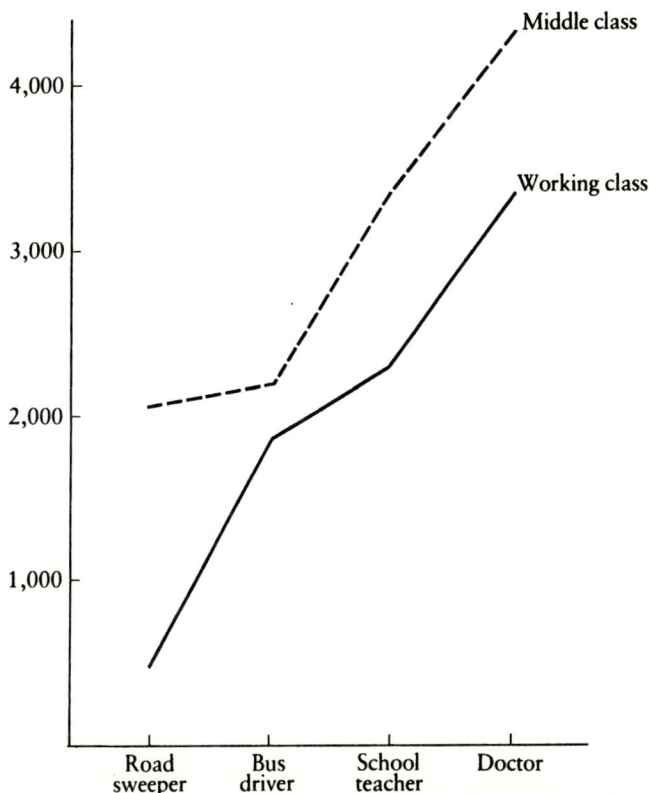

Figure 4.3 France: estimates of *monthly* incomes in French francs as a function of social class backgrounds (ages 7–11)

The number of explanations was linearly related to age but higher at each age amongst the middle-class sample.

Next we looked at the kinds of justifications offered; there are many different kinds of input that can be used to justify differences in outcomes. Particularly notable here (see Table 4.4) were Scottish—American differences in the content of justifications. For example, differences in amount of education acquired are more frequently used by American middle- and upper-middle-class children to justify differences than by Scottish children. Table 4.5 gives the results from a second British study (Dickinson, 1984). Here we see that the range of explanations begins to increase at twelve years, with skills, study and qualifications emerging as significant categories, though the latter two are substantially more prevalent among the middle-class children.

Last, and perhaps most dramatic, were the findings concerning what children believed the incomes actually to be (Figures 4.1, 4.2 and 4.3). In all three countries the income estimates of middle-class children differ from those of working-class children. In Britain and America the most striking aspect of this difference is the greater degree of income inequality perceived by middle-class children. The anomalous finding in the French data concerns the working-class children's estimates for road sweepers. We shall suggest a possible explanation for this later.

What can be concluded from these results generally? On the face of it equity theory is supported; a majority of children do refer to differential inputs to justify differential outcomes. Likewise, a cognitive developmental interpretation of commitment to the contributions rule is supported; what age-related effects there are appear to be in the direction of increasing support for this rule. However, we believe there are various reasons to doubt that a cognitive developmental interpretation of equity is entirely appropriate here.

First it cannot readily account for differences in beliefs about the extent of income inequalities. It might be argued that these differences reflect the fact that more middle-class children have reached the level of proportional equity (Hook and Cook, 1979). Thus working-class children are simply producing the appropriate rank ordering of incomes, while middle-class children have moved on to estimations of relativities. If this is the case, namely that middle-class children are simply further along the same developmental path, then differences between middle and working class should be of the same order as those between older and younger children. They are not. In these studies we found no relation between age and the degree of income inequality perceived.

Second, the assumptions of the equity principle are untenable here. Children, and indeed most adults, are seldom in a position to decide on the relative pay of different occupations; they are confronted with an established system of remuneration and can do little more than react to the fairness of its outcomes. Nor are they in a position to perform the kinds of computation equity theory requires, given that inputs for different jobs are seldom simple, quantifiable, precise and known. It also seems unlikely that children are somehow comparing the inputs and outcomes in different occupations and concluding that the results accord with the requirements of the contributions rule. For if this is so it is difficult to see how children with very different beliefs about the relative outcomes could come to such similar conclusions about the fairness of the result.

It is also difficult to see why children on opposite sides of the Atlantic should have such different views about the kinds of input that justify these inequalities, if they are operating only according to the principles of equity. One would have to assume either that the inputs are indeed different in Scotland and North America, or else that what counts as an input varies from one culture to another.

Third, the theory of cognitive development assumes that social life presents individuals with problems – such as problems in how limited resources should be allocated – and the individual solves these by the application of reasoning in terms of internalised principles. But income inequality is not a *problem* in this sense; on the contrary, it is a solution, an institutionalised, long-standing practice for which well-developed justifications exist.

This brings us to what we believe is a more fruitful perspective from which to interpret these findings. In one of the last articles Tajfel wrote (Tajfel, 1984), he argued that people react quite differently in deciding the justice of exchanges among individuals within groups and those between groups. In the former, considerations of equity may be relevant. In the latter they are not. Instead individuals refer to powerful and dominant social myths to justify the privileged position of their own group in society or else to account for its underprivileged position. In Moscovici's (1984) terms, these myths are 'social representations', shared belief systems generated by social groups and varying as a function of each group's own position within society.

When we ask children about such matters as why certain income levels or differences exist, it is unlikely that we are simply accessing their own moral judgement capacities, constructed according to universal laws of cognitive organisation and discovered by us in this kind of research at varying stages of completion. It is more likely that we are also accessing their understanding of their culture's framework of legitimations for the status quo: children are repeating society's justifications. There is nothing objective about rewarding people with higher incomes if they take jobs that require longer periods of training, or about paying them more if their jobs involve helping others or if their jobs are more difficult. Nor is there anything inherently causal in these facts. The connections are made by social convention; they are decisions about social values, and they cannot be predicted from universals in human cognitive organisation. In other epochs and other cultures other and different connections have been made.

Hence, we would argue these children are providing us with social representations, beliefs shaped by the social groups to which they belong. Thus, in this series of studies there are indications that income differences are supported in Scotland and North America by somewhat different social myths.

It seems that the Scottish middle class, and to a lesser extent the American, are more inclined than their working-class peers to organise their knowledge of occupations in terms of social classes. But this complication points to perhaps the most important conclusion about social knowledge that we have to offer: such knowledge, like the wealth to which it refers, is unequally distributed in society. And knowledge about the socio-economic and class structure of society is distributed among people in terms of their own social class position. Children growing up in the middle class have more differentiated representations of inequalities and more extensive justifications for these, and are more committed to them. This inequality of knowledge appears to be particularly marked among the Scottish children.

The idea that social classes differ, not in opinions about the legitimacy of the status quo, but in the degree to which dominant social myths are elaborated and shared, is consistent with Mann's (1970) analysis of the evidence from studies of adults. Thus working-class children, like working-class adults, share less extensively and completely in the systems of social representations that serve to explain and justify social inequalities; what they do not do to any significant extent is develop oppositional or critical ideologies.

Finally, Tajfel (1984) made two points about the consequences of social categorisation which may explain why, in the case of incomes, middle-class children should perceive a greater spread. The first is that when social phenomena are categorised we tend to perceive greater differences between categories on any dimension on which the phenomena may be ordered. The second consequence is that individuals will themselves belong to one of the social categories they compare. When people compare their own social category with others they tend to emphasise any difference that favours their own category and de-emphasise any difference that does not. Income differences generally favour the middle class and so the middle class–working class difference will be perceived to be greater by middle-class than working-class children, but only if the difference is perceived to be legitimate. Interestingly, those middle-class children in the Scottish sample who regarded the income differences as unfair also perceived the gap between the earnings of middle-class and working-class occupations to be smaller than those who regarded these differences as fair. The effects of perceived group membership may also explain the French results. Road sweepers in Paris are commonly North African, and the white working-class children in this sample may well have regarded North Africans as a subordinate group, whereas the middle-class children would not make this distinction among working-class occupations.

Conclusions

Piagetian or constructivist developmental psychology has proceeded on the assumption, which it has then sought to confirm, that there is a finished structure to social knowledge which is universal, and that all individuals progressively recreate this structure for themselves in the course of their own development. They differ only in the stage of reconstruction they have reached. In this chapter we have argued that the construction is a joint enterprise, involving children and their societies, and one in which the outcome and not just the pace of development will vary from one social group to another. Moreover the knowledge structures that societies build in children's minds are also distinguished in important ways by their content. As a first step towards these conclusions we have provided examples of some variations in the content of children's knowledge about institutional and economic relations that are associated with the different social and cultural groups to which they belong.

References

Adelson, J. (1971). The political imagination of the young adolescent. *Daedalus*, 100, 1013–50.

Berti, A. E. and Bombi, A. S. (1988). *The Child's Construction of Economics*. Cambridge: Cambridge University Press.

Billig, M. (1987). *Arguing and Thinking*. Cambridge: Cambridge University Press.

Connell, R. W. (1977). *Ruling Class, Ruling Culture*. Cambridge: Cambridge University Press.

Damon, W. (1977). *The Social World of the Child*. San Francisco: Jossey Bass.

Dasen, P. and Herron, A. (1981). Cross-cultural tests of Piaget's theory. In H. C. Triandis and A. Herron (eds.), *Handbook of Cross-Cultural Psychology*, vol. 4, *Developmental Psychology*. Boston: Allyn & Bacon.

Dickinson, J. (1984). Social representations of socio-economic structure. Paper given at the British Psychological Society London Conference, 1984.
 (1987). The development of representations of social inequality. Unpublished doctoral thesis, University of Dundee.

Doise, W. (1989). Attitudes et représentations sociales. In D. Jodelet (ed.), *Les représentations sociales*. Paris: PUF.

Doise, W. and Mugny, G. (1984). *The Social Development of the Intellect*. Oxford: Pergamon.

Duveen, G. and Shields, M. M. (1985). Children's ideas about work, wages and social rank. *Cahiers de psychologie cognitif*, 5, 411–12.

Emler, N. (1987). Socio-moral development from the perspective of social representations. *Journal of the Theory of Social Behaviour*, 17, 371–88.

Emler, N. and Dickinson, J. (1985). Children's representations of economic inequalities: the effects of social class. *British Journal of Developmental Psychology*, 3, 191–8.

Emler, N. and Glachan, M. (1985). L'Apprentissage social: perspectives récentes. In G. Mugny (ed.), *Psychologie sociale du développement cognitif*. Berne: Peter Lang.

Emler, N. and Luce, T. (1985). Social class background and perception of occupation-related income differences in middle childhood. Unpublished MS, University of Dundee.

Emler, N. and Ohana, J. (forthcoming). Studying social representations among children: just old wine in new bottles? In G. Breakwell and D. Canter (eds.), *Empirical Approaches to Social Representations*. London: Oxford University Press.

Emler, N., Ohana, J. and Moscovici, S. (1987). Children's beliefs about institutional roles: a cross-national study of representations of the teacher's role. *British Journal of Educational Psychology*, 57, 26–37.

Enright, R., Enright, W., Manheim, L. and Harris, B. E. (1980). Distributive justice development and social class. *Developmental Psychology*, 16, 555–63.

Flavell, J. and Ross, L. (1981). *Social Cognitive Development: Frontiers and Possible Futures*. Cambridge: Cambridge University Press.

Furth, H. (1978a). Children's societal understanding and the process of equilibration. In W. Damon (ed.), *Social Cognition*. San Francisco: Jossey Bass.

(1978b). Young children's understanding of society. In H. McGurk (ed.), *Issues in Childhood Social Development*. London: Methuen.

(1980). *The World of Grownups*. New York: Elsevier North-Holland.

Homans, G. C. (1961). *Social Behaviour: Its Elementary Forms*. London: Routledge & Kegan Paul.

Hook, J. and Cook, T. (1979). Equity theory and the cognitive ability of children. *Psychological Bulletin*, 86, 429–45.

Jahoda, G. (1979). The construction of economic reality by some Glaswegian school children. *European Journal of Social Psychology*, 9, 115–27.

(1984). The development of thinking about socio-economic systems. In H. Tajfel (ed.), *The Social Dimension*, vol. 1. Cambridge: Cambridge University Press.

Kohlberg, L. (1976). Moral stages and moralization: the cognitive developmental approach. In T. Lickona (ed.), *Moral Development and Behaviour: Theory, Research and Social Issues*. New York: Holt, Rinehart & Winston.

(1984). *Essays on Moral Development*, vol. 2: *The Psychology of Moral Development*. New York: Harper.

Laupa, M. and Turiel, E. (1986). Children's conceptions of adult and peer authority. *Child Development*, 57, 405–12.

Leahy, R. (1981). The development of the conception of economic inequality. I. Descriptions and comparisons of rich and poor people. *Child Development*, 52, 523–32.

(1983). The development of the conception of economic inequality. II. Explanations, justifications, and concepts of social mobility and change. *Developmental Psychology*, 19, 111–25.

Mann, M. (1970). The social cohesion of liberal democracy. *American Sociological Review*, 35, 423–9.

Moscovici, S. (1976). *Social Influence and Social Change*. London: Academic Press.

(1984). The phenomenon of social representations. In R. Farr and S. Moscovici (eds.), *Social Representations*. Cambridge: Cambridge University Press.

Ohana, J. (1987). French children's estimates of weekly incomes. Unpublished Manuscript, EHESS, Paris.

Piaget, J. (1932). *The Moral Judgement of the Child*. London: Routledge & Kegan Paul.

Siegal, M. (1981). Children's perceptions of adult economic need. *Child Development*, 52, 379–82.

Snarey, J. (1985). The cross-cultural universality of socio-moral development: a critical review of Kohlbergian research. *Psychological Bulletin*, 97, 202–32.

Tajfel, H. (1984). Intergroup relations, social myths and social justice in social psychology. In H. Tajfel (ed.), *The social dimension*, vol. 2. Cambridge: Cambridge University Press.

Tisak, M. (1986). Children's conceptions of parental authority. *Child Development*, 57, 166–76.

Tisak, M. and Turiel, E. (1984). Children's conceptions of moral and prudential rules. *Child Development*, 55, 1030–9.

Turiel, E. (1983). *The Development of Social Knowledge*. Cambridge: Cambridge University Press.

Weber, M. (1947). *The Theory of Social and Economic Organisations*. New York: Free Press.

5

Social representations of childhood: an implicit theory of development

Maria D'Alessio

Introduction

One of the most intriguing aspects of childhood is the manner in which it is located within particular socio-historical contexts. Each culture *invents*, or constructs, the child as a social object in its own terms. Viewed from the perspective of its social construction our current conception of 'childhood' centres around the image of the 'unfinished child'. This image is the product of a particular historical context, though one can also see signs of change and conflict in current constructions of childhood. Nevertheless, the idea of the unfinishedness of the child has long provided the basis for theories of child development. Nietzsche (1986) proposed a view of childhood as immaturity, and, more recently, Gesell (1943) suggested that the unfinishedness of the human child could be explained by the psychological complexity of human nature, which requires experience to realise its possibilities. Perfectibility, if it is conceived of as a realisation of potential, implies educability, and, consequently, a long childhood. Others, like Wallon, construe childhood as an evolutionary product which grows longer in duration with the developmental transformations of living beings. The higher up the evolutionary scale one goes, the more complex are the structures of action typical of a given species and the longer its period of childhood.

Common to all of these conceptions of childhood, however, is a view of the adult as providing the norms from which to make judgements about the child. The adult as a norm is the pivot at the centre of the social relations which necessitate the construction of the child's own normality, since the adult is also at the centre of the process of socialisation. Yet, as Merleau-Ponty (1964) pointed out, childhood as an object of knowledge occupies an ambiguous position. From one point of view childhood is remote from the adult observer, yet it is also something so familiar that it is always very difficult to distinguish between what is considered to be the child's behaviour and behaviour which actually depends on our adult presence. Nevertheless, the cognitive difference in power and strength between the adult and the child is so marked that the hypothesis of a 'relationship' of reciprocal exchange between adult and child has rarely been entertained.

Socio-developmental psychology is particularly interested in analysing the symbolic processes contributing to the elaboration of the socio-cognitive frame of reference which informs behaviour. Many researchers have been interested in discovering *how* adults order their ideas about children, the *origins* of the theoretical elements informing these representations, and *what* influences educators refer to when justifying their own actions.

The study of the social representation of the child examines the way in which adults construct and maintain the idea of the normal child, a process which rests upon a particular ideological base. The interplay of anchoring and objectification which Moscovici describes as the formative processes of social representation calls to mind a similar relationship between assimilation and accommodation in Piaget's theory. One could compare anchoring with assimilation in so far as they are both concerned with placing an object in a frame of reference, while accommodation would be determined by the objectification of the representation and the consequent relationships with other objects already existing in the individual cognitive world. Yet this comparison ought not to be taken too strictly, for there are also important differences which need to be recognised. Anchoring and objectification are always set in a social context, and they do not regulate the production of knowledge in the same dynamic way as Piaget suggests for assimilation and accommodation. At the same time, Moscovici is also concerned to distinguish social representation from the static transmission of blocks of thought suggested by Durkheim's (1898) account of collective representations. The social representation of childhood depends on both collective elaboration and the dynamic possibility of real, personal interaction on the part of the adults with individual children.

From the stereotype of the child to the social representation of childhood

Studies by De Grada and Ponzo (1971) and by D'Alessio (1977) have pointed out the importance of the cultural component in the construction of the idea of childhood. In these studies the responses given by adults in interviews about the skills and abilities of children from the age of two years and upwards are considered as 'stereotypes' or 'prejudices about childhood'. That is, such ideas were considered as prejudicial attitudes which also include

71

a disposition to action (Asch, 1952). Childhood, in fact, readily lends itself to being an object for the construction of prejudices by adults, combining as it does the characteristics of an easily identifiable minority group with little power and a great capacity for both self-attribution and the confirmation of prejudiced ideas. These studies also demonstrated a correlation between dogmatism as a personality characteristic and prejudicial attitudes towards the child, prejudices which even extended as far as considering the child as a negative element in belief systems (De Grada and Ponzo, 1971; D'Alessio, 1977).

While explanations in terms of personal motivations may clarify the structure of individual mental processes, they do not explain how the specific contents of the stereotype are historically determined and transmitted. In recent years there has been a shift away from a consideration of individual mentality as the basis for the formation of ideas and stereotypes (as, for instance, in Allport, 1954, and Rokeach, 1960) towards a consideration of the processes of social representation in which stereotypes are recognised as ideas shared by members of social groups and shaped by the ways in which groups construct and organise an understanding of the world they inhabit. In formulating the concept of social representation, Moscovici (1984) has drawn on the contribution of Durkheim (1898), though this concept also has links to more recent developments in social theory such as Berger and Luckmann's (1966) discussion of the construction of social reality.

In relation to the specific issue of representations of childhood, the advantage of adopting an approach based on social representations is that as well as providing a common frame for the expression of individual and group representations, this perspective also enables us to broaden the context in which representations of childhood are considered. No longer confined to the areas of logic, mathematics or knowledge relative only to the world of material and physical objects, the child is recognised as the centre of a wider process of socialisation in which the child's understanding of social relationships is not separated from the representation which adults have of childhood. It becomes possible therefore to consider both the development of representations and the representations of development within a unified framework. In this way, the cognitive and dynamic elements interact in the reconstruction of social reality; individual experience is confronted with, and related to, the collective conceptualisations of adults as they construct the social reality of childhood.

Following the model of social representations, we can consider childhood as an unfamiliar object and then trace the manner in which it is familiarised as adults communicate, represent and classify child development. In constructing their social representations of childhood adults formulate an implicit theory (cf. D'Alessio, 1987) which provides the basis for a constellation of attributions about childhood. In this sense the theory of attribution (Heider, 1958) provides a framework in which to consider the data furnished by our investigations. This framework directs attention to questions of causality in implicit theories, in terms both of the 'internal–external' locus of control and of 'stability–instability' on a temporal plane. From this point of view we can consider the recent research of D'Alessio (1977, 1987) and Emiliani (Emiliani, Zani and Carugati, 1981; Molinari and Emiliani, this volume) in terms of the attributive style adopted by subjects as they reconstruct the causal relations between the competence of children and the educative roles of parents.

Whether we talk, as we have done in the past, simply of stereotypes and prejudice, or as we more commonly do today in terms of representation and attribution, the theme of the ideas which adults formulate about children always allows us to consider these socio-psychological productions in relation to the specific cultural contexts in which actors enact their representations or beliefs. Representation in this sense refers not only to ideas which can be communicated verbally, but also to the ways in which adults act towards children. In whichever way these representations are expressed they contribute towards the objectification of the adults' image of the child. Yet the child is never reduced to a purely passive presence: they too are active in their relations with adults, and the impact of their activity provides a source of feedback on the adults' ideas. However, the simplified and rigid characteristics of stereotyped representations are associated with a tendency to seek instances of confirmation in interactions with children. Even though the 'real' child may not correspond to the adult's objectified representation, their activity when interacting with the adult may exercise little direct influence on these representations, the more so when the adults' representations are so rigidly anchored as to be no more than stereotypes.

Our ugly newborn

The responsiveness of adults towards babies represents one of the crucial points of ethological theory. Following the numerous observations of the link between the signals emitted by the young of various species, and the subsequent response on the part of the adult, Lorenz, in 1943, proposed a widening of the theory of imprinting to include the visual appearance of offspring, particularly such characteristics as the head (enlarged with respect to the body), relatively short limbs, rounded and prominent cheeks, and so on. The appearance of these childlike characteristics is held to stimulate maternal feelings.

While subsequent studies have examined the reactions of many species to the appropriate stimuli for attachment behaviour, they have been more ambiguous in clarifying the essential figurative characteristics of the newborn, and the cultural and personal circumstances which render those elements more or less significant (Berman, 1980; McCall and Kennedy, 1980). Paraphrasing an expression of Hochberg (1964), we could say that we know less about the stimuli which make possible the link between the human adult and the child than we know about certain types of fish.

An important contribution from within the ethological tradition is Huckstedt's (1965) investigation of reactions to two types of children's heads: one normal and one exaggerated. A 'prototype', with the accentuation of the characteristics preferred by the adults (for example, encephalisation of the head with extended forehead and crown), was preferred aesthetically to the profile of an actual newborn baby. Two principal objections to Huckstedt's model (1965) have been noted by Roman researchers (De Grada and Ponzo, 1971; Panier Bagat et al., 1974, 1977; D'Alessio, 1977):

1. The ethological model does not explain how the usual figurative characteristics of the newborn, which although they are not accentuated are nevertheless part of the prototype, can not only be rejected, but even perceived and defined as 'ugly';

2. Just as unsatisfying is the interpretation in terms of a prototype when one obtains from mothers statistically significant responses of aesthetic preference for the profile with more hair (older newborns) in comparison with the actual newborn baby with little hair.

Our interpretation, which is strictly linked to the theoretical model elaborated by undervaluation of the small child, was to explain the negative aesthetic judgements obtained by Huckstedt on the profile of an actual newborn baby as a specific attribution dependent on adults' beliefs about the child and their more general negative representation of the child. In our empirical investigations, we presented the profiles of actual newborns and of infants with the enlarged heads typical of encephalitics, both types being presented in drawings with and without hair (see the examples in Figure 5.1). The results obtained from numerous samples of university students inexperienced with babies showed a significant preference for the encephalitic profiles. This preference indicates that for adults the prototypical newborn is a baby whose head has an enlarged forehead and crown compared to those of an actual newborn infant. This prototype was judged to be not only good-looking, but also real, capable of stimulating affection, and so on.

The ambiguity in adults' choices can be seen in their responses to the image

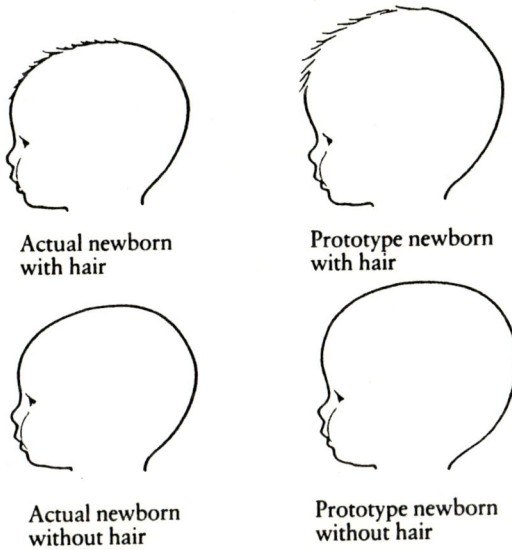

Figure 5.1 Stimuli figures of actual and prototypic newborns

of the newborn with hair, an image which they preferred. Yet this positive aesthetic judgement of 'good-looking' (attributable to the presence of hair) was accompanied by a judgement that it was also a 'false' image, in that it did not depict an actual newborn. Confronted with the profiles of actual newborns subjects judged the image of the baby without hair as ugly and false, while the image of the baby with hair was judged to be good-looking but not true. The perception of the newborn fluctuates between aesthetic undervaluation and negation.

The excessive differentiation between the perception of the actual newborn baby and the prototype cannot be attributed only to the recognition of those exaggerated signals which stimulate protection. In our opinion it is not only a matter of preference but of the very limited aesthetic evaluation of the newborn by the adult, which is a consequence of a more general attitude of ambivalence and erroneous evaluation of the average child. In addition, other studies have shown a gender difference in these patterns of judgements, with women showing a greater responsiveness to the pictures of babies.

The impact of experience

The results reported in the previous section were based upon subjects who had had little direct contact with children, so a question arises about the effect of experience on aesthetic judgements of babies. Does the pleasure attributed to the picture stimulus depend upon general cognitive structures which transcend the purely figurative content of the picture by drawing on elements of experience with babies? Does one find more pleasure in and feel more tenderness towards a profile of a baby's head when one actually holds the baby in one's arms, or before or during pregnancy? And after such direct experiences with babies will one continue to find pleasure in the profile? Finally, as the number of one's own children increases, does one find more pleasure in the profile of the newborn?

A longitudinal study of mothers of first borns through the months before and after delivery showed a statistically significant improvement (on a seven-point scale) of aesthetic evaluation, liking and tenderness for the newborn in the months after delivery (Panier Bagat et al., 1974, 1977). However, women who had had more than one child did not show any variation in their judgement after later pregnancies. Both groups of mothers showed a consistent preference before and after delivery for the pictures of older babies (four and eight months) compared to a newborn. From this preference it can be seen that it is the older baby which provides the prototype from which judgements are made about the actual newborn. The age which the sample attributes to the profiles of the babies, whether they are real or false, is on the average six to seven months. Finally, there is a negative correlation between the degree of pleasure expressed for the prototype figure and the judgement given by a mother about her own child. The more distorted her mental representation of the newborn, the more disappointing a mother will find her own child, while the mother who finds pleasure in her own newborn views the prototype less highly.

It was also possible to investigate the effect of professional experience with children by comparing the responses of obstetricians who were mothers with those of obstetricians who were not mothers. It is the latter group who judged the actual newborn 'somewhat ugly', giving it an average aesthetic score of less than three (on a seven-point scale), while the average score of obstetricians who were also mothers was five. Thus, professional competence added to personal experience seems to encourage a realistic attitude: the prototype is judged false, and although the score given to the actual newborn increases it is still not preferred to the prototypic infant.

The prototypic infant is generally chosen as true and more pleasing than the newborn; the 'prototype' child (eight months) is similarly preferred to the normal child; the normal child (eight months) preferred to the encephalitic newborn; and the encephalitic newborn preferred to the actual newborn. There is, then, a graded scale of judgements of trueness and aesthetic pleasantness running from the actual newborn at the bottom to the prototypic child of a certain age at the top who is at last enjoyed and accepted by the adult as it really is. Thus one can see in these results a denial or negation of the actual status of the newborn, a flight from reality which echoes a general trend in western culture which is oriented towards the school-aged child rather than the neonate.

We are in the presence of a structure of dominance, which is only moderately influenced by possible 'reference patterns' derived from personal experience. The predominant representations reflect the images which are most widely shared socially and which are reinforced by advertising and the mass media as well as literature. Thus, it is no wonder that variable experience and familiarity with children produces, at best, a provisional 'suspension' of the stereotype.

This structure of aesthetic dominance is not only typical of our own culture. Research with both Massai and Eritrean subjects also showed a preference for the profile of the child over that of the actual newborn. Indeed, the actual newborn was often considered to be less good-looking than the head of a donkey, provided that this head was an encephalitic prototype (D'Alessio, 1977).

Recent research (Ninio, 1979; Parke et al., 1980; Keller et al., 1984) concerning adults' naive theories of the infant has concluded experience is less formative than cultural factors. These studies were undertaken with different aims and methodologies from our own, and although they draw on interviews with mothers of very young children, these subjects were selected at a moment which, as we will see, produced a temporary but relevant effect of the newborn on the mothers' ideas.

The 'normal' child in the representation of adults

Sternberg (1985) points out that implicit theories of intelligence are different from the explicit theories developed by experts. They are belief systems, and as well as analysing the progressive elaboration and subjective arrangement of information in these systems, they also need to be investigated in relation to their social context. The role of the social dimension in the process of cognitive elaboration makes it seem simplistic to suggest that parents are simply *incapable* of generating a realistic knowledge of the small child. It is equally inappropriate to interpret behaviour according to the metaphor, which is often used in the literature, of a mother who is limited to *responding* to her child's initiations. The social representations which inform adults' ideas about child development and their actions towards children are complex combinations of specific knowledge, stereotyped images and prejudicial attitudes. These elements can all be seen in adults' perceptions of children and their 'naive' or implicit theories of childhood.

Research on adults' ideas about children's cognitive development has had a certain success in recent years as the gap between developmental psychology and social psychology has been bridged. Cross-cultural investigations of the opinions of mothers about their children have underlined the role attributed by educators to a series of social behaviours related to childhood and dependency (Kohn, 1969; Goodnow, 1984; Goodnow et al., 1986). Hess (1981) compared Japanese and American mothers and noted that Japanese mothers manifested expectations of more precocious development in the areas of emotional maturity, indulgence toward adults, good manners and independence. American mothers, on the contrary, present stereotypes consistent with a culture which appreciates verbal assertiveness and social competence with peers. They stressed the importance of asserting one's rights and taking the initiative in a group game. Loevinger (1959) has also demonstrated the impact of social class on the elaboration of naive 'theories'. It is clear that the ideal child is not the same in different cultures or social classes.

Stereotyped evaluations of the performances of pre-school-age children by adults were described by Ponzo in 1958, and subsequently elaborated through further investigations by our Roman group. The approach of these studies was to describe a task to subjects and ask them to say at what age they thought the average-normal child would become able to master it. All the items were drawn from standard developmental scales (Gesell Scales, Gille Mosaic Test, WISC Scale), which made it possible to compare subjects' responses with the population norms of the scale items. This was done in order to determine the representation of the reference pattern commonly used by the adult. Thus, it is the cognitive–perceptive norm, the idea that the adult has about the child, that will be compared with the expressed 'objective norm' or with the results obtained from the tests of children in research.

The image of the average-normal child which emerges from subjects' expectations is the expression of a stereotyped vision corresponding to adults' social representations. When evaluating the possible competence of a child, adults used as a practical description a reference pattern which organises the explicit knowledge they possess (Ponzo, 1958). This is the case no matter how much or how little explicit knowledge they possess. In addition to such reference patterns, adults also have recourse to normative values. In our culture many forms of behaviour are evaluated on the basis of norms rather than direct observation of the actual development of the child. It is, of course, primarily chronological age which articulates normative developmental

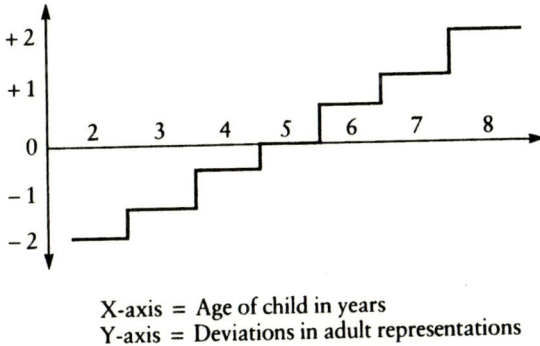

X-axis = Age of child in years
Y-axis = Deviations in adult representations

Figure 5.2 Systematic deviations in adult representations of children's competence

values; at x months something is normal, at y months something else, and so on. Chronological age is the external criterion we use to evaluate the development of children and to compare one child with another, judgements which always carry social and pedagogical implications.

A series of questions referring to children aged two to eight years were presented to approximately 2,000 adult subjects, who were asked to indicate the age at which they thought the normal child would be able to master each task (De Grada and Ponzo, 1971; D'Alessio, 1977). Items from the same set of standard developmental scales were selected for the questionnaire with a view to making the presentation of the question as simple as possible. In addition items which referred to behaviours which could have been directly observed were excluded. This was done to encourage, as far as possible, responses in terms of subjects' intuitive representation of the average child rather than responses which drew on some specific knowledge as a reference pattern.

The results showed an implicit model of cognitive development, which is shown in Figure 5.2. Adults' expectations of the cognitive abilities of the normal child describe a development rather like a staircase which has a landing at the floor of five to six years of age. For the preceding ages there is a significant underestimation of the child of pre-school age, and for the succeeding ages there is a systematic overestimation of the school-aged child. Like a broken clock which indicates the right time only once, this implicit model indicates an adequate comprehension of the child only once, around the age of five to six years.

Zazzo (1958) had already given a vivid description of the child of six as a 'model child'. In the eyes of the adult, children at this age are at the peak of childhood. They correspond to the child who is described in psychology

Table 5.1 *Comparison of adult expectations and population means for children's performance*

Item	Sample Mean	Standard Deviation	Population Mean	Z	P
1	3·8	1·40		13·21	< 0·001
2	4·2	1·52	2	11·07	< 0·001
3	4·2	1·48		12·86	< 0·001
1	4·2	1·59		8·78	< 0·001
2	4·8	1·54	3	7·55	< 0·001
3	4·6	1·91		7·21	< 0·001
1	4·7	1·09		2·19	< 0·05
2	4·1	1·40	4	0·75	n.s.
3	4·6	1·60		2·05	n.s.
1	5·3	1·54		1·69	n.s.
2	4·8	1·41	5	1·60	n.s.
3	4·7	1·46		1·37	n.s.
1	6·2	1·37		0·79	n.s.
2	5·7	0·94	6	0·43	n.s.
3	5·6	0·91		0·19	n.s.
1	6·0	1·00		− 10·15	< 0·001
2	5·6	1·18	8	− 8·74	< 0·001
3	5·3	1·16		− 9·03	< 0·001

manuals, and who is implicitly opposed to adults. In making a comparison with the adult Zazzo argues that we do not think of the three-year-old, who is too far removed from the adult, or of the school child whom we require, rightly or wrongly, to have problems and discipline similar to ours, but of the child who is on the threshold of entering school.

Zazzo's hypothesis of the 'model child' of six does not exclude our hypothesis of an articulated representation of the child, even if it does not correspond to the implicit models of older and younger children. The age of five to six years is representative of the child on the threshold of social responsibility, and provides the link between two evaluative trends which go in opposite directions.

Actual experience with the child

Children of pre-school age are systematically 'underestimated' by adults whose reference model construes them as 'incomplete and incapable little ones'. What impact does actual experience with a child have on this model?

Do adults' ideas change with increasing familiarity with the children's real abilities?

When their little Giovanni is born, for example, Signora and Signor Rossi, who *know* how incapable the little child is in general, nevertheless witness his 'feats' each day. They are then faced with the discrepancy between the achievements of their particular child and their reference pattern about the competences of infants in general. For the most part parents resolve this discrepancy by construing their child as exceptional with respect to the norms.

We all know how amazed new parents are to have a child so...*special*. Other children are incapable, but John is different...his competence, which is *so* exceptional compared to that of the average child, is shown off to everyone. Parents' tales about their children's abilities are accepted, however, with condescension by their interlocutors, who *know* that it is the parents' love for their children, and not the actual experience of the new father and mother, which is exceptional.

Thus, even the breach opened by the actual child in the prejudices of their own parents as they demonstrate their real competence does not succeed in modifying the stereotyped representation of childhood to which their parents, as members of the adult community, refer. Actual experience only effects a provisional and temporary modification of the prejudiced conception of childhood. Among all the subjects we interviewed the only mothers who did not commit errors were those who had a child of two to three years old at the time of the interview. Yet even such mothers returned to the social representations of childhood within a few years and, again, systematically underestimated the pre-school-aged child's abilities in tasks such as the suitable arranging of wooden blocks or the building of a bridge, and so on. The influence of familiarity with the child was investigated by other colleagues, who also found that mothers were able to evaluate their own children fairly adequately.

'Actual experience', however, is only one component of the representation of childhood, and one that is so sensitive to the particular social context that it has little impact on the representation of childhood in general. Actual experience does not modify the general idea of the small child; what influence it does exert is limited to the parent's relationship with their own child. Familiarity with their own child is represented by parents in terms of an exceptional situation, bombarded as they are by so much input coming from the child, who is the centre of attention. Children in this sense impose their exceptionality on their parents through the stimulus of their own activity. But this activity on the part of children produces only a temporary ripple in their parents' representations of childhood. As when a stone is dropped into a lake the ripples gradually subside, so by the time their child has grown older and entered school parents' ideas reassume the prejudiced topography of the social representation of childhood.

Given, then, that adults underestimate the young child, it would be interesting to consider the reasons for this refusal to recognise realities. The underevaluation prejudice may be construed in H. S. Sullivan's term as a 'parataxic distortion', an erroneous evaluation temporarily superimposed upon the actual abilities of the child. The extent of the error might be expected to diminish gradually in adults' evaluations of older children. Instead, in relation to school-aged children, the reference pattern of the adults results in an overestimation, an equal distortion of reality, though in the opposite direction (Ponzo, 1958; De Grada and Ponzo, 1971; D'Alessio, 1977; D'Alessio and Ortu, in press a and b).

Attributing to children abilities superior to those they actually possess implies a concern which induces frustration because of its disproportion to reality. In the case of the school-age child we can again recognise the familiar remarks of adults, though they have now become complaints. There is the teacher who says 'this child could do better' and the perplexed parent who notes that 'He was so clever when he was little, but now he's having problems; he used to be the first to do everything.' Again the interlocutor will show a friendly face, but deep down they *know* that this Johnny is far from being a genius: he must be quite slow if he cannot resolve problems and difficulties that other children of this age easily solve.

The reference pattern, although stereotyped, is not uniform across all the possible performances of the child. The 'expectations' of adults, in some areas of behaviour, even go in the opposite direction. Dell'Antonio (1977) found not only that there is a difference in adults' expectations before and after six years, but also that within age levels expectations vary for different abilities. Representations of the two- to three-year-old child, for example, also include expectations of precocious control of the sphincters and autonomy in eating or climbing the stairs or performing simple tasks. While the five- or six-year-old child seems too young for logical or manual abilities, they will never be young enough to fit the model we have defined as 'comfortable' for the adult.

The trend from under- to overestimation in the representation of child development (see Figure 5.2) suggests that the reference pattern which adults use is complex and takes into account not only the adults' ideas, but also their behaviour towards the child and the development of the child's abilities. 'Real knowledge' (personal or professional) plays a role in the reference pattern evoked by our questions, together with the norms and values which characterise typical performances.

Professional experience: teachers

The stereotype of age as an oversimplified conceptualisation of the reality of the child, is difficult to verbalise. It is rarely consciously present yet establishes a set of *universal* expectations. Like prejudice, it implies a predisposition to action in accordance with these expectations. It is also rigid and resistant to change, being only very slightly influenced by explicit patterns such as knowledge based upon experience.

In the case of elementary school teachers, the general principles of economy of stereotypes are consistent with this structure; familiarity with children does not affect the simple and stable beliefs which are applied to a school child to stimulate and encourage their development. In a study using the Gille Test (D'Alessio, 1977), teachers of 800 children in the third year of elementary school (eight years old) were asked to indicate the abilities of the pupils actually present in their classes. At the same time, the pupils' records were examined in order to compare teachers' expectations with children's performances. The results are shown in Figures 5.3 and 5.4. Although teachers were discreet judges of elementary knowledge and of the general level of education of their pupils, they all made the same error of systematically overestimating abstract–spatial and reasoning abilities. In some cases, they expected nothing less than the maximum possible performance from all their pupils.

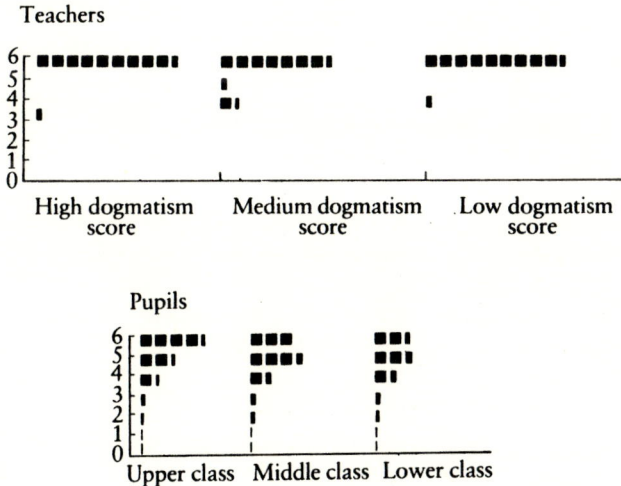

Figure 5.3 Frequency distributions of teachers' expectations and pupils' performance for the elementary knowledge items of the Gille Test

Teachers

Pupils

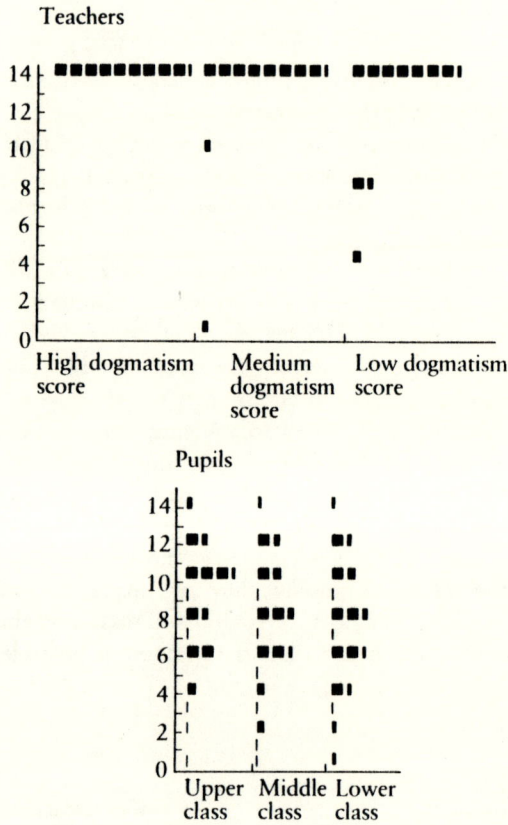

Figure 5.4 Frequency distributions of teachers' expectations and pupils' performance for the spatial organisation items of the Gille Test

In another study using items drawn from the WISC (D'Alessio, 1974), significant differences between the expectations of teachers and the ability of pupils were also observed in relation to language comprehension (Table 5.2).

Table 5.2 *Comparison between adult expectations and children's performance on verbal items from the WISC*

	N	Mean	Standard deviation	T	P
Teachers	57	49·31	10·23	5·95	< 0·001
Pupils	73	37·16	15·84		

The social context of stereotyped representations

The investigation of adults' implicit theories requires controls relating to the size and characteristics of the sample examined. The sample must be as large as possible, especially for the evaluation of the shared aspect of the representation; it must be articulated in terms of the possible differential variables both internal, such as gender, age, level of education or social class; and external, such as the particular context in which the investigation occurs, and the more general social environment.

One aspect of social research often neglected in methodology is the relationship of the setting organised for the research (questionnaire–interview, observation) to the evocation of the representation being examined. The extent to which a stereotype is shared by a group of subjects, for example, can depend on the particular demand made by the experimenter rather than the evocation of any implicit theory of reference.

The stability of the stereotype of the child is apparent from a study (D'Alessio, 1977) in which we presented questions about children's abilities to the same subjects (grouped in terms of levels of education and income) in three different ways:

(1) A *generalised questionnaire* which asked for the subject's expectation of the competence of the normal child in respect of each task.

(2) An *individualised questionnaire* which covered the same set of tasks, but presented them as the performances of a particular child whose name, age and sex were specified. In this case respondents were asked to judge whether the performance on each task was normal, advanced or delayed for that age.

(3) *Practical administration*, in which the actual test materials were shown to the adults as they were asked for their estimates of children's abilities. In this way we sought to obtain expectations based upon concrete experience with the materials (cubes of wood to join together, etc.).

The gender and age of subjects exerted very little influence on their stereotyped representation of childhood. As in other research (Emiliani et al, 1981), male adults, because they have little or no experience with children, show more rigid and erroneous beliefs. And age, if not accompanied by experience or if not evaluated together with more specific personality traits, such as dogmatism, also has little influence, even in the case where those imagining the behaviour and abilities of younger children are themselves youngsters of eleven to fourteen years of age (D'Alessio, 1977 and D'Alessio and Ortu, in press b). Different levels of education and income are key variables in social psychological research. Questionnaires are always presented in a particular socio-linguistic idiom, and this often makes it

Table 5.3 *Variables influencing parental ideas about children's cognitive competences*

Independent variable	Influence on dependent variable	Direction
Age and sex of parents	n.s.	
Number of children	n.s.	
Social class	n.s.	
Children's sex	$P < 0.05$	Girls undervalued
Administration	$P < 0.01$	Fewer errors with practical administration
Personality	$P < 0.05$	More dogmatic, more errors

difficult to compare the results obtained from subjects of different levels of education. At times, indeed, implicit theories and social representations seem to be distributed through the population according to the contours of social class. However, our results showed no differences between subjects with an elementary education and those with a higher education.

The gender of the stimulus children which subjects are asked to judge does, however, influence the responses. Even less is expected from two- and three-year-old female children than from males of the same age. The relative underestimation of female children compared to males also persists after the age of six (though this undervaluation of female children carries the small benefit that they will be less over-valued than males). As in other areas of life, girls are the object of a double stereotype, since they are both children and female.

The only manipulation which reduced estimation error was the presentation of the items through *practical administration*, and even in this case only very slight reductions were observed. For three out of the twelve items, a perceptible decrease in errors was noted, although the error was not eliminated.

Overall, therefore, the social representation of childhood which we have described is widely shared; its distribution is independent of the gender, age and socio-cultural level of respondents.

Finally, subjective personality structure was also examined as an influence on the representation of the child. De Grada and Ponzo (1971) hypothesised a relationship between the way the adult intuitively imagines the average normal child, and the general organisation of their beliefs along the dimension of the open and closed mind as proposed by Rokeach (1960). To the extent to which it is the *how* more than the *what* which is thought to explain authoritative behaviour, it should not be difficult to demonstrate that some educational practices and opinions, apparently founded on noble ideas, are actually vehicles for the educational dogmatism of adults.

Using the generative dimensions and parameters proposed by Rokeach, two scales were constructed which present the adult–child relationship in terms of an opposition between 'positive beliefs' (the adult) and 'negative beliefs' (the child and newborn). The items were presented as seven-point Lickert scales running from a more (7) or less (1) dogmatic way of establishing a relationship with a child or educating the child. The items covered a range of themes, from the perception of the newborn as irrelevant to the adult they will become, to the adult's dogmatic accentuation of the differences between the adult and the nursing infant, and a variety of ways in which experience is selectively restructured to avoid contact with facts, events and ideas which are incongruous with one's own system of beliefs. Examples of the items are:

(a) It is not the nursing infant which is important, but the adult that it will become.

(b) The nursing infant is an instinctive being, the adult is a rational being; this is why it is so difficult to understand the newborn.

(c) Each thing has its own time. Intelligence must be formed gradually. There is no need for the nursing infant to learn too soon things which it must learn in the future.

(d) In educating her child, a mother may not know what she is doing, but if she does it with love, she is never mistaken.

(e) It is good not to spoil newborns with simpering affection and blandishments, but to get them used to receiving only indispensable attention.

Personality structure, as investigated by Rokeach's model of the open and closed mind, seems to have very little influence on the actual expectations of children's abilities. Once again, the idea of childhood is independent of personality organisation. The more dogmatic subjects think that there is no difference between people who are more dogmatic and people who are less dogmatic in the prediction of child behaviour, while the less dogmatic subjects think that beliefs may be articulated according to mentality.

Conclusion

The research reviewed in this chapter offers abundant evidence that adults' ideas about children's abilities are organised as a social representation of childhood. As such these representations are not merely formal ideas, but directly connected to the social contexts in which people act. It is important, therefore, to try to make explicit the dynamic between action and representation.

The experience which adults have with their own children can be read as moments in which new data can be anchored to existing schemes. This involves both the recognition that their own children belong to the category of small, incapable children and a comparison of their children's activity with their representation of the competence attributed to this category of children. But adults, as we have seen, underestimate the abilities of small children, so that the outcome of this dual process of recognition and comparison will be the confirmation of both the general stereotype and the exceptionality of their own children. Once anchored in these ways the adult's conception of their children will be objectified in their actions towards the children.

The model of social representation proposed by Moscovici in terms of anchoring and objectification thus incorporates the continual interplay of the ideas, norms and values which justify the objectification. In this sense it represents an extension of the Piagetian model of cognitive dynamism in terms of assimilation and accommodation. Yet the incorporation of norms and values within the model also suggests that it will be very difficult to modify the social representation of a group of young people. They will be relatively impervious to concrete information about children's actual abilities, even if the information is presented through a technique similar to cognitive dissonance (Ponzo and Ercolani, 1983).

The model which I think shows the development of the social representation of child development is that of individual persons who are immersed in their social context and, therefore, as they grow up, engaged in reconstructing the ideas, beliefs and opinions of their community. The real dynamic moment occurs when the individual acquires actual experience of children through the birth and growth of their own children. At this point they are bombarded with a wealth of information through their relationship with their children.

There will be changes and adjustments in the adults' representation until, with the passage of time, their children grow up and become part of the adult community. In the course of this process the individual's experience with their children will entail less and less exposure to information contrasting with the general idea, the social representation of the average child. Gradually, therefore, discrepant ideas will become less significant for the individual, and their beliefs will restabilise in terms of the social representation.

Thus, social representations can be relatively impervious to individual diversity and elasticity; they are constructed through mechanisms of rationalisation which are sufficient to absorb interpersonal mutations.

Moscovici's introduction of the theory of social representations offers the prospect of an account of the social transmission of knowledge which steers a course between the abstract model proposed by Piaget and the static model of Durkheim's sociology.

References

Allport, G. W. (1954). *The Nature of Prejudice*. Cambridge, Mass: Addison-Wesley.

Asch, S. (1952). *Social Psychology*. New York: Prentice-Hall.

Berger, P. and Luckmann, T. (1966). *The Social Construction of Reality*. New York: Doubleday.

Berman, P. (1980). Are women more responsive than men to the young? A review of developmental and situational variables. *Psychological Bulletin*, 88, 668–95.

D'Alessio, M. (1974). Sopravvalutazione dello sviluppo del linguaggio del bambino normale e dogmatismo educativo. *Psicologia sociale e dello sviluppo*, 3.

(1977). Contributions to E. Ponzo (ed.), *Il bambino semplificato e trasparente*. Rome: Bulzoni.

(1987). Construendo l'infanzia. In *Il bambino incompiuto*, pp. 53–60. Rome: Bulzoni.

D'Alessio, M. and Ortu, F. (in press a). *Parents' Ideas about Children: A Greek and Italian Comparison*.

(in press b). *The Different Representation of Ability of Male and Female Children in Greek and Italian Subjects*.

De Grada, E. and Ponzo, E. (1966). Fattori personali associati con l' 'ottimismo–pessimismo' nella valutazione di capactià del bambino 'normale'. *Rivista di Psicologia*, LX, 55–70.

(1971). La normalità del bambino come pregiudizio dell'adulto. *Psicologia sociale e dello sviluppo*, vol. 1. Rome: Bulzoni.

Dell'Antonio, A. M. (1977). Il bambino obbediente e non pensante. *Psicologia sociale e dello sviluppo*, 6, 275–94.

Durkheim, E. (1898). Représentations individuelles et représentations collectives. *Revue de métaphysique et de morale*, 6, 273–302. (English translation in E. Durkheim, *Sociology and Philosophy* (New York: The Free Press, 1974).)

Emiliani, F., Zani, B. and Carugati, F. (1981). From interaction strategies to social representation of adults in a day-nursery. In W. P. Robinson, (ed.) *Communication in Development*. London: Academic Press.

Gesell, A. (1943). *Infant and Child in the Culture of Today*. New York: Harper.

Goodnow, J. J. (1984). Parents' Ideas about Parenting and Development: a review of issues and recent work. In M. E. Lamb, A. L. Brown and B. Rogoff (eds.), *Advances in Developmental Psychology*, vol. III, pp. 193–242. Hillsdale, N.J.: Erlbaum.

Goodnow, J. J., Knight, R. and Cashmore, J. (1986). Adult social cognition: implications of parents' ideas for approaches to development. In M. Perlmutter (ed.), *Cognitive Perspectives on Children's Social and Behavioural Development: Minnesota Symposia on Child Development*, vol. 18, pp. 287–324. Hillsdale, N.J.: Erlbaum.

Heider, F. (1958). *The Psychology of Interpersonal Relations*. New York: Wiley.

Hess, R. D. (1981) Approaches to the measurement and interpretation of parent–child interaction. In R. W. Henderson (ed.), *Parent–Child Interaction: Theory, Research and Prospects*. New York: Academic Press.

Hochberg, J. E. (1964). *Psicologia della percezione*. Milano: Martello.

Huckstedt, B. (1965). Experimentelle Untersuchungen zum 'Kindchenschema'. Z. *exper. angew. Psychol.*, 12, 421–50.

Keller, H., Miranda, D. and Gauda, G. (1984). The naive theory of the infant and some maternal attitudes: a two-country study. *Journal of Cross-Cultural Psychology*, 15, 165–79.

Kohn, M. L. (1969). *Class and Conformity*. Homewood, Ill.: Dorsey.

Loevinger, J. (1959). Patterns of parenthood or theories of learning. *Journal of Abnormal and Social Psychology*, 59, 148–50.

Lorenz, K. Z. (1943). Die angeborenen Formen möglicher Erfahrung. *Zeitschrift fur Tierpsychologie*, 5, 235–409.

McCall, R. B. and Kennedy, C. B. (1980). Attention to babyishness in babies. *Journal of Experimental Child Psychology*, 29, 189–201.

Merleau-Ponty, M. (1964). Leçons du 1949. *Bulletin de Psychologie*, 18, 2–3, 109.

Moscovici, S. (1984). The phenomenon of social representations. In R. M. Farr and S. Moscovici (eds.), *Social Representations*. Cambridge: Cambridge University Press.

Nietzsche, F. (1986). *Human, All Too Human*. Cambridge: Cambridge University Press.

Ninio, A. (1979). The naive theory of the infant and other maternal attitudes in two subgroups in Israel. *Child Development*, 50, 976–80.

Panier Bagat, M. and Ponzo, E. (1974). Prototipo infantile e rifiuto del neonato, contributo di ricerca. *Psicologia sociale e dello sviluppo*, 3, 47–67.

Panier Bagat, M., Ponzo, E. et al. (1977). La potenziale gradevolezza del neonato: maternità ed esperienze con figli altrui. *Psicologia sociale e dello sviluppo*, 6, 94–114.

Parke, R. D., Hymel, S., Power, T.G., and Tinsly, B. R. (1980). Fathers and risk: a hospital-based model of invention. In D. B. Swain, R. C. Hawkins, L. O. Walker and J. H. Penticuff (eds.), *Exceptional Infant*, vol. 4. New York: Brumer-Mazel.

Pichon, E. (1947). *Le Développement de l'enfant et de l'adolescent*. Paris: Delachaux et Niestle.

Ponzo, E. (1958). Le prestazioni dei bambini di età prescolare nella valutazione di adulti. *Infanzia Anormale*, 191–216.

Ponzo, E. and Ercolani, A. P. (1983). Lo stereotipo di sottovalutazione dell capactià infantili. *Età Evolutiva*, 15, 56–64.

Rokeach, M. (1960). *The Open and Closed Mind*. New York: Basic Books.

Sternberg, R. J. (1985). *Beyond I.Q. A Triarchic Theory of Human Intelligence*. Cambridge: Cambridge University Press.

Zazzo, R. (1958). L'evoluzione psicologica del fanciullo da due a sei anni. In M. Debesse (Italian trans.), *Psicologia dell' età evolutiva*. Rome: Armando.

6

What is in an image?
The structure of mothers' images of the child and their influence on conversational styles[1]

Luisa Molinari   Francesca Emiliani

Introduction

We frequently resort to the use of vivid images, aware as we are of their explicative power: we search our minds for them to explain a concept or idea which, because of its abstract nature, may not be readily understood. We are also aware that employing an image not only results in a simplification of information but also makes the concept familiar by relating it to our listener's knowledge of everyday life. Everyday language and knowledge are particularly rich in images precisely because they merge and accomplish this transformation from concept to image.

The notion of the use of images, as Abric (1987) has recently pointed out, has a long history in the psychological literature, though in terms of a perceptual model in which the image is seen as a reflection of the outside world with a clear separation between the subject and the object. Our interpretation of the image derives from the concept of representation, and assumes a constitutive relation between subject and object. In these terms the image is not a mere reflection of the object as such, but a product of complex relations, either real or imaginary, objective or symbolic, which the subject projects into a specific object.

From a cognitive point of view a representation may be assimilated within a mental framework which Zajonc (1968) described as a form of interdependence between cognitive elements which affects motivation, attitudes, emotion and behaviour. The notion of social representation, as Abric (1987) observes, involves a much more complex process, a total reconstruction of reality in its psychological, social and ideological aspects.

[1] We should like to thank the Italian Ministry of Education, the National Research Council and the Regione Emilia Romagna for their support for this research.

Social representations provide a way of thinking about and interpreting one's daily life. They are conceptualised as a form of knowledge influenced by social factors at more than one level, namely the daily context in which individuals and groups live, the communication which is established between them and the codes, values and ideologies connected to specific roles or social statuses.

Moscovici (1981, 1984) views social representations as a modern version of common sense, defining them as theories of common sense regarding prominent aspects of social life. The term 'common sense' currently embraces two different forms of knowledge: first-hand knowledge rooted in tradition and consensus and the more recent kind deriving from a 'recycling' of scientific knowledge into a form accessible for everyday use. It is the latter type which more fully becomes imaginative thinking, precisely because one of the processes involved in this transformation, namely figuration, entails the substitution of images for concepts. In this process, the image can no longer be characterised as a more or less precise or elaborated reflection of the outside world, as a reproduction of the world. On the contrary, the image needs to be understood as the result of a process which is both cognitive and social at the same time.

The image in these terms is the iconic aspect of a representation which expresses the shared reconstruction of a specific social reality. In a study on the representation of the body, Jodelet (1976) illustrates clearly the relationship between the iconic and the symbolic aspects in social representation. The female sex is defined as the 'holy tabernacle of life'. This image abounds with meanings and ideas: the womb is described as a 'tabernacle', an object which is necessarily associated with religion; 'holy' denotes that which is forbidden and 'life' indicates the fact that the female sex is devoted to reproduction. Indirect references to this image were found in the way the women interviewed expressed their relationship to sexuality by resorting to descriptive, symbolic and even normative elements furnished by the group to which they belong. The iconic matrix is necessary in order to *anchor* the symbolism attributed to the human body to a religious support; the images, moreover, provide a vivid example of the *objectification* characteristic of social representation.

Objectification means reabsorbing an excess of meanings into tangible form. This process is intrinsic to the structuring of any social process, but in the case of social representations it takes the form of a central figurative nucleus constructed through a selection of information and results in the *naturalisation* of the object. The selection of information and, as a consequence, the structuring of the central nucleus, is heavily influenced by the social position of individuals in everyday life and by the communications in which they engage.

The studies by Chombart de Lauwe (1971) on the social representations of childhood also provide evidence of the presence of typified images of the child in the collective imagination. These images are built around a bipolar nucleus: the myth of authenticity as opposed to what is viewed as non-authentic, that is, spontaneous and free from normative conditioning. This image crystallises a mythical outlook on the child, and in the process the child becomes a symbol of a world of values and for this very reason unreal. These images of an 'idealised child', separated from social reality, provoke unreal expectations, not without risks for the child, and convey a way of seeing the child more as a future man or woman than as a being in formation.

In a recent study (Emiliani and Molinari, 1987) we found the typical characteristics of objectification in mothers' description of their own children. What emerged was a concept of *character* seen as natural fact, present at birth and unlikely to be influenced by educational processes. This conviction acquired a tangible form in the mothers' descriptions of their children, because they, and in particular the mothers who were professional teachers, seemed to adopt a mainly *naturalised* and *objectified* thought. Naturalisation is a process which is triggered in the absence of a scientific and rational model to deal with elements that are conflicting, contradictory or simply too complex to explain, such as the differences between children; this is equivalent to ascribing the characteristics of the other, the child, to the mystery of biology or astrology. In the case at hand, the result of this process serves the purpose of maintaining a positive identity both as mother and as teacher, since it removes the responsibility both from mother and teacher.

How do these images of the child as symbol relate to the image of the child in daily life in the minds of adults who deal with children on a daily basis? There is no doubt that what makes the relationship between scientific knowledge, values, and the knowledge of everyday reality particularly dynamic is the intervention of direct experience. This forces us to come to terms with reality. The topic about which one is asked to express an opinion is made salient through comparison with other ideas. Such processes of comparison require socio-cognitive regulation, as Mugny and Carugati (1985) have pointed out in a study on the representations of intelligence (see also Carugati, this volume).

Conversations between children and adults provide an example of these processes. Adults are guided by a desire to promote interaction and thus adjust their responses to the immaturity of their partner. A great deal of literature exists which demonstrates how mothers and adults generally tend to adapt their language to the verbal comprehension which they attribute to children on the basis of their representation of children's knowledge and ability to understand reality. This means that in certain utterances the adults bear in mind not only their role in the interaction, the role and status of their interlocutor and the social context in which the interaction takes place, but also the norms and social conventions belonging to a given context, as well as tacit agreements relating to a shared reality. It is within these shared realities that adults construct enhanced images of the child (Gilly, 1980), and it is these images which guide their behaviour when interacting with children. In our own research with nursery-school teachers (Emiliani, Zani and Carugati, 1982; Emiliani and Zani, 1983) we found that different organisational styles and different conversational styles of the nurseries reflected different underlying images of the child. For example, in organisation-oriented nurseries constant reference was made to the 'well-socialised child', that is the child who is well adjusted to the institution, whereas in child-oriented nurseries the child's emotional needs were highlighted.

Aims and hypotheses

The aim of this study is first of all to identify the images of the child shared by a sample of mothers. More specifically, we have attempted to highlight three differing images of the child which refer to the 'child that can be influenced', to the 'desired child' and to their own child as mothers describe them in everyday life.

Our main concern is to assess whether the figurative nucleus is influenced by the social position of people in everyday life. For this reason, we chose to analyse the images of the child both of mothers who were housewives and of women who, besides being mothers, also worked outside the home. We assume that the dynamic of the dual role of mother and worker affects the development of social representations of childhood. The question here concerns the relation between social representations and social identities, because the experience of conflicts of identities constitutes a source of transformation of social representations. For example, a woman in her role as mother uses as a reference point a particular image of the child built on several traits, while in her role as worker she may find it necessary to stress different traits associated with a different image.

Secondly, as the notion of social representation links symbolic processes and behaviour, we consider whether, and to what extent, a process of symbolic elaboration may be predictive of modes of behaviour. In particular, we wish to assess the predictive potential of images of the child on styles of behaviour adopted during a conversation task between mother and child.

We advance the following hypotheses:

1. Women who carry out various activities (housewives, factory workers, office workers and teachers) construct differentiated images of the child. In this respect, we feel it is possible that the group of teachers will be distinct from the other groups, by virtue of the complexity and the conflictual elements present in their dual role.

2. The image that mothers have of their own children does not match their images of the 'desired child' and the 'child that can be influenced'. The differing degrees of adherence to these images in daily life play an important role in differentiating between mothers.

3. The image of the child in the mothers' minds guides the linguistic and communicative behaviour of the mother when she addresses her child. This is true above all in regard to the content and information necessary in order to ensure comprehension on the part of the child. Questions of syntax or semantic relations are not our concern here.

Procedure

The sample in our study consisted of 80 mothers of children from two to six years of age. These mothers came from four distinct groups: housewives, office workers, factory workers and teachers.

All the mothers in the sample completed four tasks:

(1) An attitude scale on the *degree of influence* they perceived themselves having on nineteen traits describing their children's behaviour. Examples of these traits are curiosity, cleanliness and obedience. These data provide information about the mothers' images of the child in terms of the influence they believe they can exert over the child.

(2) An attitude scale on the *degree of importance* which mothers attributed to the same set of nineteen traits. Mothers were asked to rate the importance attributed to each trait on a seven-point scale. These data are analysed in terms of the image they provide of the child the mothers would wish to have, *the desired child*.

(3) A detailed interview in which mothers were asked to describe the pleasant and enjoyable moments spent with their own child. Mothers were also asked questions about their children's behaviour during some critical events of daily life (meals, getting dressed, etc). All phrases and adjectives referring to their own children were examined and coded into the following fourteen categories:

Sociability (Sociable, likes to be with other people)
Shyness (Shy, afraid of other people)
Aggressiveness (Aggressive, rough)
Autonomy (Autonomous, does not want help)

Dependency (Does not want to be or to do things alone)
Intelligence (Intelligent, quick to understand)
Affectivity (Affectionate)
Liveliness (Vivacious, lively)
Opposition (Never listens, when he says no it's no)
Socialisation rules (Tidy, clean, well-mannered)
Emotional aspects (Sensitive, is easily offended)
Well-being (Happy, quiet)
Determination (Firm, knows what he wants)
Play (Need for play).

These data thus provide particular information about mothers' *images of their own children.*

(4) A picture book reading task in which mothers were given a booklet containing a series of pictures and asked to tell the story to their child. No other instructions were given to the mothers in order not to influence the way in which they chose to tell the story to their child. The conversations were recorded and transcribed verbatim. Our analysis is mainly concerned with the function of various phrases in the discourse within the interactive situation. The mothers' linguistic productions were coded into five categories: (1) descriptions, (2) explanations, (3) inferences, (4) questions and (5) answers. These categories were then sub-divided as follows:

(1) Descriptions

Simple descriptions of objects or events
Psychological descriptions of thoughts, wishes, emotions attributed to the character of the story (a little mouse)
Paraphrase, when one description is added to a previous one, to allow the child to refer, in two different ways, to the same object or event

(2) Explanations

Via reclassification, explanations which analyse the specific characteristics of an object and assimilate them
Causal explanations, each piece of information given with the purpose of enabling the interlocutor to comprehend a second one
Examples, which link events (or objects) familiar to the child and taken as paradigmatic with events (or objects) found in the story and considered similar to the previously mentioned objects
Indexes, some elements found in the context serving the purpose of helping the child to recognise an object as belonging to a specific class of object

(3) Inferences

Descriptive inferences, verbal productions of a descriptive kind which mention information not present in the illustrated text
Causal inferences, information not explicitly stated in the text given with the purpose of enabling the interlocutor to comprehend other information

(4) Questions

Tutorial: questions which elicit descriptive information regarding the text from the child

Rhetorical: the adult uses the illustrated text to urge the child to imagine events about to occur

Clarification requests: interrogative utterances used by the speaker to ask for explanations, confirmations or repetitions of an utterance previously produced by the listener, but which has not been perfectly understood

Extracontextual, which are not directly linked to the text but to the child's knowledge

(5) Answers

Answers, following a child's question

Emphatic reinforcements: expressions of the phatic type used to back up and emphasise what the interlocutor has said, thus encouraging them to continue

Confirmations: adult's expressions that precisely repeat words just spoken by the child

Extensions: expressions that contain some of the child's words or sentences but rearranged in a grammatically correct form and which may also introduce new semantic information

Non-responses: the speaker's phrase is left unanswered or is ignored by his interlocutor

Reliability for the codings was assessed by having three judges independently code 25 per cent of the transcripts. The inter-judge agreement was over 90 per cent.

Results

Four factor analyses (principal components) were undertaken in order to describe both the images of the child which mothers share and the conversational styles which they adopt while interacting with their children. Analyses of variance were conducted on the factor scores as a function of the mothers' type of work. In addition, correlations between the factor scores were examined and a multiple regression analysis undertaken to examine the factor scores of the images of the child as predictors of conversational styles.

Images of the child

The image of the child that can be influenced

The first factor analysis was performed on the data from the first questionnaire, which concerned the degree of influence perceived by mothers in relation to nineteen traits of children's behaviour. This analysis revealed the presence of four images of the child, as Table 6.1 shows.

Table 6.1 *Factor analysis of the degree of influence perceived on the traits of behaviour*

Factor 1 (59·9%)	
0·72	He is tidy
0·71	He is clean
0·70	He is well-mannered
0·65	He is affectionate
0·61	He is autonomous
0·60	He is able to control himself
0·59	He is sociable
0·58	He is happy
0·57	He is able to be alone
0·55	He is liked by other children
0·46	He is obedient
Factor 2 (6·1%)	
0·73	He is able to defend himself
0·70	He is tough
0·69	He is liked by other children
0·64	He is assertive
0·50	He is able to control himself
0·50	He can easily adapt to changes
0·47	He is happy
0·47	He is not discouraged by difficulties
0·36	He is autonomous
Factor 3 (4·7%)	
0·78	He is curious about things
0·68	He can easily adapt to changes
0·55	He is able to be alone
0·52	He is sociable
0.52	He is not discouraged by difficulties
0·43	He is tough
0·39	He is autonomous
0·37	He is happy
Factor 4 (4·3%)	
0·80	He does not tell lies
0·70	He is docile
0·66	He is obedient
0·45	He is well-mannered
0·42	He is not discouraged by difficulties
0·40	He is able to control himself
0·38	He is tidy
0·37	He is clean

Table 6.2 *Mean factor scores from the analysis of influence as a function of mothers' working position*

	H	FW	OW	T
Factor 1	−0·23	0·12	0·28	−0·10
Factor 2	−0·25	0·13	−0·06	0·28
Factor 3	0·02	−0·49	−0·06	0·53[a]
Factor 4	0·12	0·25	0·20	−0·19

[a] $P < 0·05$ in a one-way analysis of variance for this factor.

The first factor appears to cover a very broad range: it accounts for almost 60 per cent of the variance, and illustrates how mothers perceive their power to influence children in relation to socialisation rules (tidiness, cleanliness, obedience), sociability and autonomy. The second factor groups together characteristics of assertiveness and firmness (ability to defend oneself, toughness, self-assertion). The third factor comprises traits that describe a child as intelligent, autonomous and sociable. The fourth factor depicts a 'well-socialised child' according to those mothers who use the socialisation rules as a basic criterion.

One-way analyses of variance of each set of factor scores were undertaken with the occupational category of mothers as the independent variable (Table 6.2). Teachers perceived themselves as having a greater influence than the other groups of mothers over the child in relation to the characteristics delineated by the third factor (intelligent, sociable, autonomous; $F(3,76) = 3·26$; $P < 0·03$). There were no significant differences in the analyses of the other three factors.

The image of the desired child

The factor analysis conducted on the degree of importance attributed by mothers to the nineteen behaviour traits (the second questionnaire) produced three factors, described in Table 6.3. The positive pole of the first factor groups together the socialisation rules, while traits of autonomy and intelligence are located at the negative pole. The second factor is also bipolar, with an image of the 'silent child' (obedient and controlled) opposed to that of the 'lively child' (curious about things and happy). The third factor groups the traits of firmness around the negative pole, as opposed to a more heterogeneous collection of traits grouped around the positive pole, including the importance of cleanliness and traits which place the child in relation to peers (liked by other children and able to defend themselves).

Table 6.3 *Factor analysis of the degree of importance attributed to the traits of behaviour*

Factor 1 (12·8%)	
0·58	He does not tell lies
0·56	He is well-mannered
0·41	He is tidy
0·39	He is docile
−0·63	He is autonomous
−0·40	He can easily adapt to changes
−0·35	He is curious about things
Factor 2 (8·8%)	
0·71	He is able to defend himself
0·37	He is obedient
−0·59	He is curious about things
−0·55	He is happy
Factor 3 (8·4%)	
0·53	He is clean
0·50	He is able to defend himself
0·45	He is liked by other children
−0·59	He is assertive
−0·49	He is able to be alone
−0·47	He is not discouraged by difficulties

Table 6·4 *Mean factor scores from the analysis of importance as a function of mothers' working positions*

	H	FW	OW	T
Factor 1	0·27	0·16	0·04	−0·58[a]
Factor 2	0·07	0·28	0·05	−0·43
Factor 3	−0·13	0·21	0·14	−0·18

[a] $P < 0.05$ in a one-way analysis of variance for this factor.

One-way analysis of variance on the factor scores (Table 6.4) showed a significant difference on the first factor between housewives, who express agreement with the positive pole (that is the rules), and teachers who agree with the negative pole ($F(3,76) = 2.90$; $P < 0.05$). This indicates that housewives consider important, and therefore desire, a child who meekly obeys the rules, while teachers desire an autonomous and intelligent child.

There were no significant differences among the groups of mothers in analyses of the factor scores of the other two factors.

Table 6.5. *Factor analysis of the spontaneous references to their own child*

Factor 1 (16·1%)	
0·75	Dependency
−0·80	Intelligence
−0·57	Liveliness
Factor 2 (12·4%)	
0·68	Well-being
0·57	Play
−0·60	Emotional aspects
−0·59	Determination
Factor 3 (10·8%)	
0·64	Socialisation rules
0·63	Affectivity
−0·75	Opposition
−0·37	Sociability

Table 6.6 *Mean factor scores from the analysis of mothers' spontaneous references to their own child as a function of their working position*

	H	FW	OW	T
Factor 1	−0·32	−0·11	0·13	0·41[a]
Factor 2	0·18	−0·04	−0·16	−0·04
Factor 3	0·03	−0·08	−0·29	0·36

[a] $P < 0.05$ in a one-way analysis of variance for this factor.

The image of one's own child

The third factor analysis, carried out on all the spontaneous references made by the mothers while talking about their children in the course of interviews, also produced distinct images of the child (Table 6.5).

On the first factor the item of dependency is contrasted with the items of intelligence and liveliness, indicating that those mothers who describe their own children as dependent are not the mothers who use terms such as 'vivacity' and 'intelligence'. The second factor contrasts characteristics relative to the well-being and playfulness of the child to traits of firmness and specific emotional responses, namely sensitivity and touchiness. Finally, the third factor again refers to the socialisation rules alongside traits of affectivity, as opposed to the descriptions of a sociable and rebellious child.

The analysis of variance of the factor scores for the first factor (Table 6.6)

101

Table 6.7 *Significant correlations between factor scores*

	1	2	3	4	1	2	3	1	2	3
INFLUENCE										
Factor 1										
Factor 2										
Factor 3					−0·37					
Factor 4					0·24					
IMPORTANCE										
Factor 1										
Factor 2										
Factor 3									−0·20	
REAL										
Factor 1										
Factor 2										
Factor 3		0·17								
	INFLUENCE				**IMPORTANCE**			**REAL**		

indicates that it is teachers who focus on dependency, and housewives who make greater use of such terms as 'vivacity' and 'intelligence' (F(3,76) = 2·37; P < 0·08). No significant differences emerged on the last two factors.

Relations between different images of the child

On the whole, the results of the factor analyses confirm the first hypothesis we put forward, that women engaged in different types of work have distinct images of the child. It is the teachers, in particular, who revealed the most interesting mental framework involving the play of different images. Correlations between the factor scores from the different analyses were then examined to explicate the relationships between these various images.

The first factor on the degree of importance is positively correlated to the fourth factor of influence (r = 0·24; P < 0·02) and negatively correlated with the third factor of influence (r = −0·37; P < 0·002). In terms of images, we find that the meanings of the traits considered as important match the meanings of the traits on which mothers feel able to exert an influence; that is to say, mothers who regard the socialisation rules as important for the development of the child also perceive themselves as being able to influence the child in respect of these rules. The same is true for the traits of intelligence and autonomy.

The same relationship between importance and influence does not hold for the mother's image of her own child: in fact, we find that the third factor of influence, which portrays an intelligent, autonomous and sociable child, is

Table 6.8 *Factor analysis of the categories of mother–child conversation*

Factor 1 (26·7%)	
0·76	Tutorial questions
0·76	Confirmations
0·72	Extensions
0·71	Extracontextual questions
0·67	Clarification requests
0·65	Empathic reinforcements
0·65	Rhetorical questions
0·55	Non-responses
0·45	Examples
Factor 2 (11·9%)	
0·79	Psychological descriptions
0·71	Descriptive inferences
0·64	Causal inferences
0·64	Simple descriptions

positively correlated to the third factor of the image of one's own child ($r = 0·17$; $P < 0·07$). In other words, the mothers who feel that the sociability and intelligence of a child can be influenced do not describe their own children using these terms, but refer to the socialisation rules and traits of affectivity.

Moreover, the third factor in the analysis of importance is negatively correlated to the first factor in the analysis of the image of one's child ($r = -0·20$; $P < 0·04$). This means that those who attribute importance to traits of autonomy and firmness actually highlight dependence on adults when talking about their own children. In addition, those who consider cleanliness and relations with peers important describe their child as intelligent and lively.

These results confirm our second hypothesis, which posed the question whether the differing degree of adherence of the images to daily life played a role in their differentiation.

Conversational styles

The factor analysis carried out on the categories used to study mother–child verbal interaction produced two different conversational styles, namely a 'dialogical style' and a 'narrative style' (Table 6.8).

The dialogical style is characterised by the use of questions (all the four types of this category are found in the first factor) and by the use of confirmations and of clarification requests to the child's utterances. In this style, we also find examples that indicate the attempt of the mothers to insert the daily knowledge of the child within the story. By using a dialogical style, the mother 're-enacts' the vignettes with the child, in an effort to insert within the story elements taken from daily life (extracontextual questions and examples), thus allowing the child to participate actively but at the same time monitoring the child's comprehension.

Within the narrative style, there is a predominance of elements of a descriptive type, of objects or events, or of wishes and emotions, and elements of an inferential type. In this case, it is the mother alone who controls the 'retelling' of the story, using simple modes of discourse (descriptions) or more complex ones (inferences, especially causal inferences). With this conversational style, the mother does not test the child's comprehension of the story, but rather adopts a more didactic approach, aimed at teaching and conveying knowledge.

In a final analysis, multiple regressions were undertaken to examine the capacity of the factor scores obtained from the analysis on the images of the child to predict the conversational styles. Separate analyses for dialogic and narrative style were undertaken for each of the three sets of factor scores.

The results of this analysis show that the mothers who stress the importance of intelligence and autonomy make a greater use of the narrative style (Beta $= -0.24$; $P < 0.04$). The same is true for those who perceive themselves as able to influence the same traits of autonomy, intelligence and sociability (factor 3 of influence, Beta $= 0.25$; $P < 0.03$). The narrative style is adopted by those who describe their own children in terms of emotional responses and firmness (Beta $= -0.32$; $P < 0.005$).

On the whole, these results enable us to state that having a dominant image of an Intelligent and Independent child favours the use of a narrative style in a reading-book task. Drawing upon the correlations among the factors, we feel we can state that particular images of the child guide the conversational styles utilised by the mothers during verbal interaction with their own children.

Conclusion

Our investigation was focussed on the study of images as *vivid* aspects of representations. Images are located at the crossroads of ideas, attitudes and feelings, and they guide the mothers' behaviour. Nevertheless, images as well as thoughts appear to be contradictory and discrepant: what is thought of as desirable does not always correspond to reality.

In their study on intelligence, Mugny and Carugati (1985) define social representations as ensembles composed of apparently contradictory discourses, the contradictions emerging not only between different groups but also within the same group. Our data confirm this model; there is no doubt that mothers refer to a multiplicity of elements, some of which may be inconsistent with others. From this point of view it may be of interest to trace some of the modes of discourse which emerged from our data, and in particular the findings regarding the teachers. In our opinion, what is crucial to their position is a discordance between the characteristics which they seem to appreciate in a child (intelligence and autonomy) and the way they describe their child as being dependent upon adults.

This discordance in teachers' representations of the child needs to be considered in the context of other aspects of teachers' social representations. In the analysis of other parts of the interviews with this sample of women (Emiliani and Molinari, 1987, 1988) we found that teachers are less in agreement than the other groups of mothers with the traditional division of parental social roles within the family. We found that they demand a direct and active involvement from their husbands in the home and with the children. They stressed the need for an open negotiation of conflicts, and were not inclined to overlook any problems which might arise.

Alongside this debate about parental social roles, teachers also showed a less rigid attitude towards educational conceptions, especially compared to housewives. Teachers do not seem to be worried about early toilet training, nor do they desire a tidy, clean and obedient child; on the contrary, they indirectly welcome a greater freedom of action and expression in their own children. It is precisely this autonomy in the child, characterised by an attitude of curiosity and adaptability towards the world, that teachers consider to be important and which they believe they are able to influence. In contrast with this, these teachers describe their own child in terms of dependency, which is experienced as painful by both the mother and the child. At this point the question to be asked is whether these women's myth of their own child as 'Autonomous and Intelligent' will become an obstacle to their understanding of their child's real need for relations, attachments and even dependence, especially given that the teachers are at the same time active and inclined to a degree of self-assertion within the family and the professional world.

A similar contrast can be found in the analysis of the conversational styles. Once again, those mothers who refer to the image of the Autonomous and Intelligent child seem to adhere to the narrative style in which the mother does not consider it necessary to monitor the child's comprehension of the story, but takes for granted that the child is able to retain and understand the information, even abstract information, which she provides. The definition of the child's level of comprehension, and therefore of their cognitive skills, derives from the representations which adults construct of them. Using the image of the child who 'understands' as a reference, the mothers choose to use a narrative style, by means of which they describe, explain and teach without involving the child in the retelling of the story. In the interactive situation, the child is relegated to a passive role: the 'Real' interacting child never becomes an active interlocutor of the story-telling.

References

Abric, J. C. (1987). *Coopération, compétition et représentations sociales*. Cousset: DelVal.

Chombart de Lauwe, M. J. (1971). *Un monde autre: l'enfance; de ses représentations à son mythe*. Paris: Payot.

Emiliani, F. and Molinari, L. (1987). Family environment and social representations of childhood. Paper presented at the Symposium on development reconstructions of social representations, Brighton, April.

   (1988). What everybody knows about children: mothers' ideas on early childhood. *European Journal of Psychology of Education*, 1, 19–31.

Emiliani, F. and Zani, B. (1983). Strategìe interattive e rappresentazioni sociali in operatrici di asilo nido. *Età evolutiva*, 14, 90–5.

Emiliani, F., Zani, B. and Carugati, F. (1982), Il bambino e l'asilo nido: immagini a confronto. *Giornale Italiano di psicologìa*, 9, 3, 455–68.

Gilly, M. (1980). *Maître-élève: rôles institutionnels et représentations*. Paris: Presses Universitaires de France.

Jodelet, D. (1976). *La Représentation sociale du corps*. Paris: Cordes.

Moscovici, S. (1976). *La Psychanalyse, son image et son public*. 2nd edn. Paris: Presses Universitaires de France.

   (1981). On social representations. In J. P. Forgas (ed.), *Social Cognition: Perspectives on Everyday Understanding*. London: Academic Press.

   (1984). The phenomenon of social representations. In R. M. Farr and S. Moscovici (eds.), *Social Representations*. Cambridge: Cambridge University Press.

Mugny, G. and Carugati, F. (1985). *L'Intelligence au pluriel*. Cousset, Fribourg (Switzerland): DelVal. (English translation forthcoming: *Social Representations of Intelligence*. Cambridge: Cambridge University Press.)

Zajonc, R. B. (1968). Cognitive theories in social psychology. In G. Lindzey and E. Aronson (eds.), *Handbook of Social Psychology*. Reading, Mass.: Addison-Wesley.

7

The acquisition of reflexive social emotions: the transmission and reproduction of social control through joint action[1]

Gün R. Semin and Kalliroi Papadopoulou

Introduction

In recent years there has been a considerable change in the way emotions have been conceptualised (Averill, 1974, 1976, 1980; Harré, 1986, inter alia). Underlying these more recent developments is a view of emotions as culturally and historically situated social practices. They represent essentially social psychological approaches to emotionality influenced by comparative work. Indeed there is a complementary resurgence of such work in anthropology as well (for example, Lutz, 1989). There is, however, another important issue that has remained a relatively open question, namely how such social practices are culturally transmitted from one generation to another. This invites a developmental perspective on social constructionist approaches. One interesting facet of combining these two perspectives is that it also permits a better understanding of the social origins of adult emotionality. This chapter is a preliminary contribution towards an understanding of how emotions are transmitted and the social-developmental origins of adult emotionality.

A feature of the changes that take place in early childhood is the acquisition of gradually more differentiated categorisations of self, others and the world, reflecting the appropriation of culture. Such is the case with emotions too, where one of the essential outcomes of socialisation is the acquisition of the naming rules applying to social practices in different situations. For example, in situations where embarrassment or guilt are the culturally informed and appropriate 'names' for the outcome of a social episode, the young child may respond in culturally uninformed and therefore 'inappropriate' emotional concomitants to the event. In the case of a transgression, this may take the form of anxiety due to an actual disciplinary response from a socialising agent

[1] The writing of this chapter was facilitated by an ESCR grant (No. R000231104) to the first author.

or at later stages anxiety as an anticipation of such a disciplinary response. Later on, one may witness internalisation of the disciplinary reaction to the event that caused the transgression. Thus, early concomitants do not serve as culturally relevant or informed identifiers for the social situation in question. However, the internalisation of such social practices, namely transgression–disciplinary action, along with the abstraction processes imposed by social interaction in general (i.e. communicative demands), leads to the emergence of a novel response to the same situation which may be embarrassment or guilt. To label the emotional experience in the situation as a 'response' is, however, not accurate in that what is taking place is a re-representation of the meaning of the interactive conduct in situ as a function of internalisation which in turn changes the nature of the interaction, and so on. All this can be seen as a dialectical process. Thus, internalisations actually transform the nature of the situation and therefore the nature of the interaction. The processes of re-representation within evolving classificatory schemata from early childhood to early adolescence may eventually result in what is termed by the language community in this instance embarrassment. The end of such acculturation is generally defined when cultural standards are performed, since no further social demands exist to disequilibriate the nature of interaction.

Thus, one of the features of the process of cultural acquisition is the modification of interactive and interpretative routines and rules. Such routines or rules which involve naming, classification and inferential reasoning as cognitive activities and representations constitute the one side of a coin that is otherwise imprinted with the interaction or social practice in situ. What is crucial in this context is that there is a gradual refinement of the emotion repertoire from early childhood to early adolescence as a function of the differentiated interaction rituals that characterise the differences in situations and the beliefs that socialising agents hold with respect to the 'abilities and competences' of the child (cf. chapters by Molinari and Emiliani and D'Alessio in this volume). Something rather interesting takes place, namely that the discretisation of emotion by culture constitutes a marriage of emotion to generic situations. Thus, distinct interaction rituals become identified with distinct emotions rules. An understanding of adult emotionality is therefore incomplete without an explication of the emotion representations which in fact stand for internalised interaction routines for specific types of interaction sequences in distinct situations grouped together by language games as belonging to the same class of situations.

The aim of this chapter is to examine the acquisition of such interaction rituals and illustrate critical features of the theoretical model with empirical work deriving from a specific emotion, namely embarrassment. This empirical illustration is achieved by investigating the beliefs of a critical group, namely mothers,[2] in situations where their child commits a *faux pas*. Mothers constitute an essential link in the social interaction that shapes children's emotional repertoires. What do they think their likely reactions and emotional experiences would be in situations involving *faux pas*? What do they think their child would do and experience in such situations? More importantly, why do they say the things they do? The last question constitutes the critical link between the theoretical model derived from Vygotsky's work and the empirical study reported in this chapter. The ninety mothers from whom the data are drawn were selected on the basis of their child's age, namely ten each from the age groups four to twelve. Half of the respondents' children were male and the other half female. The theoretical framework for this empirical investigation is a model of socio-emotional development extrapolated from Vygotsky's work. In concluding this section we shall elaborate briefly on the choice of emotion.

Embarrassment, the particular emotion singled out for illustrative purposes, is a 'negative' reflexive social emotion (Shott, 1979). Other examples of reflexive social emotions are guilt, shame, pride and vanity. The importance of this general class of emotions is that they entail self-reactions to internalised and accepted social standards (variously named conscience, superego, generalised other, etc.), which are abstractions acquired in the course of interaction, namely culturally supplied conventions, rules and moral values. They entail a special dynamic in contrast to primary emotions (Tomkins, 1962, 1963). They involve two special features in contrast to other emotions. First, a central process for the elicitation of negative reflexive social emotions consists in how one's self is perceived to appear to significant others as a consequence of particular actions. The actions in question are real or imagined social transgressions.[3] Second, these emotions are self-directed, are 'punitive' and check 'deviant behaviour'. Therefore, they constitute efficient control instances within individuals, and keep their behaviour compatible with the rules, social conventions and moral values of the society within which they live. This self-monitoring function of these social emotions makes them important social psychological mechanisms through which individuals become socialised into the ways of their culture.

[2] The sample consisted of ninety mothers of a predominantly working-class background, recruited through the local primary school. They were asked to fill in the questionnaire in terms of a specific child (for instance, their five-year-old daughter), which enabled us to include equal numbers of mothers of children at each of the nine age levels ranging from four to twelve years, and of both sexes.

[3] This does not mean that intentional or unintentional social transgressions always lead to a reflexive social emotion, but simply that a necessary condition for their experience consists in evoking a 'perceived public self-image', which is always negative (cf. Semin, 1981, 1982; Semin and Manstead, 1981, 1982). It is also possible that reflexive social emotions are experienced, without the person having committed a social transgression, i.e. empathically.

In the context of emotional development and socialisation reflexive emotions occupy an important position because child-rearing without the acquisition of such emotions would be a very difficult business. If children did not eventually acquire any self-generated notions of social and moral accountability to keep their activities in check; if they were not to develop a sense of responsibility towards accepted social norms, rules and conventions; or if they did not acquire self-monitored social control (self-control), then the socialising process would be difficult and time-consuming if not impossible. Reflexive social emotions play a central role in contributing to the self-monitoring of conduct. In the absence of self-monitored control one would have to rely on external monitoring methods, such as physical force, punishment, deprivation, withdrawal of external rewards, withholding of love and approval, etc. These would obviously necessitate continual vigilance. This, however, is both impractical and impossible. The relations between children and their parents thus have a particular significance for the acquisition of reflexive social emotions.

Theoretical background to the acquisition of emotional representations

Recently, studies of human emotions have considered the importance of situated, constitutive practices and the role that social rules, conventions and language play in the shaping of emotional experiences (Averill, 1980; Harré, 1986). Inevitably, such orientations have meant an increased sensitivity to the socio-cultural context of human emotions.

Social rules and conventions are of paramount importance to the interpretation, expression and arousal of emotion. If this were not so, one could not account for the diverse but orderly manifestations of sadness at funerals, merriness at parties, happiness at weddings, anxiety at rites of passage, exhilaration at carnivals, or for the historical differences of emotions within our culture (for instance, Lewis, 1936) or the differences in types of emotions cross-culturally (for example, Elliot, 1960; Geertz, 1973; Levy, 1973; Lutz, 1989; Newman, 1960; Rosaldo, 1980, inter alia). Even primary emotions are subject to cultural influences, such as 'display rules' (Ekman, 1972, p. 225) which govern their expression.

The general approach adopted here is one in which, as C. Geertz puts it, 'not only ideas, but emotions, too are cultural artifacts' (1973, p. 81). This means that 'every cultural system includes patterned ideas regarding certain interpersonal relationships and certain affective states, which represent a selection from the entire potential range of interpersonal and emotional experiences' (H. Geertz, 1959, p. 225). Thus the present orientation subscribes to the view that the way in which one interprets one's emotions and to an extent what one feels are guided by one's culture, its social rules, and conventions about feelings and emotions which govern the interpretation of social situations.

Although the importance of biological factors is not denied in such approaches, what is of focal concern is the role socio-cultural factors play in the acquisition, shaping, experience and expression of emotions. Emotions are viewed as social constructions, the meaning and function of which are to be found in the cultural system of which they are part (Averill, 1980; Gordon, 1981; Hochschild, 1979; Lewis and Michalson, 1983; Lewis and Saarni, 1985; Scheff, 1983; Shott, 1979).

One's social milieu contributes heavily to how one comes to know when to substitute, inhabit or modify expressive behaviours for certain emotions. How and when to express emotions are important feeling rules that all members of a culture learn (Hochschild, 1979; Lewis and Michalson, 1983). It is clear that adults have a good knowledge of emotions and the situations linked with them, even in cases where they have no prior direct experience with a particular situation. This knowledge is a result of the socialisation of cultural rules concerning situationally appropriate emotions. It has also been indicated that children as young as four years old can identify the emotional response appropriate to certain simple situations (Borke, 1971; Lewis and Michalson, 1983; Shantz, 1975). Thus quite early in life, children acquire the knowledge that many situations are associated with particular emotions. Studies dealing with such issues from a developmental perspective have indicated an increase in children's application of display rules with age (see, for instance, Saarni, 1982).

While it has been established that children acquire knowledge about the relationship between emotional states and situations, the processes involved in the socialisation of this knowledge are not clear. Indeed, Lewis and Michalson (1983) note that 'it is the case that children learn early in life that many situations are associated with particular emotional states, expressions and experiences. The specific socialization rules that govern the acquisition of this knowledge have not been determined' (p. 188). It has been suggested that learning (direct or indirect) as well as empathy may be involved in children coming to know how other people experience emotions in certain situations, and that social experiences of children with significant others play a very important role (Lewis and Michalson, 1983). The mechanisms involved in the transmission of such knowledge have, however, to our knowledge not been investigated.

The theoretical model

The issue is to elucidate the social psychological processes contributing to the acquisition of reflexive social emotions. Our general assumption is that the incorporation of language and representational mediation into the child's activity radically transforms early forms of mental and affective functioning. Indeed, most contemporary theories of social and cognitive development rest on the general premise that increasingly sophisticated forms of mediation (for example, metacognitions, Brown, 1978; Flavell, 1978, 1979, 1981; representations, Mandler, 1976; semiotic mediation, Vygotsky, 1981b; Wertsch, 1984, 1985) allow the developing human to perform more complex operations on objects, relationships or social concepts from an increasing spatio-temporal distance and abstraction. In our specific context, representational mediation refers to the acquisition of social representations pertaining to reflexive social emotions. The mastery of culturally supplied social representations affords the child the experience, informed use and understanding of these emotions. This type of focus is also consistent with the growing interest in 'metacognitive' processes, which control, direct and regulate other socio-cognitive and affective processes.[4]

The particular approach adopted here relies substantially on Vygotsky's work. He regards such mediation (see Vygotsky, 1981b) as social in two senses. First, representational mediation as a psychological tool is social, since it is the product of cultural evolution and the socio-cultural milieu. By addressing the question of emotional development as a cultural one the social plane of development is directly introduced (cf. Vygotsky, 1981b, p. 164). Furthermore, the introduction of culture through language changes the structure of socio-emotional functions. 'It does this by determining the structure of a new instrumental act just as a technical tool alters the process of natural adaptation by determining the form of labour operations' (Vygotsky, 1981a, p. 137). This particular transformation 'occurs when speech and practical activity, two previously completely independent lines of development, converge... As soon as speech and the use of signs are incorporated into any action, the action becomes transformed and organized along entirely new lines' (Vygotsky, 1978, p. 24).

The second sense of 'social' refers to the 'localised' nature of social phenomena. Processes of representational mediation are observed in social

---

[4] This view is closely related to Flavell's reference to 'social cognitive enterprises' which 'include all intellectual endeavours in which the aim is to think or learn about social or psychological processes in the self, individual others or human groups of all sizes and kinds' (1981, p. 272). Monitoring such enterprises is viewed as occurring 'through the actions and interactions among four classes of phenomena: metacognitive knowledge, metacognitive experiences, goals and actions' (cf. Flavell, 1981, p. 273).

practices manifested in face-to-face communication and social interaction. Children's experience involves social activity in the sense that they participate in 'interpsychological functioning', namely concrete social settings involving one or more persons. These two meanings in which activity is social are combined in a great deal of the child's early experience because this experience consists of joint (i.e. interpsychological) activity with more mature members of a culture who typically define and regulate the child's activity in accordance with socio-cultural patterns. This means that much of the child's access to socio-cultural processes and structures is necessarily mediated through interpsychological processes. Indeed, the capacity for social self-regulation can itself be seen as growing out of social interaction.

As Vygotsky notes, 'Any function in the child's cultural development appears twice, or on two planes. First, it appears on the social plane, and then on the psychological plane. First, it appears between people as an interpsychological category, and then within the child as an intrapsychological category. This is equally true with regard to voluntary attention, logical memory, the formation of concepts, and the development of volition' (Vygotsky, 1981b, p. 163), and also, we would like to argue, with emotional development. For Vygotsky, then, later individual functioning is heavily influenced by social origins, i.e. social activity. Tikhomirov (1977), for example, notes in Vygotskian tradition that 'the fundamental law of the ontogenesis of goal formation can be formulated as follows. The processes of establishing and carrying out goals are initially divided up among people, and then they are united in the activity of a single person. The process whereby one person sets a goal for another can conditionally be called "external goal formation", and the process whereby the person sets his own goal can be called "internal" goal formation. Thus the ontogenetic law can be reformulated as the transition from external to internal goal formation' (p. 11). Basically, the adult and the child have a distributed responsibility on the basis of who is in charge of the representational monitoring of social situations. These types of consideration are also to be found in part in work on social-cognitive development (e.g., Youniss's, 1980, 1984, concept of 'reciprocity').

Adult representations of children's competences, abilities and their capacity for emotionality enter the shaping of the situated adult–child social interactions in a formative manner. Such representations typically define and regulate this interaction in accordance with socio-cultural patterns. This means that much of the child's access to socio-cultural processes and structures is mediated through the joint action between parents and their child (the adult–child constellation in general and the mother–child constellation in particular). This is largely because of the child's relative lack of social self-regulation and the mother's particular definition of her own role in situations with her child. In this context the mother–child social constellation acquires a very specific meaning. One can regard the mother analytically as entering the child–mother dyad in a twofold manner: once as herself and then as a component of the mother–child dyad, namely as 'another' social individual constituted by 'joint action' (Wertsch, 1985; or 'interpsychological functioning', Vygotsky, 1981b, inter alia). This basically means that the mother in completing the child reproduces a social identity for the child and in doing so defines herself in an 'extended' manner, i.e. inclusive of the child's actions. She has what one may call an 'extended identity'. However, in order to be able to complete the child as a social and cognitive being she must entertain specific 'theories' (representations) which may be tacit but are essentially 'psychological'. These concern what the child ought to be and what they are (cf. Bruner, 1978).

There is a growing tradition in the developmental psychological literature which suggests that children should not be viewed as isolated in their development. They are routinely completed as cognitive and social beings by mature members of their culture, in particular their mothers. More recent work on cognitive development and problem solving also takes such a perspective, with reference to the importance of 'joint action' in the emergence of self-regulated problem solving (see, for example, Edwards and Mercer, 1987; Rogoff and Wertsch, 1984).

From such considerations about the distinctive features characterising the adult–child interaction it is possible to develop a specific model of the representational mediation processes governing emotional development. We shall illustrate the model with an example from the domain of reflexive social emotions.

It is argued that the mother and the child constitute a social unit in social interaction, in which the mother presents a complementary component to the child's actions. We shall refer to these complementary social actions as 'joint action'. One of the central features of joint action is that the mother completes the social activities of her child as a function of her representations concerning her child's abilities, capabilities and social competence. These will obviously vary as a function of those competences and abilities which the mother deems her child should actually begin to master at the specific developmental stage which the child is in (this is akin to lay conceptions of the 'zone of proximal development': cf. Cole, 1985; Vygotsky, 1981b).

Joint action has a special social psychological significance when examined from the mother's point of view. This arises simply because the mother receives a different type of social identity through her acquired responsibility to complete acts of her child in private and public contexts. The dyadic unit

Culturally supplied theories about child – abilities, social competence, etc.	Idiosyncratic theories about children's abilities, social competence

Mother's representations
of her child's abilities
etc. which monitor her
interaction with her child

J O I N T
A C T I O N
    Representational Mediation
(The patterns of joint action
involving complementary
functions)

The child's emerging
representational world

Figure 7.1 The model of joint action

while on the one hand being engaged in one of the most important activities of passing on cultural forms also represents an unusually tight social unit which is highly integrated in its actions. In essence, the mother, through being the constant complementing actor in joint action, regards the joint action as part of an integral presentation of her 'self'. Diagrammatically, the type of general model we are proposing here is to be seen in Figure 7.1. The factors contributing to the emergence of the child's representational world as a function of joint action are outlined in this figure.

In its early stages 'joint action' is largely other-regulated, i.e. by the mother. With the development of the child the main changes occur because of the internalisation of joint action and the consequent increase in self-regulation of the child as a function of its developing representational world. This would be correlated with a decrease in the degree to which the mother takes responsibility[5] for the child's actions, and also a diminution in the definition of the mother's extended identity.

From the point of view of the child there is an emerging world of social conventions and rules regulating proper conduct. This is a consequence of the various social interactional processes which change their structure and shape as a function of the mother's representations. Such changes are in large part facilitated through the organising and enabling functions of language in which the child is developing its proficiency. The specific social interactional patterns which emerge constitute external guide-lines regulating social

[5] At least in the case of 'good mothering'. Continuing to provide external regulation when the child is capable of self-regulation would constitute over-protective attitudes on the part of the mother.

interaction in circumscribed concrete incidents. The internalisation and generalisation of such incidents are largely mediated by language (Wertsch and Stone, 1985). As Vygotsky suggests,

In order to transmit some experience or content of consciousness to another person, there is no other path than to ascribe the content to a known class, to a known group of phenomena, and as we know this necessarily involves generalization. Thus, it turns out that social interaction necessarily presupposes generalization and the development of word meaning, i.e. generalization becomes possible in the presence of the development of social interaction. Thus, higher, uniquely human forms of psychological social interaction are possible only because human thinking reflects reality in a general way.
(1956, *p.* 51)

Diagnosing the model empirically

An appropriate empirical examination of this framework would require a series of case studies based on observational work and detailed idiographic ethnographies with an analysis akin to textual demonstrations. A more economical version of such an empirical demonstration is to identify key concepts in the theoretical model and examine these key concepts in a diagnostic manner cross-sectionally. Inevitably such quantitative evidence will not prove to be as strong as one wishes, because one is relying on self-reports (in this case on mothers' self-reports and reports on what they believe their children would experience and do in diverse situations). Nevertheless, if the key concepts in the model are fruitful, then some evidence should be obtained supporting the overall framework.

Let us isolate the essential elements in this model. First of all, we proposed here, for the first time, a concept of 'extended identity' for the 'mother' which is derived from Vygotsky's notions of 'interpsychological functioning' and 'zone of proximal development', namely the mother defines her 'identity' in social situations with her child as a result of not only her actions but also those of her child. Let us illustrate a typical incident with an hypothetical vignette. *Imagine a mother at the supermarket with her child during the rush hour. To help her with the shopping the child offers to get the drinks while the mother is getting something else. Accidentally, a bottle slips out of the child's hands and crashes on the floor with a loud noise and breaks.*[6]

Now, with the particular theoretical framework advanced here, if the mother defines her identity in an extended manner, i.e., inclusive of the child's

---

[6] This is the description provided to mothers, except that it was worded in the self-perspective for them. Furthermore, they were asked to answer the degree of applicability of sixteen emotion terms on five-point scales with the ends termed 'not at all' to 'extremely'. The critical dependent variable was embarrassibility. The same applies for the emotionality they were asked to report for their child.

actions, then for mothers with younger children, who have not acquired the social practices associated with the appropriate emotional display (cf. Semin and Manstead, 1982), the mother should display embarrassment. This would be one of the elements which would result from the complementarity of the actions which are postulated by the extended identity construct. Before we explicate this and document the evidence relating to it there is one prior assumption, namely that younger children do not display or experience embarrassment in such situations, whereas older ones do. Indeed, when the ninety mothers were asked what their child would feel in precisely such a situation where the item on embarrassment was concealed among a range of sixteen different emotions, there was a highly significant correlation between age and degree of embarrassment ($r = 0.31$), and this was even higher if the mother's embarrassment was partialed out ($r = 0.42$). The critical question is what the relationship between the child's and mother's embarrassment is as a function of the child's age. If the mother and the child constitute a joint activity unit and thus the child's activities are regarded as part of her identity by the mother, then in situations involving *faux pas* there is an interesting problem. One member of the unit, namely the younger child, who is the origin of the *faux pas*, is unable to master the culturally informed social practices appropriate to the social situation. The other (the mother) is. She, however, has to compensate for the other element in this unit which constitutes her extended identity and therefore engage in embarrassment displays. The mother duly reports experiencing this state. She certainly acknowledges, as the positive correlation with age suggests, that younger children are not capable of embarrassment displays.[7] Now, the critical question is the correlation between the degree of embarrassment reported by mothers for themselves in such a situation as a function of their child's age. This turns out to be in the expected direction ($r = -0.11$), and the strength of this relationship is revealed even more strongly if one controls for variations in their child's embarrassment, i.e., if one partials out embarrassment ascribed to the child ($r = -0.31$), which shows that the less the child displays emotion, the more the mother does.

Another way of examining this relationship more directly in terms of the postulated relationship between the child and the mother is to examine the difference between the reported embarrassment of mother and child (i.e. the score obtained by subtracting the embarrassment reported for the child from the embarrassment reported by the mother) as it relates to age. As expected this correlation is negative and highly significant ($r = -0.41$). All this suggests

[7] An analysis of variance with Age, Sex and Birth Order (first versus later) as the three between subjects factors on this variable resulted in only one significant main effect for Age ($F_{(8, 72)} = 3.01$; $P < 0.01$). Indeed, on all the relevant analyses reported throughout this chapter there were no sex effects either as first- or higher-order effects.

that when the child is regarded as unable to display the appropriate emotion in a situation, the mother, as the model postulates, reports that she displays the necessary emotion for the person who is the source of the transgression thus providing for a unified but extended sense of identity.

The other collaborating set of evidence comes from three further variables which highlight the changes in the meaning mothers ascribe to the incident as a function of their child's age. First of all, they think that the older their child the less likely it is that the incident will be perceived as the mother's fault ($r = 0.42$).[8] Indeed, they think that the public will in general have a more negative evaluation of the mother when the same incident happens to a younger child than an older child. The responses to the item 'You should pay more attention to your child' and the incident 'was just an accident' correlate -0.36 and 0.25 respectively with age. It is not surprising that the meaning of the incident changes for the mother as a function of her child's acquisition of the social practices appropriate for the situation. With an older child the mother is more likely to regard the public as considering the event as an accident, as not her fault, etc.

There are, however, different facets to this set of findings. How does the child eventually acquire the culturally informed emotion practices? What are the interactions that take place between mother and child which are eventually internalised to form what we as adults know as embarrassment?

If the model advanced earlier is accurate, then we should find the following results. Visualise the earlier vignette in the supermarket. The mother witnesses the incident. The younger child, as we know, is as yet culturally uninformed. The mother duly displays embarrassment, thus engaging in the culturally appropriate display which publicly signals apology (Semin and Manstead, 1982). The emotion in question, as we argued in the Introduction to this chapter is 'self-punitive'. The critical ingredient in the situation, the causal source of the incident, is probably finding the situation even quite 'rewarding' – all the fuss and excitement! Indeed, an essential part of the mother's extended identity, namely the young child, has not experienced any self-punitive emotion. The mother, however, has punished herself by experiencing this emotion and displayed her discomfort publicly, thus reaffirming her belief in the rules and mores of her community. There is a bit of her identity which requires correction, and this is the child. Therefore, it is very likely that she will engage in punitive or corrective action in order to complete the public apology of her full persona which includes her child, namely a constitutive part of her extended identity.

[8] All three questions were answered on five-point scales, with the scale ends anchored as 'Not at all' and 'Extremely'. The overall question was 'In your opinion, what would the people standing nearby think about *you*?' The three critical sub-questions were: 'Nothing, it was just an accident'; 'You should pay more attention to your child while in public places'; and 'It wasn't your fault.'

118

Table 7.1. *Correlations of responses to vignettes with age*

	Vignette 2	Vignette 1
1. *Correlations with age*		
Embarrassment difference score	−0·34	−0·41
Reported embarrassment for child	0·31 (0·40[a])	0·31 (0·42[a])
Self-reported embarrassment for mother	−0·03 (−0·16[b])	−0·11 (−0·31[b])
Vignette 2		
2. *Reasons for child's embarrassment and age*		
because she realised she did something wrong	−0·17	
because she made a fool of herself	0·34	
it was an accident	0·16	
she did it although she knew she was not supposed to do it	−0·22	
too young to be aware of wrongdoing	−0·17	
she is careless	−0·10	
3. *Mother's reactions as they relate to her embarrassment*		
scold the child	0·26	
tell the child off	0·31	
explain why her behaviour was wrong	0·25	
get very cross	0·31	
be sad	0·25	
laugh it off and tell her not to worry	−0·24	

[a] Mother's embarrassment partialed out.
[b] Child's embarrassment partialed out.

One of the further elements of the same study consisted in an additional vignette which was included to examine the same reflexive social emotion, namely embarrassment.[9] The results for the questions which were identical to those asked about the earlier vignette are presented in Table 7.1. The pattern of these findings is very similar to the other vignette in the questionnaire. However, the interesting part of the results in Table 7.1 concerns both the reasons for the child's action leading to the incident and the activities of the mother that are associated with her degree of embarrassment.[10] The second major assumption made here (aside from the concept of extended identity) concerned the internalisation of interpsychological processes, i.e. the nature

[9] In this case the vignette provided to the mothers was the following: 'Imagine a situation where your child wasn't paying attention to what s/he was doing and as a consequence spilled her/his soup or drink on the table cloth while you were eating at a restaurant or somewhere you were invited for a meal.'

[10] All the items in Table 7.1 under 'Reasons...' and 'Mothers's reactions as they relate to her embarrassment' are responses to three-point scales. There are obvious problems for using such scales; nevertheless, given the diagnostic nature of the reported study, it is worth noting that the correlations are all in the expected direction and relatively strong.

of the interaction between child and mother is gradually internalised, giving rise to changes in the meaning of both the situation and the nature of the emotional experience. These in turn lead to different reactions to the situation producing different interpretations by the mother, etc. Elements of this dialectic are outlined in Table 7.1, in that the mother's embarrassment is correlated with increased likelihood of 'punitive' actions such as scolding, telling the child off, telling the child what it did wrong, etc. However, these are precisely the interactions characterising the early child's experience of the situation which in their internalisation give rise to the reflexive social emotion in question, namely embarrassment. The child internalises these reactions. As we mentioned in the preceding theoretical section, the specific social interactional patterns are not only internalised but generalised largely by the help of language and the requirements imposed on the use of language and the communication of some experience or content of consciousness to others.

To summarise: two types of evidence are presented for the model advanced here concerning the acquisition of reflexive social emotions. The first source of empirical evidence concerns the notion of extended identity. We find here that the nature of the social interactions in a mother–child dyad influences the mothers' reported emotional experience and their perception of themselves. That is, when children are younger and thus uninformed about culturally appropriate classifications, responses and names for the outcome of a social episode which involves an unintentional transgression, then our results suggest that the mother is very likely to display the emotion appropriate to the situation. As we proposed, she is also more likely to engage in 'corrective' actions towards her young child. It is the internalisation of the nature of the social episode, the nature of the social interaction (with the correction actions of the mother), which constitutes the crux of what is acquired as embarrassment.

Conclusions

Our research strategy was a diagnostic one which attempted to highlight some of the constructs central to the theoretical model that was advanced. Consequently, two issues remain open. The first problem relates to the nature of the data, both in terms of their strength (magnitude, amount of variance explained, etc.) and their nature (i.e. correlational evidence). The second one concerns the empirical examination of the central constructs in the theory which remain unexamined. A related problem is the applicability of the model to the social domain.

There are a number of extraneous circumstances which suggest that the model is quite robust in producing the results described above (see, for instance, Table 7.1). One of them is, as we have already noted in n. 2, the socio-economic and educational background of the sample of mothers we employed for whom the self-completion questionnaire might not have been the optimal method. Furthermore, in Vignette 2 a number of the items were three-point scales, which do not allow for an optimal examination of the constructs in question. Finally, the strength of the findings, irrespective of magnitude, is underlined by the fact that all the postulated theoretical relationships in the model as well as their directions are matched perfectly by the obtained empirical data.

The second problem concerns the empirically unexamined assumptions on the one hand and the generality of the model in the social domain above and beyond the acquisition of reflexive social emotions on the other. Of these one of the chief questions remains an exacting empirical examination of the sequential relationship between: (a) social interaction; (b) the internalisation of social interaction; (c) the process of generalisation and abstraction. In the case of embarrassment this takes the form of (a) a social interaction involving a transgression incident – mother's corrective and/or disciplinary actions; (b) internalisation of this interaction sequence. This internalisation is accompanied by (c) a gradual acquisition of culturally informed 'naming' rules which leads to a generalisation from the concrete to the abstract, i.e. detaching the incident from particulars, such as parental disciplinary actions or anticipation thereof to social practices in different situations, namely embarrassment in the abstract. In a diagnostic cross-sectional study only certain elements of this extended process can be captured. A further feature of this model is that the end-result of the acquisition of such social emotions presents problems when analysed synchronically. The present approach to what are essentially social psychological problems highlights in our view one such problem.

It is certainly the case, as can be seen in diverse treatments of adult embarrassment, that there is no developmental reference to the nature of this emotion. However, what is quite interesting in this context is that in the process of acquiring such reflexive emotions the terms which stand for specific, concrete and repeated social interactions get detached from these referents. On the one hand, the process of internalisation tends to a transformation through indexing such social episodes. Thus, a name or a category begins to stand for an interaction episode. What is more, such naming or classification tends to lead to the ascription of the specific to a known class of phenomena. This generalisation process, proposed by Vygotsky, but also to be found in Grice's work (1975), leads to a detachment from the origins of the experiences which are critical in the emergence and acquisition of this type of emotion and *its dynamics*. What remains in such a process is an individual response, which when analysed merely from a

121

synchronic adult point of view misses the social origin of the emotions in question – the emotion in question is in fact a re-representation of a specific social interaction – the interpsychological – which through language and the nature of language in social interaction is detached from its origins. We therefore often make the mistake of ascribing the origins and nature of the emotion to the individual and engaging in an individual-centred analysis which essentially remains reductionist and therefore ignorant of their social origin. This, however, is often, if not invariably, the result of a synchronic formulation of problems.

Finally, we should address the question of generality – however briefly. The choice of the specific emotions in the development and examination of the model in question was not purely by coincidence, but by design. This is because the emotions in question present instances of secondary emotions which refer not only relatively to salient moments in mothers' lives which are therefore well remembered or observed, but also instances where the nature of the actions they engage in are important. The situations associated with the emotions in question are relatively clearly identifiable in terms of the potential sequences of interactions in the episode and where general normative pressures exist about 'right' and 'wrong'. It may therefore be the case that applications of the model to other domains may prove to be more cumbersome in terms of identifying the relevant parameters that constitute the formative interpsychological stage.

Overall, this model adopted from Vygotsky provides, in our view, an avenue to examine more clearly a number of issues which have been voiced in social psychology over the last two decades, namely a clearer understanding of social psychology in terms of social relations. Simultaneously, it is our hope that the adaptation of Vygotsky's framework to issues which have remained predominantly social psychological and thus synchronic in terms of their analytic boundaries allows an alternative avenue towards explicating the social and diachronic origins of socio-emotional practices in adulthood.

References

Averill, J. R. (1974). An analysis of the psychophysiological symbolism and its influence on theories of emotion. *Journal of the Theory of Social Behaviour*, 4, 147–90.

(1976). Emotion and anxiety: sociocultural, biological and psychological determinants. In M. Zuckerman and C. D. Spielberger (eds.), *Emotion and Anxiety: New Concepts, Methods and Applications*. Hillsdale, N.J.: LEA.

(1980). A constructivist view of emotion. In R. Plutchik and H. Kellerman (eds.), *Emotion: Theory, Research and Experience*, vol. 1: *Theories of Emotion*. NY: Academic Press.

Borke, H. (1971). Interpersonal perception of young children: egocentrism or empathy? *Developmental Psychology*, 5 (2), 263–9.

Brown, A. L. (1978). Knowing when, where and how to remember: a problem of metacognition. In R. Glasser (ed.), *Advances in Instructional Psychology*. NY: Halsted Press.

Bruner, J. (1978). Learning how to do things with words. In J. Bruner and A. Carton (eds.), *Human Growth and Development*. Oxford: Clarendon Press.

Cole, M. (1985). The zone of proximal development: where culture and cognition create each other. In J. V. Wertsch (ed.), *Culture, Communication and Cognition: Vygotskian Perspectives*. Cambridge: Cambridge University Press.

Edwards, D. and Mercer, D. (1987). *Common Knowledge*. London: Methuen.

Ekman, P. (1972). Universals and cultural differences in facial expressions of emotion. *1971 Nebraska Symposium on Motivation*. Lincoln, Nebr.: University of Nebraska Press.

Elliot, R. C. (1960). *The Power of Satire*. Princeton, N.J.: Princeton University Press.

Flavell, J. H. (1978). Metacognitive development. In J. M. Scandura and C. J. Brainerd (eds.), *Structural Process Theories of Complex Human Behaviour*. Alphen a. d. Rijn, the Netherlands: Sijthoff and Noordhoff.

(1979). Metacognition and cognitive monitoring. *American Psychologist*, 34, 906–11.

(1981). Monitoring social cognitive enterprises: something else that may develop in the area of social cognition. In J. H. Flavell and L. Ross (eds.), *Social Development*. Cambridge: Cambridge University Press.

Geertz, C. (1973). *The Interpretation of Cultures*. NY: Basic Books.

Geertz, H. (1959). The vocabulary of emotion. *Psychiatry*, 22, 225–37.

Gordon, S. L. (1981). The sociology of sentiments and emotions. In M. Rosenberg and R. H. Turner (eds.), *Social Psychology: Sociological Perspectives*. NY: Basic Books.

Grice, H. P. (1975). Logic and conversation. In P. Cole and J. Morgan (eds.), *Speech Acts: Syntax and Semantics,* vol. 3. New York: Academic Press.

Harré, R. (1986). *The Social Construction of Emotions*. Oxford: Blackwell.

Hochschild, A. R. (1979). Emotion work, feeling rules and social structure. *American Journal of Sociology*, 85, 551–75.

Levy, R. I. (1973). *Tahitians*. Chicago: University of Chicago Press.

Lewis, C. (1936). *The Allegory of Love*. Oxford: Oxford University Press.

Lewis, M. and Michalson, L. (1983). *Children's Emotions and Moods*. NY: Plenum.

Lewis, M. and Saarni, C. (1985). *The Socialization of Emotions*. NY: Plenum.

Lutz, C. (1989). Morality, domination, and understandings of 'justifiable anger' among the Ifaluk. In G. R. Semin and K. J. Gergen (eds.), *Everyday Understanding: Social and Scientific Implications*. London and Beverly Hills, California: Sage.

Mandler, G. (1976). *Mind and Emotion*. New York: Wiley.

Newman, P. L. (1960). 'Wild man' behaviour in a New Guinea Highlands Community. *American Anthropologist*, 66, 1–19.

Rogoff, B. and Wertsch, J. V. (1984). *Children's Learning in the Zone of Proximal Development*. San Francisco: Jossey-Bass.

Rosaldo, R. I. (1980). *Knowledge and Passion*. Cambridge: Cambridge University Press.

Saarni, C. (1982). Social and affective functions of nonverbal behaviour: developmental concerns. In R. Feldman (ed.), *Development of Nonverbal Behaviour*. NY: Springer Verlag.

Scheff, T. J. (1983). Toward integration in the social psychology of emotions. *Annual Review of Sociology*, 9, 333–54.

Semin, G. R. (1981). *Unabsichtliche soziale Überschreitungen und ihre sozialpsychologische Bedeutung: Berichte aus dem Arbeitsbereich Psychologie*, ed. H. Luck. Hagen: Universität Hagen.

(1982). The transparency of the sinner. *European Journal of Social Psychology*, 12, 173–80.

Semin, G. R. and Manstead, A. S. R. (1981). The beholder beheld: a study on social emotionality. *European Journal of Social Psychology*, 11, 77–86.

(1982). The social implications of embarrassment displays and restitution behaviour. *European Journal of Social Psychology*, 12, 367–77.

Shantz, C. U. (1975). The development of social cognition. In E. M. Hetherington (ed.), *Review of Child Development Research*, vol. 5. Chicago: Chicago University Press.

Shott, S. (1979). Emotions and social life: a symbolic interactionist analysis. *American Journal of Sociology*, 84, 1317–34.

Tikhomirov, O. K. (1977). The concepts of 'goal' and 'goal formation' in psychology. In O. K. Tikhomirov (ed.), *Psychological Mechanisms of Goal Formation*. (1977). Original in Russian, quoted in: J. V. Wertsch, Adult child–interaction and the roots of metacognition. *The Quarterly Newsletter of the Institute for Comparative Human Development*, 2, 1, 15–18.

Tomkins, S. S. (1962). *Affect, Imagery and Consciousness*, vol. 1: *The Positive Affects*. NY: Springer.

(1963). *Affect, Imagery and Consciousness*, vol. 2: *The Negative Affects*. NY: Springer.

Vygotsky, L. S. (1956). *Izbrannie psikhologischeskie issledovania (Selected Psychological Research)*. Moscow: Izdatel'tsvo Akedemii Pedagogicheskikh Nauk. (Cited from Wertsch and Stone, 1985.)

(1978). *Mind in Society: The Development of Higher Psychological Processes*. Ed. M. Cole, V. John Steiner, S. Scribner and E. Souberman. Cambridge, Mass: Harvard University Press.

(1981a). The instrumental method in psychology. In J. V. Wertsch (ed.), *The Concept of Activity in Soviet Psychology*. Armonk, NY: M. E. Sharpe.

(1981b). The genesis of higher mental functions. In J. V. Wertsch (ed.), *The Concept of Activity in Soviet Psychology*. Armonk, NY: M. E. Sharpe.

Wertsch, J. V. (1984). The semiotic mediation of mental life: L. S. Vygotsky and M. M. Bakhtin. In E. Meertz and R. J. Parmentier (eds.), *Semiotic Mediation: Psychological and Sociocultural Perspectives*. NY: Academic Press.

(1985). *Vygotsky and the Social Theory of Mind*. Cambridge, Mass.: Harvard University Press.

Wertsch, J. V. and Stone, C. A. (1985). The concept of internalization in Vygotsky's account of the genesis of higher mental functions. In J. V. Wertsch (ed.),

Culture, Communication and Cognition: Vygotskian Perspectives. Cambridge: Cambridge University Press.

Youniss, J. (1980). *Parents and Peers in Social Development.* Chicago: University of Chicago Press.

(1984). Moral, kommunikative Beziehungen und die Entwicklung der Reziprozität. In W. Edelstein and J. Habermas (eds.), *Soziale Interaktion und soziales Verstehen.* Frankfurt a. M.: Suhrkamp.

8

From social cognition to social representations in the study of intelligence[1]

Felice F. Carugati

Introduction

The last decade has seen a growing interest in such topics as indigenous psychologies (Heelas and Lock, 1981), implicit theories (Leyens, 1983) and everyday ideas (Goodnow, 1981). The assumption underlying this research has been that lay perspectives are crucial to an understanding of prevailing patterns of action and of organising knowledge in individuals. As yet, however, there has been little attempt to ask broader theoretical questions such as how we are to account for the genesis of lay conceptions, or what their relation might be to scientific theories. The latter question is particularly interesting, as many argue that theories in the social sciences represent elaborations of everyday language, and that it is a mistake for social scientists to believe that they can have a perspective on social life which transcends the boundaries of a common-sense understanding of a culture.

In fact, Semin (1987) argues that there is an overlap between ordinary language models of psychological realities and various social scientific models; an overlap which indicates that the scientific structures are idealised abstractions and are both the *preconditions* and *consequences* of references to topics such as intelligence, drug addiction or development in everyday discourse. One implication of these considerations is that empirical analyses in social psychology presuppose a common-sense understanding of the social world which investigators share with their subjects. To rephrase Semin (1987, p. 340), the scientific investigation of topics such as learning or development takes as its starting point the conceptual edifice of a common-sense understanding of intelligence and particularly the origins of interindividual differences, i.e. a detailed knowledge of the way people of a specific culture

[1] I am grateful to the Italian Ministry of Education and National Research Council for their support for the research reported in this chapter.

think of this phenomenon. Without such prerequisites it seems impossible for an investigator to use, for example, the term '*intelligence*' in a culturally sensible manner.

The scope of this chapter is twofold: first, I shall consider the current state of the art of both scientific and lay approaches to intelligence and its development; second, I propose to challenge these views by means of the 'lost concept' of social representations.

Intelligence as social cognition

Recent scientific contributions

A recent influential contribution to a scientific perspective on the study of intelligence is Sternberg's (1985a) triarchic theory of human intelligence. It combines three different lines of research and proposes a specific sub-theory for each one: contextualist, experiential and componential. Briefly stated, the contextualist sub-theory stresses that intelligent behaviour is largely defined by the socio-cultural context in which it occurs. The experiential sub-theory postulates that for a given task a contextually adequate response does not show the same degree of 'intelligence' across respondents. The degree of intelligence required by a particular task cannot be determined independently of the individual responding to it but depends on the point in the continuum of individual experience on which the task is placed, particularly when subjects have to cope with a relatively new task, or when they are automatising their performance on a given task. In other words, it is impossible to define *a priori* whether a task requires intelligence. The componential sub-theory outlines the structures and mechanisms underlying intelligent behaviour: metacomponents, performance components and knowledge-acquiring components.

In the contextualist sub-theory, intelligence is construed in relation to the socio-cultural world. This sub-theory stresses the potential series of contents which may be defined as intelligent; the central issues concern which behaviours are considered as intelligent, and where and when they occur as well as who produces them. The experiential sub-theory considers intelligence in relation to both the external and internal world of subjects: the principal issue here is to determine when a given behaviour is judged to be intelligent against the continuum of a particular individual's activities. The componential sub-theory considers intelligence in terms of the internal, cognitive world of the subject and seeks answers to questions about how intelligent behaviour is generated; this sub-theory describes the potential series of mental mechanisms underlying intelligent behaviour independently of their specific contents.

The main thrust of Sternberg's theory is apparent even from this brief summary. He wants to account for both relativistic and universal aspects of a 'general' theory of intelligence. If contextualist and experiential sub-theories are viewed as relativistic, the mental mechanisms described in componential sub-theory are universal. In other words, the content (*which, when, where* a behaviour is considered as intelligent) is acknowledged as relativistic; the form (mechanisms) as universal. Although there is much of great interest in this attempt to construct a new general theory of intelligence, it still remains an 'individualistic' theory. The social is by no means viewed as constitutive of any mechanisms, but only as the 'scenario' in which various kinds of information processing are accessed by individuals. Rephrasing the title of an earlier paper by Sternberg (1980), we can acknowledge that 'all individualistic theories of intelligence are right almost'. But for such theories to generate a corpus of scientific knowledge a tremendous amount of work would still remain to be done, and indeed it may never be finished, for as Sternberg himself notes, 'no one kind of theory, unit of behaviour, or methodology can give a complete account of human intelligence in all its aspects...' (1980, pp. 12–13).

An even more sceptical conclusion may be drawn from *Mechanisms of Cognitive Development*', edited by Sternberg (1984). Reading this collection of essays brought to mind the Rashomon illusion of multiple perspectives on the same event. Although each author begins by acknowledging the challenge set by the editor, no shared conceptualisation of cognitive mechanisms emerges from this collection. It is difficult to find common ground among the contributions in their basic conceptions of cognitive mechanisms; each author has a different point of entry into the developing system. The image of the child which emerges from these theories is of a rational, decontextualised isolated mind of limited knowledge, without interests, feelings, attitudes or world-views.

In his review of the book Sigel (1986) asks himself and his readers why developmental psychology continues to wallow in diversity and fragmentation not only of subject matter but also in terms of the way in which the organism is studied. Why do we still lack a common vocabulary? Why has the grand theory of Piaget (even though his shadow falls in varying degrees across most of the book's chapters), no less than Freud's, been unable to generate a coherent and systematic theory which would be generally accepted? Why do psychologists continue to devise minitheories denoting what they view as important and then proceed to study childhood in terms of the miniworlds they themselves have created? The issue is as old as the science of psychology: 'what else is new, except the details?'.

The changing patterns of scientific conceptions of intelligence are also considered in another recent collection of essays (Fry, 1984). Five themes are identified in these discussions. First of all, there is a contextualist view in which intelligence is understood as being embedded in particular socio-cultural and ecological contexts. Intelligence is thus viewed as a complex mixture of ingredients which can differ from one socio-cultural milieu to another. A second theme is that of cultural relativism in which the meanings of intelligence are defined and explained in terms of different world-views. The third theme presents an ecological reconceptualisation of intelligence which stresses the dynamic relationships between the actor and the environment, with the actor engaged in problem-solving, goal-directed activities both in the ecological niches of their culture and within the culture as a whole. The fourth theme concerns Piagetian stage theory and its impact on the meaning and assessment of intelligence and cognitive development, particularly in western psychology. After a discussion of the methodological problems of using Piagetian tasks to measure general cognitive level in cross-cultural research, attention is once more drawn to the cultural relativism of intelligence, be it from a Piagetian or any other perspective. Finally, the fifth theme represents an important shift away from conceptualising intelligence as a quality people possess in varying degrees towards regarding it as a judgement which people make of what constitutes intelligent functioning. This theme is elaborated through considerations of a variety of issues related to the process of judgement. These include the rules and protocols underlying the display of intelligent behaviour, both by persons judging and by those being judged; the strategies used by those being judged to evade evaluation; and the developmental aspects of judgements, rule acquisition and protective strategems.

It is very noticeable that in this collection there is little discussion of the themes of the classical debates on intelligence. Controversies about the relative importance of nature and nurture, or whether intelligence is static or dynamic, are noticeably absent. Indeed, the idea of context free, general laws of intelligent functioning is not much in evidence. The 'alternative views' of intelligence outlined in this book focus on the way in which people are judged to be intelligent or stupid rather than trying to define just what intelligence *is*. Each theme, in fact, considers the assessment of intelligence in situations combining both formal testing and everyday judgement. This perspective leads into a consideration of other related issues. Are teachers, for instance, explicitly aware of their implicit views of what constitutes intelligent functioning in their students? What are the social, verbal and cognitive attributes of *intelligent* students at various levels of the educational system?

Felice F. Carugati

Implicit and explicit theories of intelligence

Sternberg's (1985a) distinction between explicit and implicit theories of intelligence suggests a complementary way of exploring the phenomenon of intelligence. If explicit theories have to be invented by scholars (and they have been successful in inventing, for example, differential, cognitive and even triarchic theories!), implicit theories can only be discovered in so far as they exist in some form in people's minds. Neisser (1979) argues that there can be no process-based definition of intelligence; rather the *intelligent person* may be viewed as 'a prototype-organized Roschian concept...There are no definitive criteria of intelligence, just as there are none for chairness...It is a resemblance between two individuals, one real and the other prototypical' (p. 185). Thorndike is acknowledged as the first psychologist to express such a view when he (1924) defined intellect as the quality of mind which distinguished Aristotle, Plato, Thucydides and the like from most Athenian idiots of their day, or as the quality which distinguishes the lawyers, physicians and scientists reputed to have the greatest ability from their contemporaries classified as idiots (p. 126).

Even if, as Neisser maintains, implicit theories of intelligence 'exist' in people's minds, the question remains whose notions in particular are to be used as sources of information. One source which can be used is the notions of 'experts' on intelligence, and perhaps the best-known collection of such notions is that produced by the editors of *The Journal of Educational Psychology* (1921). They interviewed fourteen experts including Terman, Thurstone and Thorndike himself. Viewed narrowly, there seem to be as many definitions as there are experts who gave interviews. Viewed broadly, however, two themes at least seem to run through several of the definitions: the capacity to adapt to one's environment and the capacity to learn from experience. These are themes which run through the history of developmental psychology; one need only recall the history of genetic psychology from Baldwin to Piaget!

Thus there is something of a paradox in so far as experts sometimes disagree among themselves about what intelligence is (Sternberg, 1984), while at other times they seem to agree on at least some of the defining characteristics of intelligence (as in the 1921 symposium). One explanation for this paradox may be that experts have accentuated the diversity and fragmentation of their work, as a consequence of some kind of *logic of development* of scientific theories. A complementary explanation may be that experts tend to disagree among themselves in the course of inventing scientific theories (or even *must* disagree, in order to produce and maintain professional distinctiveness!), while converging in their views when called upon to explain themselves to lay persons or amateurs. A third explanation for the diversity of scientific conceptions of intelligence would be that science is not a unitary discourse. The investigation of intelligence as an educational phenomenon has different aims and objectives from the investigation of intelligence as a problem for cognitive science.

Sternberg et al. (1981) suggest that implicit and explicit theories of intelligence are theories of different things. They see implicit theories as theories of *word usage* while explicit theories tell us what intelligence *is*. While this suggestion seems appealing at first sight it elides the question of the relationship between implicit and explicit theories. Indeed, when Sternberg in a more recent paper compares lay conceptions of intelligence and wisdom with explicit theories, he recognises that correlations of scores from these two kinds of measures show both convergent and discriminant validity (Sternberg, 1985b). Thus implicit theories *do* correspond substantially to explicit theories. We need, therefore, to consider the dynamics between explicit and implicit theories. I want to argue that they are not so much theories of different things as two different starting points for talking about the phenomenon of intelligence. In a social psychological perspective the multiple discourses about intelligence (either implicit or explicit!) may be viewed as part of the wider process of the symbolic construction of shared reality which constitutes, at any given time, the historically constructed 'objective knowledge' both of social groups (experts and lay people) and individuals. From this perspective the considerable overlap between implicit and explicit theories is no longer surprising: indeed, its absence would have been more surprising. Experts as much as lay persons are participants in the symbolic construction of reality; they too are informed by the implicit theories elaborated in this process. Yet Sternberg does not discuss the implicit theories of experts in this wider perspective. Implicit theories appear to rise in a vacuum. Intelligence is defined as a concept or prototype and implicit theories are seen in a framework of an individual psychology of cognitions about social stimuli. But these stimuli are taken as given, and the social dynamics which produce such stimuli remain untheorised. The main effect of this individualistic perspective is to present a view of lay conceptions or everyday understanding and the overlap between implicit and explicit theories as a product of the activity of *individual* minds confronting the *social* world.

In this sense Sternberg can be seen as adopting a *social cognition* approach to the study of lay conceptions of intelligence. This is an approach which has gained considerable prominence in recent years (see for example Carugati, 1989b), but it is easier to clarify the main points of this perspective by considering Sigel's (1985) work.

Lay theories as belief systems

Sigel's starting point is the notion of belief systems introduced by Rokeach (1954, 1980) but he stresses a more cognitive approach in which beliefs are seen as cognitions based on knowledge and accepted as truth. Knowledge is used here in the sense that individuals know that what they espouse is true or probably true, and evidence may or may not be deemed necessary; or if evidence is used, it forms a basis for the belief but is not the belief itself (Sigel, 1985, p. 348). Beliefs are seen as arising from social experiences (though this process is not itself discussed) and as coming to define an individual's psychological reality; beliefs may be organised in domains (such as the political, social, or religious) with different degrees of relationships among them.

Beliefs are thus conceived as analogous to schemata, with boundaries defined in terms of the varying probabilities that new information can be assimilated and existing knowledge reorganised. Beliefs may also vary in terms of such dimensions as concrete-abstract (for instance: the belief that children learn through direct instruction contrasts with the belief that children learn through self-regulation). Using such schemes to create hierarchical levels of beliefs may well help to solve some of the problems of predicting consequent behaviours, since direct links can be drawn between some sets of beliefs and actions more than others. Someone who believes that children learn through direct instruction is likely to act towards children in a different way from someone who believes in self-regulation. As this example illustrates, beliefs are considered as guides to action. Actions can be initiatives or reactions to particular classes of events. Beliefs guide not only the action, but also the choice of events to which to react. While beliefs appear in the context of behaviour, the range of actions is limited since actions are never free of situational constraints. Thus observations of actions may provide only a limited understanding of an individual's beliefs.

From this very brief summary of Sigel's conception, it can be seen that a parent, like the person in the street, is held to acquire knowledge by processing the information which reaches them from the outside world through 'schemata'. Our emphasis on the singular form of *parent* and *person* has to be stressed, because the perspective of belief systems (notwithstanding its wide use of the plural 'parents') is actually concerned with individual perception and the logical analysis of information held by each parent about the development of their own child. In this sense, Sigel shares the postulate of social cognition theories in assuming that the *individual* is the seat of psychic reality and that any *category* of people is derivative.

This assumption has several implications. A parent, like the person in the street, is conceived as a *thinking machine* more or less biased in their judgements about others by their belief systems or implicit theories; such beliefs are considered distinct from corresponding scientific theories. In addition a parent is construed as being relatively impervious to their own experience. Indeed, experience has a contradictory theoretical status in the model: it is conceived as a source of beliefs, but once established a belief system is quite impervious to new experience. Finally, reality, the source of information, is viewed as natural, non-social. The source of biases is located in the thinking machine, with some allowance made for variations in so far as the machine may be biased by emotional factors such as anxiety or affect.

Social representations: at the crossroad of the sociological and the psychological

It is not necessary in the context of this book to describe in detail the theory of social representations since the Introduction and Moscovici's comments serve just this purpose. As an approach to the phenomenon of intelligence the theory of social representations provokes a number of questions. How does the man in the street as a naive scientist differ from the professional rational–logical scientist? What is the impact of socio-economic and cultural influences on everyday ideas about intelligence? However, in the remainder of this chapter I shall be less concerned with such specific questions than with emphasising the important reversal of theoretical perspective brought about by considering the social representation of intelligence. It is no longer the nature of individually gathered and processed information which is the focus for our research, but the sociogenesis and ontogenesis of implicit theories or everyday ideas.

I must stress that the perspective of social representations implies more than simply changing the wrapping on the conceptual structure of theories of social cognition. Theories of social cognition use lay conceptions or implicit theories to explain observed biases, errors and imperviousness to new information. Clearly, a notion of bias or error implies the presence of an ideal model of intelligence, and, indeed, in such theories it is scientific thought which is held to represent the highest stage of intellectual development. This is the force of Sternberg's argument that implicit theories are theories of word usage, while explicit theories are supposed to tell us what intelligence *is*. From the perspective of social representations the central issue is no longer a matter of identifying biases or describing intercultural differences, but of analysing the sociogenesis and ontogenesis of symbolic reality, of studying the articulation of the individual and the collective.

Social representations, in fact, can be regarded as operating in some ways as the inverse of scientific thought, the ideal model of intelligent behaviour. It is not important that this ideal is never actually achieved in scientific practice. What matters is the actual model of the hypothetico-deductive formulation of knowledge (which is held to construct the reified universe of scientific signs) which is predominant. This contrasts with the manner in which social representations are formed. These develop in the many divergent areas of our lives where the scientific model is not dominant, or in areas which resist the application of the scientific model. These areas constitute what Moscovici describes as the consensual universe, in which things are more agreed than demonstrated, and where the rules of scientific thought are supplanted by imperative or negotiated obligations which are the products of collective formulations (see the Introduction above). In this universe every social actor (groups and individuals) contributes to a greater or lesser degree to the elaboration of a collective understanding. Social representations, in fact, fulfil specific functions; by constructing our everyday experience at the semiotic level, they help us to justify our attitudes and actions, as well as to anticipate and influence them. These socio-cognitive constructions are more concerned with confirmation than falsification; their conclusions are more important than their premises, and their functioning stems from a certain conservatism. Nevertheless they can be changed or transformed. In some sense, social representations can 'develop'; they can be re-elaborated as social actors encounter new experiences linked to new social positions.

Social representations are socio-cognitive principles which are activated in decision-making situations and by specific social positions. They can and do vary between individuals, groups or social categories. Such variation is also the reason why we should talk about *social representations*, in the plural form, rather than simply about *social representation* in the singular (at least when we consider their *structure*: see the Introduction to this volume). Recognising a plurality of social representations also marks a contrast with social cognition theories which claim to study *the* representation of the world.

Moscovici (1981) suggests that the primary function of social representations is to enable people to cope with the *inexplicable* by integrating strange or unfamiliar phenomena and cognitions into the *familiar*. This, for example, is what psychoanalysis does, when it 'provokes' an ideological system or a religious ethic (Moscovici, 1976). It must be stressed that social groups do not all respond to the same sorts of unfamiliarity, or to the same degree.

People may have ideas about all kinds of social stimuli, such as child development (Goodnow, 1981), for instance, or the characteristics of childhood (Chombart de Lauwe, 1979) or economics (Berti and Bombi, 1988). But the collection of these ideas does not constitute social representations *per se*. We need to grasp the sense in which these ideas correspond to the familiarisation of something unfamiliar, and this means studying categories of people who have specific reasons for constructing, sharing and transforming representations. What might these reasons be?

Let us take parents and teachers as a concrete example: for these social categories, the representation of intelligence and development is by no means simply a matter of the unsolicited gathering of *free information*. Parents and teachers have to cope with a central question: *where do interindividual differences between children in intelligent behaviour and ability come from?* This very ancient question has been the source of endless controversy through the centuries and it has intrigued philosophers, scientists and every kind of *maître à penser*. The continuing controversy shows that intelligence is one of the most predominant positive values of western society. No wonder therefore that both lay people and scientists have continually constructed and reconstructed a polysemantic discourse around this kind of *idolum tribus*.

As I noted earlier, in discussing these issues among themselves scientists appear to be circling around the topic in such a way as to produce a fragmentation of their theoretical models while converging on a *common-sense* definition (adaptation to environment) when addressing a lay audience. However, parents and teachers (who form part of the scientists' lay audience) have neither the freedom nor the time to circle around the theme in the manner of scientists or to wait for the ultimately true scientific model to emerge. Every day, parents and teachers are concerned with the success and failure of children in school; they need to be able to make and communicate their evaluations of the children to each other and they also have the responsibility for deciding on any remedial action. As with any group of people confronted with the unfamiliarity and the relative inexplicability of certain issues, parents and teachers may feel a gap between the information at their disposal and the information they need to generate an adequate explanation. Earlier studies of social representations have considered the unconscious (Moscovici, 1976), illness (Herzlich, 1973) and the mentally ill (Jodelet, 1983) as unfamiliar themes; in the present case it is interindividual differences between children which confront parents and teachers as an unfamiliar theme which they need to familiarise in order to be able to communicate about the topic. Parents and teachers as social groups are very sensitive to the salience of questions about the origins of interindividual differences and, at the same time, because of concrete and everyday problems concerning intelligence and development they need to be able to make practical decisions about these issues. These two factors may work convergently in organising specific representations of intelligence and development.

From this point of view, social representations are not merely mental reconstructions of varied stimuli but organising principles of these reconstructions. Thus the tension between the *strange* and the *familiar* tends to be resolved wherever possible in favour of the familiar, by a kind of socio-cognitive principle of economy. Social thought does not operate analytically, or on the analysis of variance model, but progresses by analogy, looking to confirm conclusions rather than to validate the premises of the discourse.

Intelligence as social representations

The social cognition model takes for granted that parental belief systems are individual constructs, a pattern of schemata used by individuals to process information. Consequently, parents and teachers are studied as categories *per se*, and a psychology of individual differences elaborated which describes variations between parents or teachers, or adults in general. In contrast to this model I want to sketch the outline of a research programme in which we have tried to consider intelligence as social representations.

Duveen and Lloyd in the Introduction to this book describe social representations as significant structures which enable us to identify the groups which construct them as well as the content which is represented. The originality of the social representations approach to everyday understanding stems from this effort to integrate particular processes with specific contents. In the present case, intelligence and its development is the 'social stimulus' about which we have sought to elicit the specific contents in the social representations of specific categories of people for whom such representations constitute a significant structure. For parents and teachers there is, as I noted earlier, a functional necessity to construct social representations of intelligence. For such people, intelligence is a salient and intriguing issue as well as being a phenomenon which they experience directly in their everyday *professional* life. Furthermore, they may feel a lack of information in trying to explain the apparently unequal distribution of intelligence between individuals (children and pupils) for whom they are responsible.

Moreover, social representations are significant structures in the sense that they are functional in building social identities and in negotiating identity conflicts. Concretely speaking, teachers may also be parents: as teachers they may be compelled to defend the school against the failures of pupils; as parents they are compelled to defend their own children against the school, against themselves as teachers, as it were. A second category of people affected by the dynamics of identity conflict are mothers working professionally in addition to being housewives. As housewives, they may be prone to explain intelligence and development as a product of their own direct commitment in child-rearing and as a task socially assigned to mothers; as working mothers, they may feel guilty in relation to these tasks. In both cases (parent-teachers, and working mothers) specific socio-professional positions may induce identity conflicts which can be resolved by readjusting the representations they hold of intelligence.

We do not construe such readjustments in terms of biases or errors, as the social cognition approach suggests. A social psychological perspective which regards psychological phenomena as social products suggests that perceived realities always refer to and are derived from the social context in which they are set and upon which they are predicated. The whole set of hypotheses which we have sketched in this chapter suggests that the functions and the transformations of social representations are located at the interface between the individual and the social. The unfamiliarity and inexplicability of interindividual differences need to be construed as social processes in such a way that they can generate a conflict of identities.

Intelligence and development, therefore, are by no means simply a matter of cognition or of information processing. The construction and transformation of social representations provides useful instruments for specific groups to locate themselves in social life. In this sense, the ontogenesis of social representations of intelligence may be studied at critical *turning points* of adult life, particularly, in the case of intelligence and, its development, entry into certain professions (for instance, as teachers, paediatricians, child psychologists and psychiatrists) or at the birth of children.

These considerations suggest that an interesting problem for research would be to examine how and why social representations of intelligence and development are produced by an interrelated set of social groups for each of which it is possible to hypothesise that the question of the origins of differences in intelligence will have a different degree of salience. Thus, if the choice of groups to be investigated can be made in terms of some well-grounded theoretical reasons, one can anticipate that the dynamic of familiarising the unfamiliar will operate so that the organisation of the content of representations will differentiate between the groups. The aim is to produce a theoretical supposition and a conceptual armoury with which to link the products of a 'thinking society' to the social-psychological processes involved in the production and transformation of social representations. Two main social-psychological processes need to be considered: the familiarisation of the unfamiliar and conflicts of identification (no doubt there are also other processes which contribute to the social psychology of social representations, but the centrality of these two makes them the most useful to consider in initiating this research).

In our research on the social representations of intelligence and its development (Mugny and Carugati, 1985; Carugati, 1989a) we collected information from 728 adults living in Geneva and Bologna. This sample included teachers, students (some of whom were trainee teachers) and people working in other occupations (that is, people who were neither teachers nor students). In all these categories our respondents included both men and women as well as parents and non-parents. This was clearly not a random sample of the population, but a more systematic sampling of contrasting social groups selected to test specific hypotheses.

We decided to take a broad sample of the products of the 'thinking society' about intelligence and its development. Specifically we sought general opinions on these topics as well as prototypical images of the intelligent child. We also collected information about the didactic strategies employed to cope with failure in mathematics, language and drawing. In addition we asked our respondents which sources of information they regarded as important and their views about the explanatory power of the sciences.

The choice of which 'raw material' to collect was made in order to grasp not only the richness and variety of discourses about intelligence, but also the relations between the ideas and conceptions expressed and the specific sources of information recognised by our respondents. Intelligence and its development are controversial themes in society, and the variety of social categories in our sample enabled us not only to search for a consensual discourse about intelligence, but also to examine the social logic of disagreements about particular topics and issues within this discourse. With these aims in mind we decided to employ a 'closed' questionnaire of about 200 items in this investigation rather than a more 'open' or 'free' method (such as open-ended interviews, observations or word associations). This choice reflects not only the stress which different authors have placed on the plurality of method in empirical research on social representations (see Di Giacomo, 1981; Flament, 1981; Moscovici, 1988), but also the approach to social representations sketched in this chapter. We were interested not only in describing how individuals represent intelligence, but also in testing specific hypotheses by manipulating socio-cognitive variables through the selection of particular social categories.

An extremely rich and vivid set of responses emerged in our study. The multiplicity of meanings and discourses which these adults produced ranged from the logical and mathematical model operating in science to a notion of social intelligence as the elaboration and interiorisation of norms of social conduct and values, and a view of intelligence as primarily a matter of succeeding in fulfilling the institutionally defined norms of schooling, a view which obviously covers the acquisition of a heterogenous collection of skills and values. Logical (or academic) and social (or everyday) intelligence seem therefore to be widespread co-occurrent conceptions, as almost all other studies have also shown (cf. Sternberg et al., 1981, inter alia).

The polysemous nature of popular views of intelligence agrees with the informal views of the prominent English-speaking psychologists who responded to the editors of the *Journal of Educational Psychology* (cf. the 1921 symposium on 'Intelligence and its measurement') as well as more recent scientific approaches such as Sternberg's (1985). These views contrast, however, with the more monolithic approaches (such as Piaget's) which argue for a single unambiguous meaning of the word. In this sense, the representations expressed by our sample as well as recent scientific views of intelligence seem to be closer to the classical psychometric approach.

One reason for such a similarity may be that the logic of such views is in fact homologous with the factorial structure of psychometric test scores in which the variety of dimensions of intelligence are assumed to be complementary. Moreover, this complementarity underlies a more general conception of intelligence in terms of *giftedness*, which is closely connected with the ideology supporting testing. Comparable explanations for the close similarity between the conceptions of lay people and experts have been suggested for topics such as personality (Semin and Krahe, 1987) as well as specific psychological theories (Smedslund, 1978).

In relation to intelligence, personality traits and rates of development, individual variability presents a challenge to prototypical conceptualisations. It is to cope with this variability that explanations of interindividual differences are anchored in the ideology of giftedness. In this way the unfamiliar themes of personality, character, temperament and intelligence are transformed into something familiar. In our study the ideology of giftedness is the reference point used by parents and teachers to construct explanations for differences in intelligence, differences with which they have to cope in their daily experience. Yet once anchored in this way, these explanations are also objectified as individuals are categorised as a *bright* child or a *dull* child. In the process of objectification the differences between individuals which were originally effects have been transformed into causes.

Anchoring and objectifying a representation of intelligence as a gift unequally distributed among children is also a product of a (relative) lack of competing information. Faced with the question of the source (the cause) of interindividual differences, parents and teachers are selectively affected either by a lack of specific information or by a distrust of *scientific* explanations, both of which lead them to rely on their own idiosyncratic parental and professional experience. The differences between children become all the more salient for parents and teachers because they introduce additional complications into running a family or a classroom. But there is no alternative model, including any scientific one, which offers a comprehensive explanation of these differences or any advice on the means to cope with them. The result of this is that the extremes become 'prototypes' against which the whole range of individuals are assessed; at one end of the continuum are the *brilliant* children, at the other, the *stupid* ones. Since both prototypes are extreme cases, they call for special explanations which take account of their unusual nature. Thus social representations of intelligence based on a theory of natural inequality or giftedness are functional and familiarise social experiences by confronting the unusual and actually inexplicable. The same reasoning is then applied by analogy to people in general.

A second function played by a theory of natural inequality concerns the social identity of our categories of adults. If this theory allows parents and teachers a single unifying explanatory principle using a phenomenal causality which transforms effect into cause, the principle of identity governs the socio-cognitive management of unfamiliarity; in fact distinct representations are articulated by the social groups for whom intelligence is a constitutive part of their identity. We have shown that it is primarily parents and teachers who construct their own highly complex theory of natural inequality; other people, for example, education students, are not likely to produce such an organised theory, but are more likely to share just some of the ideas belonging to such a theory. These results are quite in line with our main hypothesis that turning points of everyday life are critical in transforming scattered ideas and information into social representations, since students will not yet have been exposed to the phenomena of differences between children in the same way as either parents or teachers.

Final remarks

If we acknowledge that people live in a *thinking* society (Moscovici, 1981) which surrounds them with ideas and everyday conceptions of all kinds of topics ('social stimuli'), then we must also recognise that particular *thinking environments* are constructed from specific social experiences which may have various levels of institutionalisation (Berger and Luckmann, 1966). Even if parental experience and job entry in education are quite different in this respect, they are both significant events in the life span. These turning points may therefore be viewed as critical for the study of the ontogenesis of representations of intelligence. Rephrasing Duveen and Lloyd, I maintain that the theory of the natural inequality of intelligence supports the social identities of both parents and teachers. As we saw, education students attempt to describe the phenomena in different terms. It is only when their social identities are at stake as they enter the professional world as teachers that these people transform their social representations (cf. Ch. 9 below). This is the sense in which I want to suggest that social identities are principles governing the transformations of scattered ideas into representations.

Our own research has been cross-sectional and does not therefore present direct evidence of this ontogenesis. An adequate examination of this hypothesis requires further research. Nevertheless, formulating this hypothesis is useful in so far as it challenges both implicit and explicit views of intelligence. It suggests a need to incorporate aspects of the problem which have hitherto been ignored both by lay people and experts like psychologists, whose narrow focus on individualistic, normative and correctional approaches to intelligence have led them to try to differentiate what people view as intelligence from what intelligence *is*.

Social thought is by no means a site of incoherence and disorder: it has its own logic and rationality. The evidence I have presented here at least provisionally illustrates that this is also true in relation to intelligence. Far from dissolving into scattered ideas or an arbitrary sequence of errors in comparison with a correct theory, social representations of intelligence have a coherence of their own, and indeed, a sophisticated type of rationality. Like scientific triarchic theories, social representations of intelligence show a rationality, which may be called (following Moscovici) *cognitive polyphasia*: in Sternberg's work it assumes the form of three sub-theories, and in social representations it works as a multiplicity of different orders of reasoning and a diversity of socio-cognitive functions which accounts for the heterogeneity of the way different groups talk about intelligence.

Pursuing this line of reasoning will mean changing our habits and assumptions not only in respect of intelligence but for all those other 'social stimuli' which are the merchandise of the social cognition approach to the understanding of social life. It will become increasingly difficult to carry on talking about social cognition in the singular when it is undeniably a label which subsumes social stimuli which, in Duveen and Lloyd's metaphor, constitute only the visible tip of an iceberg whose submerged portion comprise the very processes which enable groups and individuals to construct meaningful and functional representations of everyday life.

References

Berger, P. L. and Luckmann, T. (1966). *The Social Construction of Reality*. New York: Doubleday.

Berti, A. E. and Bombi, A. S. (1988). *The Child's Construction of Economics*. Cambridge: Cambridge University Press.

Carugati, F., (1989a). L'intelligenza e le sue rappresentazioni: nuove illustrazioni sperimentale. Unpublished manuscript.

(1989b). Everyday ideas, theoretical models and social representations: the case of intelligence and its development. In G. R. Semin and K. J. Gergen (eds.), *Everyday Understanding: Social and Scientific Implications*. London: Sage.

Chombart de Lauwe, M. J. (1979). *Un monde autre: l'enfance; de ses représentations à son mythe.* 2nd edn. Paris: Payot.

Di Giacomo, J.-P. (1981). Aspects méthodologiques de l'analyse des représentations sociales. *Cahiers de psychologie cognitive,* 1, 397–422.

Ferguson, G. A. (1954). On learning and human ability. *Canadian Journal of Psychology,* 8, 95–112.

Flament, C. (1981). Sur le pluralisme méthodologique dans l'étude des représentations sociales. *Cahiers de psychologie cognitive,* 1, 423–7.

Fry, P. S. (ed.). (1984). Changing conceptions of intelligence and intellectual functioning: current theory and research. *International Journal of Psychology,* 19 (special issue).

Goodnow, J. (1981). Everyday ideas about cognitive development. In J. Forgas (ed.), *Social Cognition.* London: Academic Press.

Heelas, P. and Lock, A. (1981). *Indigenous psychologies.* London: Academic Press.

Herzlich, C. (1973). *Health and Illness.* London: Academic Press.

Intelligence and its measurement. *Journal of Educational Psychology* 12 (1921), 123–47; 195–216; 271–5.

Jodelet, D. (1983). Civil et bredins: représentations sociales de la maladie metale et rapport à la folie en milieu rural. Ph.D. thesis, Paris.

Leyens, J. Ph. (1983). *Sommes-nous tous des psychologues?* Brussels: Mardaga.

McGillicuddy-De Lisi, A. V. (1982). Parental beliefs about the developmental processes. *Human Development,* 5, 192–200.

Mortimer, J. T. and Simmonds, R. G. (1978). Adult socialization. *Annual Review of Sociology,* 4, 421–54.

Moscovici, S. (1976). *La Psychanalyse, son image et son public.* Paris: Presses Universitaires de France.

(1981). On social representations. In J. Forgas (ed.), *Social Cognition.* London: Academic Press.

(1988). Notes towards a description of social representations. *European Journal of Social Psychology,* 18, 211–50.

Mugny, G. and Carugati, F. (1985). *L'Intelligence au pluriel.* Cousset, Fribourg (Switzerland): DelVal. (English translation forthcoming: *Social Representations of Intelligence.* Cambridge: Cambridge University Press.)

Neisser, U. (1979). The concept of intelligence. In R. J. Sternberg and D. K. Detterman (eds.), *Human Intelligence: Perspectives on its Theory and Measurement.* Norwood, N.J.: Ablex.

Rokeach, M. (1954). The nature and meaning of dogmatism. *Psychological Review,* 61, 194–204.

(1980). Some unresolved problems in theories of beliefs, attitudes and values. In H. E. Howe and M. M. Page (eds.), *Nebraska Symposium on Motivation.* Lincoln: University of Nebraska Press.

Semin, G. (1987). On the relationship between representation of theories in psychology and ordinary language. In W. Doise and S. Moscovici (eds.), *Current Issues in European Social Psychology.* Cambridge: Cambridge University Press.

Semin, G. and Krahe B. (1987). Lay conceptions of personality: eliciting tiers of a scientific conception of personality. *European Journal of Social Psychology,* 7,2, 199–210.

Sigel, I. E. (ed.). (1985). *Parental Belief Systems.* Hillsdale, N. J.: Lawrence Erlbaum.

Sigel, I. E. (1986). Mechanism: a metaphor for cognitive development? A review of Sternberg's 'Mechanisms of cognitive development'. *Merrill Palmer Quarterly,* 32, 1, 93–101.

Smedslund, J. (1978). Bandura self-efficacy theory: a set of common sense theorems. *Scandinavian Journal of Psychology,* 19, 1–19.

Sternberg, R. J. (1980). Factor theories of intelligence are all right almost. *Educational Researcher,* 9, 9–13.

(1985a). *Beyond I.Q. A Triarchic Theory of Human Intelligence.* Cambridge: Cambridge University Press.

(1985b). Implicit theories of intelligence, creativity and wisdom. *Journal of Personality and Social Psychology* 49, 607–27.

Sternberg, R. J. (ed.). (1984). *Mechanisms of Cognitive Development.* New York: Freeman.

Sternberg, R. J., Conway, B. E., Ketron, J. L. and Bernstein, M. (1981). People's conceptions of intelligence. *Journal of Personality and Social Psychology,* 41, 37–55.

Thorndike, E. L. (1924). The measurement of intelligence: present(?) status. *Psychological Review,* 31, 219–52.

9

Prototypes of the psychologist and professionalisation: diverging social representations of a developmental process[1]

Paola De Paolis

Anchoring and prototypes

Social representations are construed as ways of knowing and organising reality; they provide the social psychological instruments for the construction of objects of knowledge, and in this sense they are at the core of any process of developing knowledge. The locus of social representations is social groups, and they play an essential role in developing as well as in maintaining intergroup relations. It is probably for this reason that anchoring, the mechanism which has been most widely studied in empirical surveys of social representations, has been interpreted mainly in terms of how objects become rooted in a group's system of values. While this interpretation is certainly true, this chapter also draws on other meanings of the term in presenting a study in the field of group values. The aspect of anchoring which has been considered less often concerns the socio-cognitive process of comparisons between categories in order to locate the familiar category which offers the best fit for something 'new' as a social representation is constructed about a novel object.

What I have tried to analyse in this study of social representations of the professionalisation of psychology are precisely these socio-cognitive procedures of categorisation through which anchoring takes place. These procedures result in different ways of knowing as different social groups evaluate and elaborate the same object in different ways. The point at which a particular group anchors an object in its conceptual field is influenced by the dynamic of its relations with other groups. While analysing the process of anchoring, I have also examined the intergroup relations which account for

[1] I am grateful to Gerard Duveen for his assistance in the preparation of an English version of this chapter. The research reported here was originally undertaken as part of a Ph.D. thesis, and I should also like to thank Serge Moscovici for his supervision of this work.

diverging points of anchoring in the construction of social representations about a specific object (De Paolis, 1986).

When we try to analyse the two essential functions of social representations described by Moscovici, classifying and naming, there are many established psychological perspectives from which to approach these themes. In my opinion the most useful approach for integrating cognitive processes of classification in a social psychological perspective concerned with social representations and intergroup relations derives from research into prototypes. Eleanor Rosch's (1975, 1977, 1978), and Rosch and Mervis' (1975) approach to prototypes is useful in this context in so far as it facilitates the analysis of category organisation and the processes of classification, both of which are essential to the construction of social representations. Prototype studies share a constructivist perspective with social representation theory; both stress the importance of the selection and rearrangement of salient traits in the organisation of categories. But let us look at the links between classification and social representations, and the role which prototypes can play in this framework.

In 1984 (stressing once again the status of social representations as independent variables, explanatory stimuli) Serge Moscovici wrote: 'it is the *pre-established images and paradigms* that both determine the choice and restrict the range of reactions...emotional reactions, perceptions and rationalizations are not responses to an exterior stimulus as such, *but to the category in which we classify such images, to the names we give them...*' (Moscovici, 1984, p. 61). Comparisons with previous models, with familiar paradigms in order to locate the point in the conceptual field at which to anchor something novel, seem to be necessary steps in the construction of social representations. If the problem is to comprehend something new or strange, then it is the existing familiar categories which provide the touchstone, the reference point by which the unfamiliar is recognised. The new object is located within a familiar category in order to establish its normality or deviance, and in order to integrate, if possible, and if useful, the new in the well known. More importantly for the present discussion, such comparisons do not take place with categories *per se*, but with the *prototypes* of these categories, as Moscovici has suggested on various occasions (Moscovici, 1981, 1984). This point is worth thinking about in more detail, as we have recently seen an exceptional interest in prototypes in relation to the cognition of social life. We tend to forget the limits of these approaches, but we may also have underestimated the implications of prototypes in a sociopsychological perspective.

The prototype is the best exemplar of a category; it is an image which combines the characteristics defining a category in such a way as to maximise its distinctiveness from other categories. A prototype expresses what is central to a category rather than what is peripheral. Through its prototype a category appears to be more sharply defined and even more differentiated from other categories than is the case for peripheral members of a category, where the fuzzy boundaries between one category and another often make distinctions difficult and problematic. The 'surplus' of differentiation encoded in a prototype is especially interesting, as it highlights at the same time the relations between the prototype and its own category and the relations with neighbouring categories.

I shall not describe approaches to the study of prototypes at length, but shall limit myself to a consideration of what is essential for a social psychological approach in the systematic theory of prototypes presented by Eleanor Rosch and her colleagues: the prototype accentuates the intra-categorical similarities of the members of the category and, at the same time, stresses the differences with the members of other categories (Rosch, 1975; Rosch and Mervis, 1975; Rosch et al., 1976; Rosch, 1978). In a socio-psychological perspective, these characteristics of accentuation of intra-categorical similarities and of inter-categorical differences probably have wider consequences than in Rosch's intention. She emphasises in fact the universality of principles in the structure of categories, whereas the content of categories depends on socio-cultural variations (Rosch, 1977). But, in a socio-psychological perspective we cannot limit ourselves to observing socio-cultural differences. From this perspective the structure of categories elaborated by a social group also serves to situate the group in relation to other groups. We also need, therefore, to consider the social dynamics underlying categorisations, their normative bearings, and to take into account the significance of similarities and differences between category structures for competition between social groups.

The professionalisation of psychology

An example of the play of similarities and differences in category structure can be found in the construction of social representations about an emerging profession. Comparison with previous models is in fact stressed as an important issue in professionalisation processes analysed in a sociological perspective, both by functionalist approaches (Barber, 1963; Goode, 1960) and approaches critical of functionalism (Hughes, 1958; Bucher and Strauss, 1961; Wilensky, 1964; Chapoulie, 1973).

Professionalisation has been described by Chapoulie as the process by which an occupation tends to organise itself according to the model of established professions. Other sociologists of professions give some interesting reference points for grasping a sort of prototypical process of professional-isation. Wilensky (1964), for instance, presents the conditions allowing the development of an occupational group into a profession:

Get a technical basis

Create an exclusive jurisdiction

Establish training standards in relation to techniques and exclusive jurisdiction

Get public trust.

Obviously, in reconstructing the developmental process through which any profession becomes institutionalised, we have to take into account the events which historically mark the evolution from disparate practices to the creation of a professional field and the establishment of a professional group. The points listed above are recognised as necessary conditions. The data I will present show that these conditions are indeed assumed as implicit reference points by psychologists for representing their own professional development. Nevertheless, these conditions do not apparently constitute the main focus for understanding the multiple facets that the same social object, the psychologist, assumes according to different points of view, or for the place which neighbouring professionals permit a new profession.

Data presented below show the implications of competition between professional groups in their choice of category prototype as the point at which they anchor their elaboration of representations about the emerging profession of psychologists. A second set of data concerning the social representations elaborated by psychologists themselves will be presented to account for the developmental dynamic of the internal structure of an emerging professional category. Comparisons of the different anchoring points used by psychologists and other professionals are discussed in the framework of Habermas' distinction between communicative and strategic action, the former consensus oriented and the latter success oriented (cf. Furth, 1983). I have taken strategic action as a prototype of professional activity, following the distinction which Habermas makes between *work* and *interaction* (Habermas, 1971), and used this as a frame of reference for comparing the prototypes used by different groups of subjects. We will see that, in the anchoring process, while naming may apparently be homogeneous between groups, the semantic value of naming and classification procedures diverges according to the actual and anticipated intergroup relations.

Paola De Paolis

Social representations of physicians, social workers and teachers about the psychologist

I approached classifying and the semantic value of naming in a prototypical perspective by using two different methods with the same samples of subjects.

The first method required subjects to describe the prototypical psychologist without any *a priori* definition of categories to be used. I asked physicians, social workers and teachers (315 subjects in all, from Switzerland and Italy) to produce a *free* description of the prototypical psychologist as well as of the ideal one. This two-step procedure enabled me to draw out the paradigmatic attributes of the categories as used by my respondents, and to compare their perceived and ideal psychologists. The comparison between the typical and ideal images allowed me to avoid an exclusive focus on contingent negative attributions and to grasp the dimensions which can account for the place other professionals would permit the emerging profession in an ideal context.

The second method asked respondents to use a set of predefined categories to describe the typical and the ideal psychologist. After the experimenter had collected the free descriptions, the same subjects were asked to fill out two 'identification cards', one for a typical psychologist and one for the ideal psychologist. Each card requested definitions in terms of a set of categories which included gender, age, educational training, field of work and preferred authors.

Responses to the free descriptions were summarised in semantic categories by four independent judges. The predetermined category responses were summarised in terms of frequencies. Comparisons between the two methods are interesting in so far as they show the limits of methods based on predefined categories (often used in studies on prototypes) in grasping the play of similarities and differences established by subjects in defining the core of social representations about psychologists. Indeed, the 'objective' categories employed in the second method cannot account for the hierarchy of dimensions implied in the free descriptions, or for the links between them. At the very most, they allow us to get a 'predefined dimensions' prototype.

Despite such limitations, prototypes based on predefined dimensions reveal some of the problematic issues concerning an emerging profession. Consider, for example, the categories of gender and age. High-status professionals (physicians) represent both the typical and the ideal psychologist as a relatively young woman much more frequently than do either of the groups of lower-status professionals (social workers and teachers). In representing the prototype of the psychologist generally as male, these lower-status professionals attribute to psychologists a higher status in the field of professions. Their over-estimation of masculine membership (in fact we know

148

that about 70 per cent of psychologists are women) can be interpreted in terms of an implicit legitimation of professional status. On the contrary, when physicians use the feminine and younger categories to describe the *ideal* psychologist, we can think, echoing Sullerot (1968), of an attempted devalorisation of the psychological profession.

However, these data on predefined categories are not able to show the actual similarities and differences brought into play when subjects take their own professional identity as a frame of reference for describing psychologists. Their points of anchoring become clearer in the analysis of the free descriptions.

Free descriptions

Let us begin with a few salient dimensions, used by the three groups in different proportions, as shown in Table 9.1, and displayed in Figure 9.1.

For the typical image, as well as for the ideal one, there is a focus on *personal attributes* (sensitive, well balanced, conscious of his limits). This is particularly the case for physicians and social workers, who use these personal dimensions essentially in the negative form to stress the lack of these qualities in the typical psychologist. Teachers, on the contrary, seem more concerned with helping behaviour and, for the ideal image, with ethical problems, which are based on *professional practice*. The ideal psychologist for physicians and social workers, on the other hand, is, again, mainly concerned with questions about his own sensitivity and a consciousness of his own limits. Although there is a focus on personal attributes in the prototype of the psychologist described by teachers, the members of this group register a shift in their choice of categories between their descriptions of typical and ideal images. The other professionals, by contrast, maintain their focus on personal attributes in the typical as well as in the ideal image.

The first opposition we can outline, therefore, contrasts a main focus on the *way of being*, assumed by physicians and social workers, with the focus on the *way of doing*, which is developed by teachers, especially in the ideal perspective.

These examples draw on only some of the category attributes constructed on the basis of spontaneous statements by our subjects. Many other categories have in fact been used to describe the presence or the lack of attributes of psychologists. The configuration of all these categories is more clearly integrated in two correspondence analyses (Benzecri, 1973; Greenacre, 1984) of the free descriptions of the typical and ideal psychologist. Figures 9.2 and 9.3 present plots of the first and second factors for the typical and for the ideal image respectively. Both the positions of the specific categories used by subjects and the positions of groups of subjects are projected on the co-

Attributes of the typical psychologist
Presence/lack of attributes according to the three groups

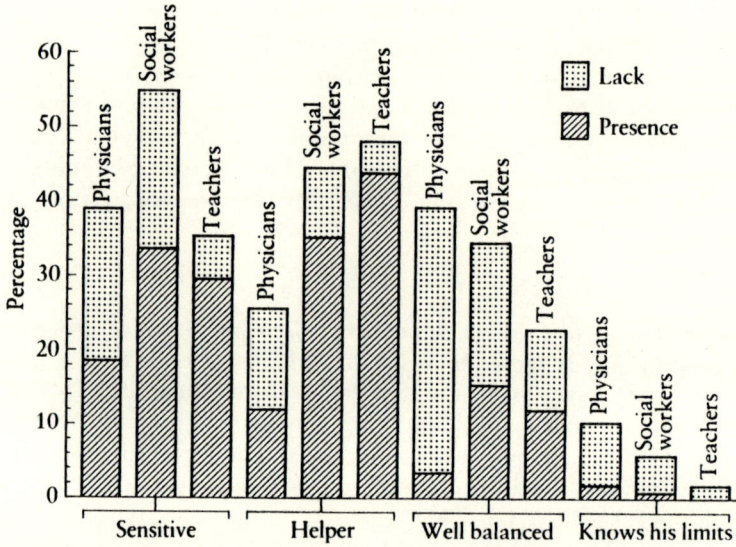

Attributes of the ideal psychologist

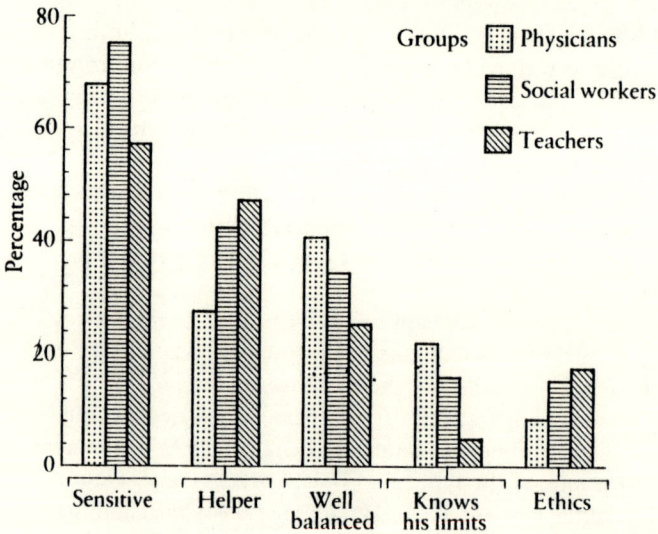

Figure 9.1 Attributes of the typical and ideal psychologist

Table 9.1. *Attributes of the typical and ideal psychologists (percentages of responses of physicians, social workers and teachers)*

Attributes of the typical psychologist

	Physicians		Social workers		Teachers	
	Lack	Presence	Lack	Presence	Lack	Presence
Sensitive	20·3	18·6	21·2	33·6	5·8	29·4
Helper	13·6	11·9	9·4	35·0	4·2	43·7
Well balanced	35·6	3·4	19·0	15·3	10·9	11·8
Knows his limits	8·5	1·7	5·1	0·7	1·7	0·0

Attributes of the ideal psychologist

	Physicians	Social workers	Teachers
Sensitive	67·8	75·2	57·1
Helper	27·5	42·3	47·1
Well balanced	40·7	34·3	25·2
Knows his limits	22·0	16·1	5·0
Ethics	8·5	15·3	17·6

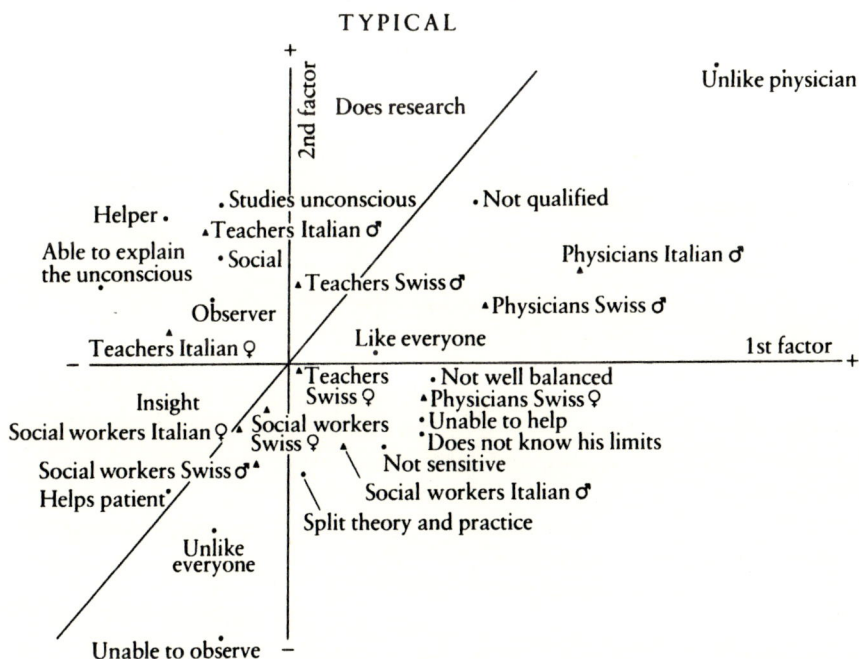

Figure 9.2 Typical psychologist: first and second factors of the correspondence analysis

ordinates of these graphs. Groups are organised according to profession, gender and nationality.

Representations of the typical psychologist

In the analysis based on the typical image the first factor, explaining 30.11 per cent of the total inertia, organises the opposition between a *lack of qualities*, towards the positive pole of the factor, versus a *potentiality of action*, towards the negative pole.

The lack of qualities is mostly expressed by Italian and Swiss physicians using categories like 'not well balanced', 'unable to help', 'not sensitive', 'does not know his limits', 'not qualified' and 'different from physician'.

The potentiality of action is mainly expressed by Italian teachers and refers to categories such as 'helping behaviour', 'find solutions', 'ability to explain unconscious dynamics' and 'observation activity'.

The second factor for the typical image explains 22·16 per cent of the inertia. It highlights a particular feature of psychological skills, corresponding to what Smedslund (1972) calls the 'magic eye'. It is the ambiguous power attributed to psychological insight, expressed here by the opposition between *professional insight* (different activities of observation applied in the clinical field as well as in research, expressed by Italian teachers) and a sort of *blindness* (the ability to observe, the presumption of being different from ordinary people which prevents the psychologist from seeing their actual problems, as well as the trap of a cleavage between theory and practice).

If we take a north-east/south-west diagonal across the plot of the first and second factors we can easily reconstitute the essential principles organising the social representations of our groups of subjects. On the one side we find the responses of *teachers*: the Italian women were more concerned with the explanations and solutions that psychologists can produce about problems of the unconscious; the male teachers, more centred on the research and study dimension. On the other side *social workers* and *physicians* share a negative image of psychologists, but not always according to the same criteria. Social workers mostly criticise psychologists' supposed superiority which hinders their practice ('unlike everyone', 'unable to observe', 'split theory and practice'...), whereas for the physicians the problem is essentially about the personality of psychologists, their lack of sensitivity, their lack of balance, their fundamental defect of not being like a physician and not even being conscious of their limits.

Is the direct comparison with their own profession a specific socio-cognitive procedure of our physicians looking for a familiar point of anchoring in the construction of their representation? This is not exactly the

IDEAL

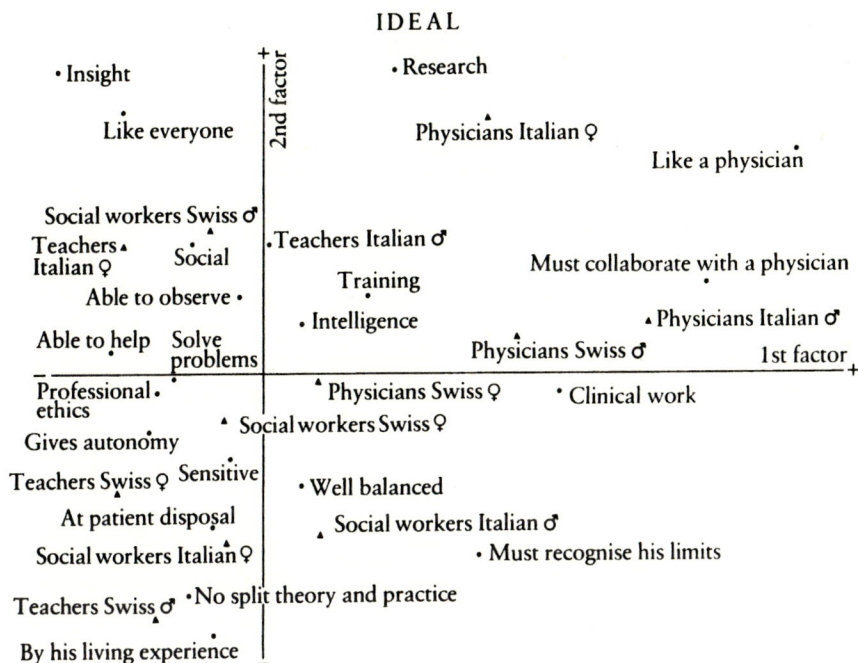

Figure 9.3 Ideal psychologist: first and second factors of the correspondence analysis

case, as is illustrated by the responses to the ideal image described in the following section.

Representations of the ideal psychologist

Let us look at the configuration of the different dimensions invoked in subjects' descriptions of the ideal psychologist. The first factor, explaining 23·9 per cent of the inertia, presents a clear opposition between *conforming* and *originality*. Towards the positive pole, we find categories such as 'must be like physician', 'should collaborate with physician', 'clinical work', 'trained' and 'conscious of his limits'. These contents are primarily proposed by physicians.

Towards the negative pole, the response configuration, primarily produced by Italian teachers, is quite simple: 'helping in the solution of problems', 'giving autonomy to the patient' and 'professional ethics'. At the core of the opposition drawn by this factor there are different representations of caretaking. There is first a clinical representation, conforming to a medical model, and this representation is dependent on physicians who stress the collaborative attitude and the consciousness of his limits in the ideal psychologist. Secondly, there is a more original representation, where psychological activities are recognised as such. The originality of this representation consists in the idea of producing welfare by promoting the autonomy of the patient. The professional legitimation of psychologists in this second representation (which is primarily elaborated by teachers) derives from the responsibility for their actions attributed to the psychologists by the evocation of specific professional ethics.

The importance of ethical issues, and the different meanings they assume in different contexts, is more clearly specified in the configuration of the second factor of this same analysis. This factor, explaining 18·5 per cent of the inertia, specifies the quality and direction of the *psychologist's insight*, a dimension that we found earlier for the typical image. Here, towards the positive pole, we find this penetrating insight formulated in such terms as the magic eye and intuition, as well as research activity. More importantly, this insight is addressed towards the exterior, the social, and the psychologist has to be discreet, like everyone, not obtrusive. On this pole of the factor we find actions and their fields of application, as well as professional ethics. This configuration describes the responses of the Italian teachers and the (male) Swiss social workers.

Towards the negative pole, by contrast, the issues are mainly centred on the insight that the ideal psychologist has to direct towards himself, towards his personal life. He has to look at his personal limits, to his personal well-being. This configuration of responses fits the Swiss teachers' and the Italian social workers' positions. In other words, on this second factor, we have an interesting opposition: on the one hand there is an opening towards a specific practice and the professional ethics connected with this practice, while on the other the ideal psychologist is drawn back to himself, to his way of being which overrides any professional perspective, an ethical sensibility here coinciding with a sort of self-effacing attitude in which the psychologist is mainly concerned with controlling his personal way of being and making good any failings without reference to professional actions.

Two groups of subjects, physicians and social workers, seek to make the ideal psychologist conform to their own professional model, whereas teachers allow the psychologist a differentiated space. In fact, teachers constitute the professional group least involved in competition for jurisdiction in this field; their prestige is less threatened by the establishment of psychologists as professionals. In this sense they can more easily invoke original dimensions specific to psychological practice than the other professionals.

The strategies used by these professionals in choosing categories for anchoring their representation of psychologists are worth examining in more detail. The strategy of the physicians consists in a process of assimilation to their own profession. As we have seen on the first factor of the ideal image, they take the medical profession as the prototype of the professional category and place the psychologist in a marginal and subordinate position, as a collaborator in clinical activity. The comparison with the typical image they produced confirms this strategy of assimilation to the familiar model, the medical one, resulting in an objectification in which the psychologist is judged as deviant.

A strategy of assimilation is also used by social workers, though perhaps in a more subtle way. In fact, they do not say 'the psychologist is (or is not) like a social worker', but they use categories like 'feeling', 'sensitivity' and 'living experience' which are at the basis of their own way of being in touch with social cases, as Le Poultier (1986) has clearly shown in his work on the cognitive strategies applied by social workers to their own professional practice.

Before I discuss this part of my data any further, it will be helpful to look at the social representations which psychologists elaborate about themselves and about their own professional development. This will allow us to compare the different categories invoked by psychologists with those used by other professionals in the field.

Social representations of psychologists about their profession

The starting point in the case of psychologists was a previous survey conducted in Italy at the end of the seventies (Palmonari, 1981; Palmonari et al., 1987). The content analysis of 140 interviews with psychologists working in different contexts was organised in a typology of four different representations, arranged on a continuum from a focus on collective to individual contexts for the activity of psychologists. The first of these representations is organised around the socio-political engagement of the psychologist. The second stresses the importance of an interdisciplinary approach to the social causes of psychological problems. The third introduces a focus on individual problems to legitimate the effort to preserve the psychologist's clinical competence. Finally, the fourth representation accentuates the individual focus so that the individual is the only object of psychotherapeutic intervention and the personal value of the psychologist is the only criterion legitimating his activity.

The prototypical contents of each one of the four representations were described in the items of a questionnaire initially administered to students of psychology in Switzerland, Italy and Paris (Doise et al., 1982; De Paolis et al.,

1983). Factor analyses conducted on the students' answers showed that subjects recognised the coherence of each representation, but at the same time they reorganised their contents in new configurations based on several oppositions between vocational issues versus professional ones.

According to these underlying oppositions between vocational and professional centration, and for the purpose of my own research, I give another interpretation of the relations between the four types. On the one hand, the second and third types (different in their focus on the collectivity or the individual) share opinions about the importance of training, the scientific status of psychology and the valorisation of specific professional skills in order to differentiate psychologists from other professionals in the field. On the other hand, the two remaining types (the more 'socio-political' and the more individualistic) share an existential vision of their activity where above all it is the personal commitment and the way of being of psychologists which defines their vocation.

This opposition between a vocational and a professional focus seems to be an essential issue in the developmental process of a new profession. In order to assess the vocational versus the professional trend of evolution, it was useful to explore with other psychologists the social representations they elaborated of the development of their own occupation.

A questionnaire of forty-four propositions was constructed on the basis of the Italian typology and administered to eighty Swiss psychologists (divided between clinical and non-clinical psychologists, as well as between those who joined the profession before 1972 and those who joined subsequently). I asked them to express on a seven-point scale their *present* degree of agreement with each statement and, at the same time and on the same scale, the degree of agreement they would have expressed at the *beginning* of their careers. Although each statement focussed on either a professional or vocational issue, these descriptions were not presented to the subjects.

Clearly, what we obtain from this procedure is not an objective reconstruction of their professional evolution, but rather the image they wish to present of their professional development, the representation of themselves as an emerging professional group or rather as a vocational one. For some of the propositions, psychologists show a *stability* of opinion (no significant differences between scores for the beginning of their career and for their present rating). For some other propositions the agreement is stronger at present than at the beginning of their career, and these I have called the *emerging images*. Finally, there is a group of propositions in which the change goes in the opposite direction: they were more accepted at the beginning but have been progressively *abandoned*. All of these propositions contribute to the map of the social representations of the professional development of

Table 9.2. *Psychologists' representations of their own professional development: stable images*

STABLE IMAGES FOR ALL PSYCHOLOGISTS

[a] Most accepted items

P   The discoveries of psychology offer the psychologist the means for unveiling various manipulations to which individuals are exposed.

P   The main satisfaction for the psychologist derives from his efficiency in the amelioration of the functioning of individuals and of relations between individuals.

P   The mastering of competences specific to psychology defines the professional identity of the psychologist.

P   It is the individual in his relations to others who must constitute the specific object of psychology.

P   In his activity the psychologist must concern himself with the well-being of the individual.

[b] Most refused items

V   The present function of psychology is to redirect attention away from social problems.

V   The motivation of psychologists should be based on a choice of a political nature.

V   The principal source of satisfaction for psychologists resides in the certainty of working for a true political alternative.

V   In our societies, the intervention of the psychologist is manipulative because it hides the true problems which are, in fact, of a political and social order.

P   The professional value of a psychologist depends above all on his integration in an interdisciplinary team; it is not very important to have a professional grouping or association.

Subjects were asked to respond to each item on a scale ranging from 1 (do not agree at all) to 7 (agree completely). The forty-four items were ranked in decreasing order according to the cumulative percentage of responses at points 5, 6 and 7 of the scale. The items marked [a] belong to the group of eleven items (25%) which were most accepted, while those marked [b] belong to the group of eleven items which were the most refused.

P = professional issues; V = vocational issues.

psychology, in which the stable images represent the core, the invariant point of anchoring, integrated with the emerging issues and deprived of less salient, peripheral issues. These three groups of issues are presented in Tables 9.2, 9.3 and 9.4.

As we can see, there is stability both for opinions widely accepted from the beginning of their careers to the present and for opinions consensually rejected all along (no significant differences on a t-test for repeated measures between 'actual' and 'beginning' answers, or on a t-test for groups between clinical and non-clinical psychologists as well as between generations of

Table 9.3. *Psychologists' representations of their own professional development: emerging images*

EMERGING IMAGES

P The psychologist must bring his contribution to the definition and analysis of the needs of different social groups.

P To be psychoanalysed only constitutes an aspect, however important, of the specific qualifications of the psychologist.

P In order to be scientific, the psychologist needs to base himself on the findings of the other social sciences.

P It is desirable that the activity of the psychologist inserts itself in an interdisciplinary project of social change.

P[a] Changing the individual in his relations to others must be the aim of the psychologist's activity.

---

[a] Only the non-clinical psychologists show a greater acceptance of this statement now than at the beginning of their careers: clinical (-0.10), non-clinical $(+0.67)$, $t(61) = 2.42$, $P < 0.02$.

P = professional issues.

psychologists). At the core of the representations of these psychologists is their agreement about confidence in psychological knowledge, efficiency, mastery of specific abilities defining their professional identity, and research in a specific area of intervention. There is a striking coincidence between these issues and the conditions which allow the development of an occupational group into a profession described by Wilensky, which were noted earlier.

The core of the representation is also constituted by the stable rejection of ideological, 'old-fashioned' positions which cannot motivate the choice of the psychologist's activity, and of arguments against the legal protection of the profession.

At this point, the opposition between vocational and professional issues already takes shape. The emerging images and the abandoned ones confirm this trend.

Table 9.3 shows the emerging images on which the growing agreement is consensually expressed between groups of clinical and non-clinical psychologists. The preponderant centration is on the delimitation of the sphere of action and on the opening towards an interdisciplinary approach.

The list of abandoned images given in Table 9.4 illustrates that more issues are now considered as being peripheral. Psychoanalytic training is no longer a central criterion for being a good psychologist, nor is the development of individual personality. Moreover, four professional issues, all of which define the psychologist merely in terms of technical skills, are less accepted now than at the beginning of the career. They must be read in connection with the stable

Table 9.4. *Psychologists' representations of their own professional development: abandoned images*

ABANDONED IMAGES	
V	To be psychoanalysed constitutes the only necessary and sufficient condition to work as a psychologist.
V	To be in analysis is to learn to neglect the social aspects of individual problems.
P	The models and techniques inherent to psychology guarantee its scientific validity.
P[a]	The training of psychologists must emphasise above all the specific technical competences of their profession.
P[b]	Only the technical competence of the psychologist enables him to help individuals to change their relations to others.
P	The main concern of the psychologist should be to underline his technical competences.
V	All psychologists must engage themselves in personal relations enabling them to alleviate the psychic sufferings of others.
V	The main motivation of the psychologist should be the development of his own personality through his work with others.
V	The main satisfaction of the psychologist is based on the satisfaction of the client, patient or consumer.
V	The main satisfaction of psychologists resides in the accomplishment of a social project to which they contribute.
V	The training of psychologists must concern above all the development of a critical analysis of society.

[a] Change towards refusal is mostly among non-clinical psychologists: clinical (-0.34), non-clinical (-1.28), $t(66) = 2.73$, $P < 0.01$.
[b] Change towards refusal is made by the non-clinical psychologists: clinical ($+0.03$), non-clinical (-0.75), $t(66) = 2.07$, $P < 0.05$.
P = professional issues; V = vocational issues.

and the emerging issues: in this sense, their decreasing scores are consistent with the growing acceptance of other disciplinary approaches.

Psychologists show a stable focus on specific attributes of their discipline as well as an increasing interest in other perspectives. Furthermore, they seem to refuse to be merely confined in a tautological validation of their discipline. They use different strategies to offer a coherent image of their professional development. There is an evident interest in overcoming differences stemming from the variety of *practices*. They try to present themselves as belonging to a cohesive group mainly centred on the acquisition and maintenance of acknowledged professional characteristics.

In this sense psychologists seem to accentuate intra-categorical similarities based on dimensions which can sharpen the profile of their fuzzy category: items which they do not consider salient for the development of their professional acknowledgement are relegated to the peripheral region of their representational field. Nevertheless, as we saw earlier, other professionals do not seem to grant them a reciprocal professional acknowledgement.

Strategies of anchoring in the development of social representations in different professional groups

As I noted earlier, Habermas' (1971; see also Furth, 1983) distinction between strategic action and communicative action, between 'work' and 'interaction', provides a useful framework in which to summarise these diverging social representations about the professionalisation of psychologists. Strategic action fits the professional model in so far as it implies:

(1) The translation of knowledge into techniques.

(2) The definition of targets.

(3) The choice of instruments and appropriate strategies.

(4) Training as the criterion of access to the mastery of techniques.

(5) Efficiency in the resolution of problems as the criterion of normative verification.

This list of attributes is common both to the dimensions valorised in psychologists' representations and the conditions for a professionalisation process described in the interactionist literature in the sociology of professions (although these conditions also emphasise the creation of an exclusive sphere of action, a point which is not explicitly stressed in this list of attributes).

Reference to these attributes in the elaboration of social representations about the psychologist signifies that they are being construed as a professional category, whereas the preponderant reference to attributes of communicative action anchors the category in an interactional context. In the latter case, values and behavioural norms can be shared in different contexts, not necessarily or exclusively in the professional one: communicative and existential attributes have a very low diagnostic power for the unambiguous identification of a professional.

Physicians and social workers invoke communicative categories in describing psychologists. Empirical knowledge, techniques and operational strategies are not at the core of their representations. The psychologist, deprived of any practice, obviously does not appear as a professional. On the contrary, the psychologist is identified in terms of interactive abilities (or the lack of interactive abilities for the typical image). There is in this representation a primacy of *being over doing*, whereas the opposite trend is evident in the responses of teachers and of psychologists themselves. In fact, teachers take much greater account of the content of psychological knowledge and its application to specific issues. They talk about practices based on such knowledge, as well as about goals and professional ethics, so that those interactive abilities of the psychologist which are evoked by teachers are tempered by considerations of strategic action. In an even stronger manner, psychologists construct the representation of their own professional development essentially on technical and professional issues, rejecting more and more dimensions centred on personal attributes or on idiosyncratic ideological choices.

The opposition between strategic and communicative action as points of anchoring for diverging categorisations determines the inclusion or exclusion of psychologists from the professional world. As we asked our subjects to talk about an occupation, we can expect references (whether positive or negative) to the professional traits which characterise the first category, which imply the inclusion of psychologists in the professional world. The choice of references pertaining to communicative action has a normative value; it is a way of excluding the 'fuzzy category' from the restricted boundaries of the professional world.

In this way, I want to underline a fundamental difference with the standard approach of prototype theory when it is limited to a consideration of cross-cultural differences without taking account of the normative and evaluative meanings of categorisations. One can only use prototype theory in social psychology if one also takes account of the content of categories, and content here refers not only to the cognitive aspects of categories but also to their normative and evaluative aspects, which will vary even within the same cultural field. Moreover, a real or supposed similarity, a potential sharing of the field of action, is likely to activate a process of comparison which leads, in a particular context of competition, to disconfirming the membership of the novel in the familiar valorised universe. As we saw earlier, this allows the well-established professionals to deny psychologists entry into the professional world by questioning their legitimacy, something which is achieved by describing the activity of psychologists in a manner which fails to constitute them as a profession.

As with any object of social representations, professions have to be placed in the developmental dynamics of relations between social groups: diverging social representations contribute to creating the conditions for the maintenance or the development of hierarchical relations between professional groups and therefore the place which any new profession could eventually occupy. The choice of prototypical attributes serves the essential goal of discriminating between categories in an intricate play of assimilation and differentiation. Sometimes, a strong assimilation becomes the shortest distance to differentiation. When the psychologist is considered as potentially threatening the distinctive sphere of action of his neighbours, any acknowledgement of professional attributes is dismissed in favour of human and relational dimensions. These dimensions are in fact less threatening and competitive, as Van Knippenberg's works (1984) have largely illustrated. The human and relational dimensions can be usefully applied in intergroup representations in order to accommodate the strange and intrusive object while preserving the distinctiveness of a specific group identity.

As long as social relations between groups determine the choice of prototypical attributes around which a category is constructed, classifying and naming cannot be considered as neutral processes. The diverging representations elaborated by physicians and social workers on the one hand, and by teachers and psychologists on the other, show once again how classification arises in the context of competition between social groups. Each group categorises the world and constructs identities in accordance with its own vested interests.

References

Barber, B. (1963). Some problems in the sociology of professions. *Daedalus*, XCII, 669–88.

Benzecri, J.-P. (1973). *L'Analyse des données*, vol. II: *Correspondances*. Paris: Dunod.

Bucher, R. and Strauss, A. L. (1961). Professions in process. *American Journal of Sociology*, LXVI, 325–34.

Chapoulie, J. M. (1973). Sur l'analyse sociologique des groupes professionnels. *Revue française de sociologie*, XVI, 86–114.

De Paolis, P. (1986). *La Résistible Ascension professionnelle du psychologue: représentations sociales d'un processus de professionnalisation*. Thèse de doctorat 3ème cycle. EHESS, Paris.

De Paolis, P., Lorenzi-Cioldi, F. and Pombeni, M.-L. (1983). Il lavoro dello psicologo: l'immagine di un gruppo di studenti di psicologia. *Giornale Italiano di psicologia*, 1, 143–61.

Doise, W. in collaboration with Mugny, G., De Paolis, P., Kaiser, C., Lorenzi-Cioldi, F. and Papastamou, S. (1982). Présentation d'un questionnaire sur les psychologues. *Bulletin Suisse des Psychologues*, 3, 189–206.

Furth, H. G. (1983). A developmental perspective on the societal theory of Habermas. *Human Development*, 26, 181–97.

Goode, W. J. (1960). Encroachment, charlatanism and the emerging professions: psychology, sociology and medicine. *American Sociological Review*, 25, 902–14.

Greenacre, M. J. (1984). *Theory and Application of Correspondence Analysis*. London: Academic Press.

Habermas, J. (1971). Technology and science as 'ideology'. In J. Habermas, *Toward a Rational Society*. London: Heinemann.

Hughes, E. C. (1958). *Men and their Work*. Glencoe, Ill.: Free Press.

Le Poultier, F. (1986). *Travail social, inadaptation sociale et processus cognitifs*. Paris: Publications du CTNERHI.

Moscovici, S. (1981). On social representations. In J. P. Forgas (ed.), *Social Cognition: Perspective on Everyday Understanding*. London; Academic Press.

(1984). The phenomenon of social representations. In R. M. Farr and S. Moscovici (eds.), *Social Representations*. Cambridge: Cambridge University Press.

Palmonari, A. (ed.). (1981). *Psicologi*. Bologna: Il Mulino.

Palmonari, A., Pombeni, M. L. and Zani, B. (1987). Social representation and professionalization of psychologists. In W. Doise and S. Moscovici (eds.), *Current Issues in European Social Psychology*, vol. 2. Cambridge: Cambridge University Press.

Rosch, E. (1975). Cognitive reference points. *Cognitive Psychology*, 7, 532–47.

(1977). Human categorisation. In N. Warren (ed.), *Studies in Cross-cultural Psychology*, vol. 1. London: Academic Press.

(1978). Principles of categorisation. In E. Rosch and B. B. Lloyd (eds.), *Cognition and Categorisation*. Hillsdale, N.J.: Erlbaum.

Rosch, E. and Mervis, C. B. (1975). Family resemblances: studies in the internal structure of categories. *Cognitive Psychology*, 7, 573–605.

Rosch, E., Mervis, C. B., Gray, W., Johnson, D. and Boyes-Braem, P. (1976). Basic objects in natural categories. *Cognitive Psychology*, 8, 382–439.

Smedslund, J. (1972). *Becoming a Psychologist*. Oslo: Universitets Forlaget.

Sullerot, E. (1968). *Historie et sociologie du travail féminin*. Paris: Gonthier.

Van Knippenberg, A. F. M. (1984). Intergroup differences in group perceptions. In H. Tajfel (ed.), *The Social Dimension*, vol. 2. Cambridge: Cambridge University Press.

Wilensky, H. L. (1964). The professionalization of everyone? *American Journal of Sociology*, LXX, 137–58.

10

Social psychology and developmental psychology: extending the conversation[1]

Serge Moscovici

Serge Moscovici

(1)

There are numerous sciences which study the way in which people handle, distribute and represent knowledge. But the study of how and why people share knowledge and thereby constitute their common reality, of how they transform ideas into practice – in a word, the power of ideas – is the specific problem of social psychology. This is by no means a secondary problem – witness the famous and conclusive remarks of Keynes:

But apart from this contemporary mood, the ideas of economists and political philosophers, both when they are right and when they are wrong, are more powerful than is commonly understood. Indeed the world is ruled by little else. Practical men, who believe themselves to be quite exempt from any intellectual influences, are usually the slaves of some defunct economist. Madmen in authority, who hear voices in the air, are distilling their frenzy from some academic scribbler of a few years back. I am sure that the power of vested interest is vastly exaggerated compared with the gradual encroachment of ideas.
(*Keynes*, 1936, *p*. 383)

The processes through which ideas are transmuted are not necessarily the province of philosophers and writers. Such processes take place in an anonymous manner; they apply to traditions, to common sense or to professional groupings, and in each case the same things could be said. They enter into relations and actions which are still in the making, anticipating what should happen and justifying it once it has happened. In more concrete terms, the theory of social representations, with which we are concerned here, was proposed in relation to this specific problem, in order to understand the encroachment of ideas on modern culture. In this sense it occupies a distinct

[1] Translated from the French by Gerard Duveen.

place in social psychology. Indeed, a growing number of researchers even wish that it should become the heart of our science. I am aware that there are many ideas which are more precise and more powerful than those which I have advanced. And many think, perhaps rightly, that the theory has insufficient roots in the motifs which govern the evolution of our field of research. But when one considers what is essential, what gives it its specificity, one does discover such roots, in a retrospective fashion. One sees, in effect, that the notion of representation made its entry into social psychology in different ways towards the end of the 1950s. This is worth recalling, so as to establish more clearly an originality which we tend to neglect. One of the reasons for returning to this idea was the necessity for checking the tendency of reducing everything to the individual, of avoiding every social idea, every collective action, on the pretext that they would ensnare us in the fallacy of the group mind. In insisting instead on the necessity of studying them, Asch argued as follows:

Social action requires that the individual participant be capable of representing to himself the situation that includes himself and others. These individual representations contain, in cases of full-fledged interaction, a reference to the fact that the other also possesses a corresponding view of the situation. These similar and mutually relevant representations in individuals provide the equivalent of what group mind theorists sought and individual psychologists denied.
(*Asch*, 1959, *pp.* 370–1)

You will recognise here a dialectic between individuals and the society which they constitute, a dialectic made possible by representations created in a collective fashion and which are shared. This notion resolves the paradox that while humans are private persons they nevertheless communicate, have a common existence, form groups and invent institutions. Who will be surprised that I invoke Heider at this point? I certainly share his interest in the knowledge of common sense and sympathise with his remarks on everyday psychology. His point of departure is the same hypothesis as that of the theory of social representations. That is to say, that a great part of everyday relations depends on unobtrusive theories and explanatory models through which people understand their experience. Such popular theories, far from being a tissue of lies and uninteresting 'representations', play an essential role in determining the kind of perceptual and inductive inferences we make and the kind of arguments and explanations which we accept. It thus seems possible to consider language and ordinary inferences as the result of processes for which one can find analogies in scientific psychology.

If this deduction is correct, then one can, for example, approach the relations between the ordinary use and the scientific use of psychological or scientific predicates, the difference being that the former is less explicit than

165

the latter. This hypothesis provides the basis for much contemporary research in cognitive psychology. While Heider considered 'popular knowledge' (in particular 'folk psychology') as a 'given' and asked questions about its structure, we see it as socially 'constructed' and are interested in its genesis. Since its primary function is to make communication possible between people, one must recognise that its cognitive properties are transformed in accord with the needs of action and communication.

The usual way of extending such a hypothesis is by recognising the constructive aspect of mental life and experience through the notion of representation. In describing the reasons why, in the course of perception, distal stimuli change and become proximal stimuli, Heider writes:

Within the organism there is, then, the constructive process of perception which leads to some event corresponding to the awareness of the object, the reality as perceived. The terms *representation* or *image* of the object have been used to describe this awareness...The constructive part of the perceptual process within the person is sometimes spoken of as involving central or higher phenomena, processes or layers, whereas the proximal stimuli entering the organism, the so-called raw material, involve more peripheral or lower layers.
(*Heider, 1958, p. 24*)

I leave it to the historians to pursue these relationships. Farr (1977) was the first to point out the links between Heider's theory and that of social representations, and what each could contribute to the other. Why has this notion not played its part fully? Why was it not recognised, as it ought to have been, by Asch and Heider? Perhaps because of the dominant interest which perception has held for social psychology. Since the turn of the century our attitude towards the notion of representation has nearly come full circle. After a period of oblivion during which the notion of representation fell into disuse, in which psychology affirmed the primacy of behaviour and of perception, people are now returning to it. Our theory presupposes in large measure the primacy of representations and asserts their social character. In effect, as the philosopher Cassirer put it, in human knowledge nothing is simply presented: everything is represented. Our perception and our thought are the products of minds which already have a shared organisation and content which, to a large extent, delimit what our immediate world of experience will be. Consequently, the organisation and the content of our mental representations have a certain autonomy in relation to the environment and the information which we receive from it.

There is something marvellously ethereal about representations, since they are transmitted from one individual to another through non-material means. At the same time they are concrete, once objectified in institutions, rituals and works of art. They can thus become social and mental causes producing physical effects, as Mauss showed in his studies on magic, or Freud in relation to hysterical paralysis. In somewhat antiquated terms Durkheim summed it up when he wrote:

There is one division of nature where the formula of idealism is applicable almost to the letter: this is the social kingdom. Here more than anywhere else, the idea makes reality.
(*Durkheim*, 1976, *p.* 236)

One does not need to accept his sociology to recognise a great truth in this abrupt formula.

(2)

I do not cite these examples to dispel the impression that the phenomenon of social representation is less idiosyncratic than it is usually thought to be, or to confer some legitimacy on the idea. Why, then? Social psychology has discovered a great variety of ideas and facts, and displayed great inventiveness in its methods. Nevertheless its history shows it to be devoid of a unified aim, of any steadfastness in relation to its object, and fickle about its concepts and interests; jumping without any apparent reason from one field of investigation to another (Moscovici, 1984). And a close examination reveals that under such diverse terms as attitudes, attributions, social cognitions, norms, lay theories, group mind, social identity, or schemas, social psychology has been turning around the same phenomenon defined in particular contexts and considered at different levels. It would be more logical, and this is a point I want to stress, for social psychology to recognise this phenomenon in its originality and to take it as its authentic object. In this book various contributors endeavour to bring this into relief. But the book itself has a much wider aim: to bring out, perhaps even to demonstrate, the profound links between social psychology and developmental psychology. Is it just by chance that they should come together around a theory of social representations? Is it simply a question of the application of the representations of the world of adults to the world of children? In my view this is not so. I see here, rather, a renewed effort which extends the range of other work and asks new questions. Indeed, one can observe that the currents of thought which have sought to explore the origins of higher mental processes in the child have been inspired by older studies of collective representations. This seems evident in the first works of Piaget. His approach was governed by the hypothesis that human thought in the more simple cultures was shaped by the collective representations shared by their members. This is also true of the work of Vygotsky and his pupils. They realised that such representations predominate in the mental life of individuals, whether they are adults or children. Above all they believed that there was strict correspondence between the transformation of societies and that of the corresponding representations. Luria is very explicit in this respect. In particular he describes the echo which they found in the studies of Lévy-Bruhl and his comparison between archaic mentality and modern mentality:

Lévy-Bruhl was the first to point out the qualitative feature of primitive thought and the first to treat logical processes as products of historical development. He had a great influence on the psychologists of the 1920's who tried to go beyond simplistic notions about the mind as a by-product of natural selection and to understand human consciousness as a product of sociocultural development.
(*Luria*, 1976, *p.* 7)

In many respects it still remains for us to show that social relations and social changes are accompanied by profound transformations of thought. One can easily discern the phenomenon which has allowed the formulation of this task and the researching of mental processes not only within the organism. An examination of the possibilities shows that two ways can be described to accomplish this task. One, which I shall call 'Bartlett's way', recommends the comparison of the representations and beliefs of groups situated at different stages of evolution. One begins with the study of the primitive group as being 'probably the best introduction to the construction of a social psychology adequate to modern needs' (Bartlett, 1928, p. 263). In particular Bartlett makes the following remark about Lévy-Bruhl:

It is first to be observed that Lévy-Bruhl's antithesis is not between the primitive and the ordinary member of a modern social group, but between the former and the scientific expert at work within his own field... The error here, as in much recent social and abnormal psychology, is not that the primitive or abnormal are wrongly observed; but that the modern and normal are hardly observed at all.
(*p.* 284)

In this perspective the modern and the normal refer to the ordinary members of a group, observed in their milieu and in relation to topics which are significant for their common life. It would be erroneous to believe that studies of sophisticated subjects in refined contexts offer any substitute. At most these would be the complement and extension of more authentic observations.

The second way, which for reasons of convenience we shall call 'Vygotsky's way', but which is also that of Piaget, passes through the child as the equivalent of a simpler and younger culture, and follows its development. This way therefore postulates that the social nature of human cognition appears in the individual's interiorisation of social experiences. Progressively, as this process develops, we can grasp the moments and operations through which the consciousness of everybody is articulated with that of their neighbours and with the culture of which they form a part. The evolution of human groups can be brought to light through the imprints inscribed in the development of an individual. The contrast between the child and the adult reflects that between the primitive and the modern, between origins and outcomes. As G. Stanley Hall put it: 'Infancy, childhood and youth are the bunches of keys to unlock the past history of the race.'

As social psychologists we have followed Bartlett's way, believing that representations provide a privileged access for observing the normal and the modern (Moscovici, 1988), which until now have not generally been the object of observations. From this point of view social psychology becomes, in the wide sense of the term, an anthropology of the modern world. But one is struck by the fact that the two ways have a common point of departure and are animated by such close underlying issues. Their different traditions and methods allow a deep similarity to show through and tie them together. It is as if social psychology and developmental psychology were concerned with the same thing, the former in space and the latter in time, the first by way of the exterior and the second by way of the interior. They are in sum the two faces of a single science, in which the one tries to resolve at the level of the group the enigma with which the other is concerned at the level of the individual. We can see that after being separated almost to the point of losing all contact, social psychology and developmental psychology (Doise and Mugny, 1984) are beginning to return to a shared line of research, as pendulums which have been separated return by themselves to the vertical. To spare the reader's patience I shall draw this historical overview to a close here. It should be clear by now that social representations are much more than just one subject among others in the psychological study of the child.

(3)

I should need more talent than I have and a greater familiarity with developmental psychology to discuss such a varied series of studies in depth. William Corsaro and Maria D'Alessio illustrate wonderfully the contrast between representations in action and the action of representations. There are several ways of approaching these phenomena. Corsaro has chosen to go from their 'solid', stable states to their 'fluid', unstable states, *in statu nascenti*. To this end he has taken children themselves as his guides, in the efforts which they make to move from one arena of life into another, from the family to school. One sees them experimenting with society and creating experimental societies, transforming what is given to them into something made by them. This process brings to light a capacity for invention, for creating their own reality, and, above all, for knowing and reconstituting at their level the world of the school into which they penetrate. This process brings out the truth of Vico's maxim, to which Marx also subscribed, that men know society because they produce it. We can see social representations taking shape in a very concrete way, in this passage from the given to the made, and the fashioning of the metamorphosis from the one to the other.

The rules themselves are inverted by the children when they engage in the forbidden gesture of bringing their own toys into school. In his joyous descriptions of these experimental societies, William Corsaro shows how the children represent and imagine alternative courses of action and relations which have the same origin and lead to the same result. One enjoys this vision of the child, denser and more authentic, at the same time both dissident and conformist, closer to our experience. But can one not also see in these various transgressions the sign of an effort which the children make collectively to re-establish the continuity with their life at home and in society in general? Their acceptance of the norm also means that they accept the break and yield to the institution.

The episode of the bank is a moment in this effort through which the children seek to establish some communication between two worlds which are not in communication. In creating this imaginary bank they transfer and transpose their knowledge of the external world into the world of the school, like scientists who move from one discipline to another. In this way the children render the strange familiar, and their representations are the means for doing so. But they also diversify their skills, and learn how to handle relationships, establish reciprocities and complicities. Besides objectified or reified behaviour, one also sees many an anchored behaviour based on mutual understanding and shared impulses. It seems that a detailed examination of their language would open up further new horizons. Yet I am aware that in such an exploration the more one grasps the details the more one multiplies the ambiguities, so that there is a risk of the facts dissolving in theory.

Maria D'Alessio brings together and compares a series of indices which give breadth and solidity to the facts. We can follow her reasoning and her conception without difficulty since they are carefully reflected through her chapter. Why, then, am I so struck by all that she has to say about the crumbling of the barriers between the world of children and the world of adults, the dissolution of childhood as a social category? Perhaps because I think I can see a facet of a more general phenomenon of our post-modern western world which has to do with the declassification of behaviours. One can establish this phenomenon in relation to the handicapped, foreigners, women, the elderly, and so on. A person may be handicapped, foreign, old or female; but what they should do or actually do ought not to be situated in a particular category, nor should they be judged as a member of a social category. In our relatively pacified society the less invasive institutions try to neutralise these differences and to make them painless. To this end there is an effort to eliminate every mark of class, every specific indication, to the extent that today one can no longer recognise the soldier as one could in the past because he wore a uniform, or a priest because of his cassock. It is as if they had disappeared from present existence. The members of these categories can no longer be distinguished by their language or their dress, and even less by their way of life. How to mark their differences, which have been made invisible, and their evidently given similarities, is one of the aspects of the crisis of representations in our epoch.

Maria D'Alessio makes us see an aspect of this declassification of behaviours in relation to the child, which is a strategic example. She describes the child as an active social subject, but embodied in a stereotype. One of the traits making up this stereotype I found particularly intriguing: the six-year-old child is just as much a model for the parents as for the psychologists. Why should this be so? The reply which comes to mind is that around this age the child manifests the ability to attribute mental states to themselves as much as to others and to represent wrong beliefs (Marvin et al., 1976). In sum the child is capable of adopting the point of view of another, not through imitation but as a function of a representation of what the other feels, thinks, etc. This development changes entirely the manner of the child's social interaction with other children and, above all, with adults. One can impute to the child a moral responsibility, and therefore a knowledge of the effects of their actions. By the age of six we are no longer speaking of an 'old' child, but a 'young' adult. This should, then, be a very important moment, the age of cognitive initiation, just as there is an age of religious or sexual initiation. The details of the lived conditions of this cognitive initiation remain to be explored.

In Maria D'Alessio's chapter, and above all in Paola De Paolis', one can see the multiple links between the notion of social representation and that of the prototype. Both belong to the same family, share the same historical origin, and are interwoven in their mental functioning. Paola De Paolis describes in a very personal way, bringing to light a new perspective, the development of psychologists in the world of professions. She shows us some of the rules of this play of representations which the neighbouring professions manufacture in order to situate, see and master our own. She is aware that representations much more than values or norms serve to define the social role of psychologists. Imperceptibly this study gives a social sense to the notion of prototype, beyond its cognitive sense. She shows that it is better adapted than the overused notions of role and even of status for expressing the behaviours and relations expected of an individual if they are to remain an exemplar of their category. Above all, in a professional society (Moscovici, 1988) such as ours, which valorises competence and expertise, it seems more exact to speak of social prototypes. That these should be the points of anchoring for shared representations, and even defined by them, is something of which I have been convinced for some time, by the evidence presented in the earlier studies of Palmonari, and now by that presented by Paola De Paolis. Nevertheless, anchoring in a prototype still leaves open the question of the diversity of prototypes.

Let us stay with this question for a moment. It is true that the most specific object, the individual, can provide a general example for a class of objects, of individuals. Now it is natural to observe that there are prototypes by default and prototypes by excess. The first kind are constituted by an element which appears common and characteristic, which has no alternatives and which is shared through uninstructed copying in a group. Such is the pre-eminence which the six-year-old child seems to have for us. The second kind of prototypes are crystallisations of an *ensemble* of ideas, qualities, practices in a single idea, quality or practice which becomes dominant and which tends to absorb the others. The atom for physics, the unconscious for psycho-analysis, the big bang for cosmology, the sacrifice for ritual are all examples of this kind.

Now, prototypes by default should have primarily a deictic value, designating only a class of objects or persons without entailing or revealing much information. Prototypes by excess, on the other hand, have a representative value because they serve as models for other ideas, qualities, etc., in a hierarchy, which resembles them to some extent. In social representations we are more concerned with this second kind of prototype. The way in which they are reworked in a collectivity and diffused in the course of time until they become a dominant motif would be worth examining. Both Maria D'Alessio and Paola De Paolis open up perspectives in this sense.

It would have been unthinkable, in a book dealing with social representations, not to have considered their semantic aspect. In their penetrating chapter, Barbara Lloyd and Gerard Duveen return to the ideas which we have just discussed, but from a different point of view. Certainly one could say that they take up these issues from the point of view of language, but in so far as this raises a question, that of understanding the ever-present problem of the nature of the arbitrary. It is certain that the arbitrariness of the sign in relation to its signified is not so remote from the arbitrariness of the prototype in relation to its class, or of the image in relation to perception or categorisation, and so on. That it is only the linguists who have defined the arbitrary and given it a theoretical bearing does not mean that others should not also consider the problem. A belief that one has been exempted from considering this issue is due to a kind of naive realism, an opaque positivism which still predominates. But the constructivist point of view brings this question clearly into the foreground. More exactly, the arbitrary is one of the essential constraints upon our thought, and the way in which we justify or mask it still remains unknown. Barbara Lloyd and Gerard Duveen credit social representations with the power to reduce the arbitrariness of the sign, but one could just as well say that of the prototype. This means that, in our society, the exemplary might be unmarried men and women; though in another society, perhaps, with a religious representation, the exemplary might be the pariah or death.

I do not wish to expand further on this point, except to underline its importance and the fact that it makes a difference for those of us who have proposed a constructivist view of social psychology. This does not excuse an ignorance of the research on the distinctions between men and women. For someone of my age it is fascinating to follow the evolution of the vocabulary of these problems, which reflects the evolution of the representation of our society itself. Until the 1970s, under the inspiration of socialist and liberal thought, people often referred to the working class, to the class struggles, to the exploitation of commodities, etc., and the building-blocks of our society seemed to be social classes. Since then, people refer more frequently to discrimination, to power, to differences of quasi-biological categories, as if the building-block of society were now a biological class defined by age, sex, ethnicity, almost race. This is to say that the proliferation of these studies seem to be part, to say no more, of a change in the representation of our society which is in progress.

Let us close this parenthesis and turn to the elegant demonstration contained in the chapter by Barbara Lloyd and Gerard Duveen. The qualification 'elegant' might seem curious, but it is not out of place: it describes an approach which is supple and rich and at the same time precise. I shall mention only two of the many comments which it evokes. The first concerns the asymmetry between boys and girls in their choice of toys. That the former choose masculine-marked toys more frequently while the latter do not choose feminine-marked toys more frequently is very striking, even if it is not surprising. But that this difference persists and is apparent in all the forms described in this chapter is of course significant. On the one hand, one can say that what is taught to children is the markings which make girls or boys of them. But what is transmitted to them is the representation of a hierarchy, in a society where boys have a positive identity and girls a rather negative identity. In effect, to choose the toys attributed to one's own gender is to affirm a distinction and a superiority, whereas not to choose them amounts to denying this distinction but recognising through this denial one's own inferiority. One can illustrate this superimposition of a difference and a hierarchy by the stylistic conventions of the English language in scientific journals. The difference is underlined by the use of 'he or she' where before one would have written simply 'he'. But the hierarchy is preserved since 'he or she' is not used randomly. If I am not mistaken, 'he' always comes first and 'she' follows, as the men walk in front of the women in the streets of Mexico. One can observe clearly in these examples how the relationship of the difference to the hierarchy, of the sign to its signified, has its arbitrary character masked by a representation. What remains to be clarified is whether mothers stress first the difference or the hierarchy between girls and boys. In addition we see once again that ingroup favouritism, that tendency to a chauvinism of petty resemblances, is determined by relations of power. What are the links between this and social identity? This would be a beautiful problem to resolve in the footsteps of Henri Tajfel.

The other comment concerns the development of the social representation of gender with age. One has the impression that the marks of what is a girl or boy, of what will be a woman or a man, appear very closely linked to language itself, verbal language and probably body language. This makes us wonder, in one sense, if there is a real development or just an adaptation to the environment. And, in another sense, when one sees the variations described by the authors, one is convinced that this development exists. But then it does not have the linear and pre-established aspect which is described for the themes of intelligence or morality. One does not become a girl or a boy by passing through stages, as one becomes reflexive or moral around the age of ten or twelve. Rather it is a question of a development which is also a differentiation with diverging but sufficiently regular lines to be interesting. All these chapters augur well for the conversation between social psychology and the psychology of the child. It is an entrancing conversation, and will become more so in the future.

(4)

What are the chances that one day we shall succeed in significantly improving our definition and our methods of studying social representations? It is difficult to respond to this question; there is a shortcoming whose origin is difficult to locate. Is it in our way of approaching the phenomenon, or in its cognitive or social nature? We have often been reproached about a certain woolliness in the theory, an evident opportunism in method, and a too idiosyncratic preoccupation with content. When I associate these deficiencies exclusively with social representations the problem seems to reside in our way of approaching the phenomenon. On other days, though, looking over the fence into the neighbours' garden, I find the strength to assert that even though they have simplified and standardised, predicted and produced series of results, they have not for all that overcome these shortcomings. One can see this in attribution theory (Fiske and Taylor, 1984; Turiel, 1983; Youniss, 1981). After so many years it remains an ensemble of propositions loosely connected with each other and with the empirical data. The more one advances the more one encounters methodological difficulties in understanding this simple fact: how do people infer causality? And as one does not seek to discover new facts the most positive and permanent aspect of these studies is to put together a survey in depth of our way of representing what is a cause or an intention. In spite of so much criticism and discouragement we have the impression that the shortcomings have not prevented us from learning a great deal. And we are not surprised, or even indignant, that more or less the same thing can be said of the notion of schema:

> The concept of mental schema pervades theorizing in cognitive psychology despite the fact that its basic meaning is indefinite, its usage by theorists is highly individualistic, and its operational connection to empirical events is tenuous.
> (*Hastie*, 1981, *p. 85*)

Yes, on those days when I look at our neighbours it seems that there is something in the complexity of the phenomenon, and that one should not underestimate it. The theory of social representations has been conceived as a function of this complexity and of the time needed to understand it. I have often said that it does not seek to explain the character of thought and social behaviour at one stroke. Those theories which present themselves as flawless and complete at the very beginning of empirical observations should be regarded with the greatest caution. Such a theory could only be the result of innocent speculation or of an undue simplification of reality according to ready-made conventions. In any case the shortcomings do not prevent us from continuing, considering the theoretical and practical necessities.

In their chapter Luisa Molinari and Francesca Emiliani rightly insist on the ambiguity of the image in general. On the one hand it provides a privileged access to an abstract idea since it is concrete and striking; while on the other hand it simplifies, caricatures and reduces the informational value of this very idea. Is this not the ambiguity of social representations themselves? Popular wisdom would have us choose the lesser of two evils. But in this case as soon as one chooses one alternative one gets the other back at a premium. With great finesse and equanimity our Italian colleagues retrace this ambiguity in a couple as turbulent as that of a mother and her child. Yet there are moments when one would like to hear the narrative or dialogic style in action, to see the living persons as in William Corsaro's chapter. Be that as it may, the

175

mothers who are also teachers constitute a distinct group, and without doubt a fascinating one. The coincidence between their profession and a family relationship displaces the social representations from the public to the private sphere, and *vice versa*, changing as the evidence shows the expectations and behaviours observed in other groups. Is it the expectations which become more ideal, or the behaviours which become more distant? Each of us who is both a teacher and a mother or father has their own reply to this question.

But the list of shortcomings is not limited to questions of definition and method. In different ways one hears that the view of people which is more or less dominant in social psychology is that of the *cognitive miser*. Here is an apt and striking expression. Cognitive miserliness is certainly no advantage, though neither is it something for which one ought to be blamed: it is neither a degradation nor a stupidity, and cannot be classified as abnormal. Many highly respected individuals in history were cognitive misers and have been chosen by their people as their heads. The fact is that, unintentionally, the theory of social representations has opted for a view of people as *cognitive prodigals*: not only because they are the creators of such things as the arts, religions, and so on, but also of psychological theories, as Heider or Freud credited them. Freud even went so far as to write:

One day I discovered to my great astonishment that the view of dreams which came nearest to the truth was not the medical but the popular one, half involved though it still was in superstition...Since under the name of 'psycho-analysis' it has found acceptance by a whole school of research workers.
(*Freud*, 1953, *p*. 635)

Above all, ordinary knowledge, common sense if you prefer, is really something other than an 'expertise' in everyday thinking. It implies a combination, sometimes deficient and sometimes overabundant, of very different types of thought and of information. It is thus distinguished from specialised or expert knowledge which, to the contrary, attempts to follow a single type of thought and to deal with a single category of information. If Hofstadter writes a book which combines music, art and logic, joining such disparate names as Gödel, Escher and Bach (Hofstadter, 1979), it is in order to explain artificial intelligence to each of us. He thus contributes to our ordinary knowledge and not to the science of this intelligence. In other words, as scientists we have to master the art of canon, of a single theme played against itself, while as people we have to master the art of fugue, an art which is usually based on one theme which is played in several voices in different ways, at different tempi or inverted or reversed. Doubtless the erudite expert mistrusts such improvisations, while the knowledgeable amateur or novice is infatuated with them, prompted by their propensity to consume words, images or information. There are both gourmets and gourmands of knowledge, but everyone must prepare their own dish. And if the recipes are the same, I mean the mental operations, one is more or less successful according to one's patience, education, practice, etc. In any case there must be a mixture of intellectual material and diverse opinions to understand and to communicate. For this reason compromise is only possible in everyday thinking, as Bartlett notes: 'There is no compromise for the thinker in the closed system and none for the experimental scientist' (Bartlett, 1958, p. 186).

It is therefore normal that representations in a society where so much knowledge is produced and consumed, like streams converging in a river, should be richer than expert theories.[2] It is to illustrate this point that I have chosen the characters from Flaubert's novel *Bouvard and Pécuchet* as models of the knowledgeable amateur scientist (Moscovici and Hewstone, 1983). Assuredly one could judge them ridiculous, but they are certainly not cognitive misers. To be sure, as medicine reminds us every day, abundance can be as injurious as penury. But, according to this point of view, if everyday thinking is flawed it is not because it applies this or that rule of inference, but because it applies it in an arbitrary way; it is not because it is biased but because it lacks bias; it is not because people allow themselves to be tempted into error by unique examples instead of taking account of statistics, but because they sometimes do one thing and at other times the opposite, according to the circumstances. These flaws are due to the necessity of combining diverse information and knowledge according to the changing relations in concrete situations. Many studies in social cognition neglect these relations and these conditions, and one can say of them what Malinowski said about the study of myths:

The whole treatment appears to us faulty, because myths are treated as mere stories, because they are regarded as primitive armchair occupations, because they are torn out of their life context and studied from what they look like on paper, and not from what they do in life.
(*Malinowski*, 1954, *p.* 110)

In my view Felice Carugati gives a masterly illustration of these issues on the basis of a concrete study. He examines the different registers in which intelligence is defined, from social representations to science. Obviously there is a continuing conversation in society about something called intelligence, in the course of which people are classified and declassified, valorised and devalorised. One cannot do without explaining intelligence, according to experience or to the place one occupies in this society. On the other hand, this

---

[2] I was pleased to note that M. Minsky made the same point in his recent book *The Society of Mind* (New York: Simon & Schuster, 1986).

conversation makes it salient, gives rise to beliefs and finally objectifies it. In this way the conversation gives intelligence a degree of reality which it is the mission of science to consecrate and guarantee. Is this a vicious circle or a virtuous one? Carugati leaves us to take care of the choice by analysing the construction of an object which we represent to ourselves and in which we are represented. Following him, one can reflect on the fact that most of the objects with which we have to deal in the human sciences – society, social class, personality, money, etc. – are susceptible to the same treatment. They are given to us in language and institutions, with directions for their use, indeed an explanation furnished in advance. And our theories are inscribed in the chain of these collective and anonymous elaborations, from which they derive their verisimilitude. In other words, one side of the coin is that they conserve the characteristics of social representations, of everyday knowledge; while on the other side they acquire them afresh, which brings our theories closer to science. They continue the same conversation, renewing the vocabulary, the meaning of the words and arguments which are exchanged. Curiously, for this reason the study of social representations becomes a condition of knowledge of scientific theories themselves. They would be a way of clearing up many persistent confusions and putting into perspective what we do know about reality. Emotion, like intelligence, is also an item of our conversation, meaning 'what is not reason' or 'what you experience as a passion'. Here the line between a belief being expressed and its being experienced is very thin.

Semin and Papadopoulou nonetheless enlarge the circle of conversation by introducing a new point of view. And I dare say a promising one. To be sure, a representation is not created without acting on our bodies and our affects as much as on our minds. But one would like to know more about this: for example, how the words which are used, Greek or French, or a piece of cloth changed into a flag, provoke the corresponding ideas and emotions. Yes, these trivial facts continue to surprise us and to arouse our indignation because we still do not know how the symbolic representation of emotion is constructed in the surroundings in which one is born and grows. Emotions impregnate a culture (do we not speak of shame-cultures or of guilt-cultures?) and are transmitted from one generation to another. We need to try to understand emotions more clearly in social psychology. We would then be better prepared to understand the way in which each individual acquires emotions and the expressive styles embedded in rules, conventions and rituals. Semin and Papadopoulou are aware of this, but, following Vygotsky, they also think that the process of interiorisation offers a short cut and a general solution. I confess to being as fascinated as they are by the ideas of this Soviet psychologist. But also puzzled, because I wonder if they are as fertile as they are believed to be. In particular I am not sure about his notion of an evolutionary metamorphosis from the social to the individual, namely, that what is experienced initially at the inter-psychological level is later found at the intra-psychological level. As the saying goes, it is too good to be true, but a surprise is possible.

By the way, I am not at all sure that this is a Marxist idea, or one which plays an important role in Marx's doctrine. To the best of my knowledge it is Freud who held it and who wished to show that in the evolution of our species one finds in psychic and interior reality what had once existed in the social and external world. In his mass psychology this is a recurrent theme, and one to which the great Soviet psychologist was not, perhaps, indifferent. Whatever the origins of this idea may be, the results of Semin and Papadopoulou are encouraging and show that it works, in particular because of the role played by language in the acquisition of reflexive social emotions. The repertoire made known through joint action seems determinant. It is possible to believe with Kripke and others that the mass of everyday representations mediating such emotions are quasi-deictic: they just point to a class of objects and reactions. How they become reflexive is our common social psychological problem. To say more about this study, which indicates a coherent direction in a very intricate field, would risk trying the patience of both these authors and the readers.

(5)

I have left to the end the study by Emler, Ohana and Dickinson, which shows us once again how artificial the frontiers are between social psychology and child psychology. Actually, it would be unseemly to discuss it, given that it is a product of some research which we have undertaken together. Yet it is not out of order to add some complementary information. In short, this research brought us together around the obvious assumption that our moral judgements correspond to a shared representation of the relations between children and between children and adults in our society. Without doubt maxims and prescriptions about what is good and bad are inculcated by parents. But children rediscover them and experiment with them in the safety of certain social relations which they represent, evaluate and discuss among themselves. William Corsaro gives us an idea of these transactions and activities. In our exploratory research, we started with children whom we knew had had two different educational and schooling experiences. We found that they formed different social representations. One of them turned out to be a 'participatory' social representation and the other an 'integrative' one. According to the former children believe that everyone has a say in any decision, authority is obeyed if one has respect *for* it, and the school itself is conceived as a *group*. The relations among children and with adults entail a certain degree of freedom of communication, flexibility of rules, openness in expression, care of common objects (books, for instance) and people, including teachers. As for obedience, this requires a measure of consensus. According to the second social representation, children see everybody as part of a system, in which decisions are made independently of each member, emphasising respect *due to* authority. The exercise of any freedom depends on the hierarchy, and one has to recognise fixed rules and apply them to avoid sanctions, otherwise the system could not function. In this sense the school is perceived as an *institution*, having the norms and values of any institution, such as the family, which everyone needs to interiorise in order to be successful.

Having assessed these representations, we asked children aged six to ten to solve a series of moral dilemmas, in the usual way. As expected we found systematic differences between moral judgements according to the type of representation, and these differences had a logical character. Just one example. One of the stories recounted the case of a pupil who wanted to borrow a book, but the teacher refused. We asked the children if this was fair and invited them to choose between various reasons offered for this refusal. Some reasons were external (for example, the book had already been lent) and others internal (for example, the child had not done enough work). Evidently, those who represent social relations in an 'integrative' manner suppose that authority and the institution are always right and that the members are at fault. These children risk doing something which is wrong. There is nothing surprising, therefore, if children with such a vision of relations in the school are significantly more likely to choose internal reasons, blaming the pupil for the teacher's refusal. There are many instances like this one, showing the close link between moral reasoning and the representation of the familiar world.

On the other hand it came as a surprise to find that differences with age were very few and even disparate. This seems to be contrary to the accumulated evidence of a regular development of moral reasoning at the rate and measure that the child grows up, and independently of the conditions in which they grow up. Without doubt this result supports the theory of representations, which considers such reasoning to be worked out in the course of intense social exchanges among children themselves and with adults. In the course of these exchanges the children's experience is drawn to particular relations that have particular meanings. But this result does not support Piaget's conception according to which moral judgement in young children begins by being determined in the bosom of the 'gerontocratic society' of adults, marked by the discipline and constraint which they impose. It is only later that children detach themselves, co-operating in the 'spontaneous societies' which they form; at the same time their moral judgement changes and progresses, taking on a more universal character. Although this explanation recognises a role for the social, it supposes that there is *a* conception of *the* child, without taking account of the specificity of relations with adults, according to the nature of institutions, as we have observed it.

In any case, it is not possible to think that these moral judgements are derived by children in isolation, from experience itself, either as observers or as participants; or that moral judgements develop at the rate and measure that children develop the intellectual abilities which enable them to abstract further from, and reason more profoundly about, the actions of which they are the witness. Not only can it be asked what sense there would be for a lone individual to articulate a rule such as 'do not kill' or 'love your neighbour', but it can also be seen that, endowed with the same intellectual capacities, children reason about a moral dilemma in different ways. Further, it can be asked why it is only with the onset of adolescence that children come to a rational moral judgement. They already have the necessary competences, since they speak and handle grammatical rules much earlier, which are much more complicated to handle than the rules of right and wrong.

The results which we have obtained, if they are confirmed, highlight an uncomfortable situation: on the one hand the theory proposed leads to a diversity without development, while, on the other hand, the established theory assumes a development without diversity. But I do not wish to enlarge any further on this subject, which would require a book to be discussed properly. If the truth be told, one problem arises above the others, and it is not so much concerned with the social or individual causes of development as with the way in which it is envisaged. Everything takes place, in numerous discussions, as though there were a class of judgements called moral given with the capacity to make judgements from the outset; and as though development followed in a linear manner from a pre-conventional stage through a conventional stage to a post-conventional stage, in which moral decisions are generated from rights, values and principles to which individuals in every culture could subscribe. It is as though there were an orderly evolution established by human nature in the approach of moral questions, with the last stage being morally superior and more pertinent than the first (Kohlberg, 1973). Obviously it is a question of a teleological evolution, in Auguste Comte's sense, which is obliged to pass through the same stages fixed in advance.

But one can also envisage development in a historical way as a process in the course of which different and autonomous domains are formed and differentiated. What comes to us from the past would then change the sense and character of the present. Thus traditional societies are distinguished from modern societies not so much because the former practise barter while the latter practise exchange, but because in the former, economic relations are confounded with familial or religious relations whereas, in the latter, economic relations are recognised as such. In this way the economy has, in the course of history, become differentiated from the surrounding setting and affirmed as a separate domain which has even taken on a preponderant character. This is particularly the case in capitalist settings, though not in socialist ones. In the same way, it could be thought that, if the types of reasoning about what we can or should do, about rule-directed behaviour in general, are precocious, their 'moral value', the fact of belonging to a particular class of judgements, emerges with time, at the rate and in so far as we acquire social experience. In other words, they are distinguished with the moral conscience which becomes autonomous, and constitutes an end in itself and sometimes predominates over everything else. One cannot speak of a movement in which one would pass from a lower to a higher stage; on the contrary, one creates and differentiates the different domains of social life. The formula 'one must respect one's parents' is not more moral than the expression 'one must respect the red light', which is no less banal. It acquires this meaning in our culture when the word 'respect' takes on an interior value for us and occupies a position in our vocabulary.

In sum, development consists in the discovery and formulation in moral terms of a certain number of points of view, of actions or of relations with others which have been or which could be expressed in other terms. It can become a distinct topic of discussion and interaction, stimulating the appearance of basic common values. One cannot speak of improvement in such reasoning about what one should or should not do, but of its autonomy in a marked domain in which every kind of reasoning or behaviour is associated with interiorised values which are shared with our fellow creatures. If such a development takes place, one should be able to see how the language used by children to resolve these dilemmas changes in a regular way with age even though there is much less variation in their judgement in this respect. It is true that the moral language of children has been little studied and that we do not have sure methods for doing so. In spite of reservations about the methods and the improvisory character of the hypothesis, we have tried to test it.[3] The story presented to children was a Dickensian one, and concerned two children, one rich and one poor; the former trusts the latter, but is, in the end, robbed and disappointed.

Without doubt morality is accompanied by a consciousness made more

[3] I am grateful to Jocelyne Ohana and Corinne Touati for their patience in the course of this simple but thankless task.

intense by the subjectivity or intersubjectivity of the judgements which it supports. Reference to the self is substituted for reference to an external authority, as in religious judgements, for example, retaining the same imperative resonance. We have established that the use of 'I' (*je*) in formulating a judgement ('I prefer', 'I find', etc.) increases, regularly with age. Whereas there were only four instances of 'I' at the age of six, there were thirty-three at the age of eight and 109 at the age of ten. That is to say, at the rate and the measure in which they grow up children appropriate and assume the judgements as being their own, in place of referring them to an external, impersonal and hence objective authority. We have also established that there is a parallel increase in the use of such expressions as 'me too' (*moi aussi*) and 'I in his place' (*moi à sa place*). What this signifies is that children identify themselves with the characters of the story, and perceive an intersubjective community with them, even if it is imaginary.

Although the use of 'I' (*je*) and 'me' (*moi*) is impressive and dependent on age, it is nevertheless related to their social representation. In fact, children who hold a 'participatory' representation make judgements in their own name four times more frequently than those who hold an 'integrative' representation. This does not mean that the nature of their judgement, as expressed in language, also changes in parallel. We can distinguish two classes in the language used to resolve the dilemmas: on the one hand a language using general and abstract terms ('one should not steal', 'that's not honest'), and on the other a language using specific and concrete terms ('Bruno was afraid', 'she wasn't honest', etc.). An examination of the frequencies shows that they do not vary significantly with age, but more according to the type of representation. Curiously, children having a 'participatory' representation make a significantly greater use of general and abstract terms, whereas children with an 'integrative' representation use specific and concrete terms. To interpret these facts we can look at another symptom: general and abstract language is used almost as frequently to express a positive (49 per cent) as a negative (51 per cent) judgement, whereas specific and concrete language is used less to express a negative judgement (29 per cent) than a positive (71 per cent) judgement about the protagonists in the story. In sum, one uses the former to express a greater severity. Thus, although 'participatory' children have a more 'democratic' and consensual vision of social relations, they are more harsh in matters of what one should and should not do. For the 'integrative' children this pattern is inverted. One finds analogies in comparing political regimes: the moralism of democratic regimes compared to the compassion and complicity of people living under authoritarian regimes. We shall not stop here.

If one examines this language more closely, one finds that formulae for expressing obligation ('one must', 'one mustn't', 'one should', 'one should not') and norms of good and bad ('it's bad', 'it's wicked', etc.) are predominant, even if they tend to diminish with age. On the other hand one sees a regular increase first of all in evaluative judgements ('that would be better'), then in appeals to values of right, fault and honesty ('it's honest', 'it's her fault'), and lastly in the spontaneous mention of such concepts as responsibility, shame and trust.

To sum up, one must admit that solutions to problems about reciprocity and obligation (Habermas, 1986) can be quite similar at all ages. This initial statement rescues us from the sterile arguments of whether or not (Turiel, 1983) institutions such as family or school exert an influence on the substance of children's experience and knowledge, and the way in which it is represented. Of course they do, given the observed differences. It should be immediately noted, however, that these problems are dissimilar at different ages. The difference is that the older children tend to make morality into an autonomous domain, a category of our culture, and interiorise it as a point of view about reality, whereas the younger ones remain at the threshold of this movement. The former are no more morally superior to the latter than the civilised are to the primitive, or men to women. Older children have a better mastery of the particular language which society puts at the disposition of everybody. They use it to communicate a judgement which is similar to that of younger children, though expressed in more rational terms.

We shall need more time before we know if the theory of social representations contributes its share to the *rapprochement* between social psychology and developmental psychology, and if it does so in a productive way. It is not sufficient to appeal to the social to overcome the difficulties evident in our science and to add to its advancement. But the studies in this book do more than appeal to the social and restore a balance. They give the impression that we are moving in a new direction. Perhaps here and there in an impulsive or clumsy way, yet we do move. And the fact that we can and do is what counts finally.

References

Asch, S. (1959). A perspective on social psychology. In S. Koch (ed.), *Psychology: A Study of a Science*, Vol. 3. New York: McGraw-Hill.
Bartlett, F. (1928). *Psychology and Primitive Culture*. New York: MacMillan. (1958). *Thinking*. New York: Basic Books.
Doise, W. and Mugny, G. (1984). *The Social Development of the Intellect*. Oxford: Pergamon Press.
Durkheim, E. (1976). *The Elementary Forms of Religious Life*. London: George Allen & Unwin.

Farr, R. M. (1977). Heider, Harré and Herzlich on health and illness: some observations on the structure of 'représentations collectives'. *European Journal of Social Psychology*, 7, 491–504.

Fishkin, J., Keniston, K. and MacKinnon, G. (1975). Moral reasoning and political ideology. *Journal of Personality and Social Psychology*, 27, 109–19.

Fiske, S. T. and Taylor, S. E. (1984). *Social Cognition*. Reading, Mass.: Addison-Wesley.

Freud, S. (1953). *On Dreams. The Complete Psychological Works of Sigmund Freud*, Vol. 5. London: The Hogarth Press.

Habermas, J. (1986). *Morale et communication*. Paris: Cerf.

Hastie, R. (1981). Schematic principles in human memory. In E. T. Higgins, C. P. Herman and M. P. Zanna (eds.), *Social Cognition*. Hillsdale, N.J.: Lawrence Erlbaum.

Heider, F. (1958). *The Psychology of Interpersonal Relations*. New York: Wiley.

Hofstadter, D. R. (1979). *Gödel, Escher, Bach*. New York: Vintage Books.

Keynes, J. M. (1936). *The General Theory of Employment, Interest and Money*. London: Macmillan.

Kohlberg, L. (1973). The claim to moral adequacy of a highest stage of moral development. *Journal of Philosophy*, 70, 630–46.

Luria, A. (1976). *Cognitive Development*. Cambridge, Mass.: Harvard University Press.

Malinowski, B. (1954). *Magic, Science and Religion*. New York: Doubleday.

Marvin, R. S., Greenberg, M. T. and Mossler, D. G. (1976). The early development of conceptual perspective taking: distinguishing among multiple perspectives. *Child Development*, 47, 62–70.

Moscovici, S. (1984). The myth of the lonely paradigm. *Social Research*, 51, 940–67.

(1988). *La Machine à faire des dieux*. Paris: Fayard.

Moscovici, S. and Hewstone, M. (1983). Social representations and social explanations: from the 'naive' to the 'amateur' scientist. In M. Hewstone (ed.), *Attribution Theory*. Oxford: Blackwell.

Turiel, E. (1983). *The Development of Social Knowledge*. Cambridge: Cambridge University Press.

Wertsch, J. V. (1985). *Vygotsky and the Social Formation of Mind*. Cambridge, Mass.: Harvard University Press.

Youniss, J. (1981). Moral development through a theory of social construction: an analysis. *Merill-Palmer Quarterly*, 27, 385–403.

Author index

Author index

Subject index

Printed in the United Kingdom
by Lightning Source UK Ltd.
106394UKS00002B/124-126